HOW TO STAY
MARRIED
&
LOVE IT!

Solving the Puzzle
of a SoulMate Marriage

Nancy Landrum with Jim Landrum

First Edition

River Publishing
Anaheim, California

HOW TO STAY MARRIED & LOVE IT!
Solving the Puzzle of a SoulMate Marriage

by Nancy Landrum
with Jim Landrum

River Publishing
P.O. Box 27433
Anaheim, CA 92809-0114

E-mail: staymarried@aol.com
Website: howtostaymarried.com

Library of Congress Control Number: 2002 190004
ISBN: 0-9719314-2-9

Printed in the United States of America
0 9 8 7 6 5 4 3 2 1

The term SoulMate™ is a trademark of River Publishing.

To Jim
Our story would have had a very different ending without your courage,
the workshops never would have existed without your vision, and
this book would have remained a dream without your belief.
Thank you for asking me... I'm so glad I said, "Yes!"

And to our children,
Teri, Karen, Steven, Peter, and Jimmy
You suffered with us but continue to humble and delight us
with your willingness to forgive, learn, and love.

About the Authors

Jim and Nancy Landrum have been awarded Masters Degrees in their respective fields—Nancy's in Psychology and Jim's in Church Music. Since 1994, Jim and Nancy have been teaching SoulMate skills to personal clients as well as hundreds of couples in their workshop, "How to Stay Married & Love It!" They continue to read and incorporate the most recent research findings and concepts into their presentations. The Landrums are frequent guest speakers at marriage functions and stepfamily support groups.

After surviving the deaths of their first spouses, Jim and Nancy were overjoyed to find each other. Their inability to resolve frequent and escalating conflicts, however, was bewildering and exhausting. They were stunned to find themselves on the brink of divorce. They sifted through mountains of material gathered from seminars, books, tapes, and counselors to find the specific communication and conflict resolution skills that were needed to save their marriage.

The Landrums believe that SoulMates are not "found" but *created* by learning and using these simple, couple-tested skills that produce thriving marriages. That belief has proven true in their own relationship as well as hundreds of marriages that have learned and used these concepts. Couples with adequate marriages as well as those in great conflict have elevated their relationships to SoulMate status by following the path mapped out by Jim and Nancy.

Although their faith is a vital part of their journey of healing and is gently reflected throughout their message, their primary emphasis is on teaching the powerful skills that enabled them create the intimacy, safety, and romance that is characteristic of a SoulMate relationship.

Table of Contents

Acknowledgments

I am more grateful than I can adequately express for:

Kay Lyou, M.A.
You reassured me I could write.
In the midst of your own enormous challenges,
your unfaltering belief in this book encouraged me.

One-On-One Book Production and Marketing
You masterfully turned vague ideas into a finished product
for which we have great pride, and enthusiastically walked us
through the maze of book publicity.

Betty Coble Lawther, LittD and Pastor Bob Fulton
Betty, you saw the possibility of Jim and I as a couple.
Bob, you taught us about communication filters
and prayed for us.

Jim and Laura Campbell and the weekly Kinship Group
You, without judgment, loved us through our darkest night.

Carrie, Colleen, Donna, and Maria
My gratitude for your love and support is boundless.
My life is so much richer with you in it.
You are the best friends ever, and forever.

Drs. Ron and Mary Hulnick
The University of Santa Monica
Your vision provided me with school the way I always longed for it to be.
The Masters Degree Program
challenged, supported, empowered, and celebrated my growth
so that many of my dreams are coming true.

Jackie Barille
Not a day goes by that we don't use or teach the concepts you gave us.

Stephanie Merritt, Ph.D., M.F.T., Cecelia Schulberg, M.S.,
Janice McNatt, R.N. Dean Whitney, M.A., R.P.T.,
Susan Simpson, Ph.D., and Colleen Callahan, M.A.
You helped me unlock the author within.

My sisters Mary, Sally, and Jean
You just assume I can do whatever I want to do,
and love me whether I do anything or not.

Participants of our Workshops
You vulnerably shared you frustrations, tears, laughter, and
deepest desires for a SoulMate marriage.
You gave us the laboratory for refining these concepts.
With incredible grace and courage, you proved our belief
that what worked for us can work for others.

My SoulMate, Jim
Two of my deepest desires were to have a great marriage and to write a book.
You have helped make both dreams a reality.

Our Heavenly Father
You heard our cries for help and answered beyond our wildest dreams.

A Note From
Jim Landrum

The very successful workshop on which the *How to...* books are based is taught by both Nancy and me; however, unless clearly noted, these volumes were written by Nancy. I have watched with amazement as Nancy has given birth to this labor of love and I believe it is a significant part of her life's work.

As we became friends in 1980, I found that Nancy was a woman of substance, wise beyond her years. Even then I said to her, "You have a book in you." Little did I know that the book would be about us and our struggles to have a great marriage!

As you read you'll see the depth of her heart, sense her compassion for those who are hurting, and understand that she brings to this work a richness of experience gleaned from her own journey of healing.

It is my hope that these concepts and skills will help you solve your own puzzle of *How to Stay Married & Love It!*

Sincerely,

Jim

Chapter 1

Divorce!

Ladies and Gentlemen, we are gathered here together
to join this man and this woman in holy matrimony…

Opening words to the
Landrum's wedding ceremony

Divorce! The word shattered the space and hung in the air between us like a red fog. Even after all the conflict we'd experienced, we were both stunned to silence by the introduction of that possibility. How could our relationship have come to this? Why wasn't it enough to love each other? We'd always heard that love and commitment were all it took to have a great marriage. We did love each other. We were very committed to each other and to our marriage. What was wrong? We'd both been through so much and were so happy to find each other. We were in our 40s. Adults. Why couldn't we resolve the conflicts that were eating away at our love and commitment like a deadly cancer?

～

Jim: I was born in Oklahoma. As I grew up I learned how a man is supposed to act by observing the men in my life. By their actions, my dad, uncles, grandfathers, and male friends all showed me that real men don't talk about their feelings. If a man gets angry, he just clams up. If he gets his feelings hurt, he doesn't let anyone know. If his wife wants to talk about her feelings, he doesn't pay much attention, because women are too emotional. When it all gets to be too much, a man explodes verbally or physically, then everything calms down again. Some marriages survive this lack of communication, but there is very little closeness.

For example, a few years ago, my mother, who is in her 80s now, told me an interesting story about herself and my dad. They had been married a few months and she thought everything was wonderful…in her words, "hunky dory." One morning she burned the toast and my dad exploded about five or six things he had been angry about but hadn't mentioned. Needless to say, she was devastated.

In 1957, I married my high school sweetheart, Dixie. I worked part time in local churches while finishing college. By 1963 we had two little girls, Teri and Karen. I was awarded my Master's Degree in Church Music from the seminary and began working full time as a Minister of Music. In 1966, when Dixie was only 27 years old, she became very ill with pancreatitis. After 13 weeks in the hospital, she returned home, but her health remained fragile.

In 1969 our family moved to California. Dixie continued to be ill occasionally, each event threatening her life and requiring hospital-ization and often surgeries. We learned that one of the things that triggered her illness was emotional upset. I avoided conflict with her by sweeping any issues under the rug. In fact, my motto was, "Peace at any price!" The circumstances reinforced my pattern of not talking about my feelings and leaving conflict unresolved.

In 1979 Dixie died, leaving me with two teenage girls, Teri and Karen, and our 7-year-old son, Jimmy.

～

I was born and reared in a small farming community in Southern California. My parents were very active in our church and they, my three sisters, and I were there whenever the doors were open. They loved God and were wonderful models of integrity and generosity, but there were also patterns of chronic conflict. Soon after high school, I married a man who I was sure would make me happy forever. Within six months I realized we were developing the very relationship struggles that I had been determined to avoid. I didn't know how to do things any differently! We worked very hard at our relationship and eventually felt ready to have our first son, Steven. Eighteen months later a second son, Peter, followed. In 1968 my husband left home to pitch in a softball game and dropped dead from a previously undiagnosed heart problem. I was 23 years old. I didn't have the inner resources to handle this trauma. It took several years to even *begin* to recover.

I wanted to remarry, but considering the future of myself *and* two little boys made me very choosy! Twelve years passed as I sat through many Little League games, enjoyed camping with extended family, and began to develop my love of teaching with the young people of my church. As the boys approached middle-school age, I decided the teen years were a terrible time to complicate their lives with the changes a marriage would bring. I felt a surge of strength and confidence, and so turned my attention to starting a small business.

In the Fall of 1980, I met Jim through a mutual friend. We began dating casually and became good friends. My determination to postpone remarriage until the boys were grown gradually dissipated as we fell in love. Our many friends and family members celebrated our wedding with us in the Spring of 1981. We had each survived the loss of a spouse, were responsible, caring persons, and were sure that we were due for some better times. We had no doubt that we were meant to be together. We were soul mates! We blissfully left for a two-week honeymoon.

Teri had married the previous summer, so there were four children waiting for us at home, Karen (17), Steven (14), Peter (13), and Jimmy (8). The day we returned from our honeymoon, the conflicts began. We had very different styles of parenting. We couldn't agree, and the children did what all children are born knowing how to do, divide and conquer! At first it was easy to kiss and make up, but the same old issues erupted repeatedly to hammer the bruised places in each of us. Every recurrence made our pain deeper and we became more sensitive. After a few years, we saw the areas of safety between us shrinking as the areas of conflict expanded.

It became impossible to share the same space peacefully. Each of us secretly feared our marriage had been a terrible mistake. The decision was made to live in separate households until all the children were on their own. That arrangement wasn't much fun, either.

In spite of our disenchantment, we didn't want to give up. The memory of the bliss we'd experienced in the beginning tantalized us. Although we knew the unique stage of honeymoon-euphoria never lasts forever, we wanted to *rekindle* and learn how to *maintain* the quality of soul-mate-love we had believed would characterize our marriage.

Finally, we seriously began to seek help.

〜

Jim: Times have changed, but when I first entered the ministry, it was the kiss of death to your career to admit you had marital, financial, or any other problems. Besides, I was convinced that Nancy was the real problem, not me. Although she had been seeing a counselor on her own for a few years, it took the stunning realization that our marriage might not make it, before I was willing to get help. Together we saw several counselors, (finally settled into working with one) read books, listened to tapes, and attended seminars. We prayed desperately, asking God for help.

~

Our patterns had driven us to such extremes that we found it difficult to implement most of the material we read or heard. Our response to a general instruction such as "Always treat each other with respect," or "Never go to bed angry," was, "*HOW*?" We agonized with the frustration of trying to put together the puzzle of a happy marriage while it was obvious we were missing some important pieces.

During those years I remember thinking often that there are such clear laws that govern the physical world…nothing can be more dependable than gravity, for instance. By cooperating with the law of gravity, I can remain safe—I can refuse to jump off a roof, for example. If I try to defy gravity, I can count on a painful consequence. I believe the universe is orderly. So, could there also be laws dictating the success or failure of relationships? If I knew what they were, I would do my best to live in cooperation with them in order to avoid the painful consequences of defying them.

Could there be laws dictating the success or failure of relationships?

We began an intensive search to find the relationship rules we were inadvertently breaking—the missing pieces to the puzzle. Over a period of about five years, we gradually collected and implemented specific, doable communication tools that helped us resolve our conflicts. We discovered other pieces, as well. Soon the puzzle of "How to Stay Married & Love It!" was solved.

Today the love and respect Jim and I have for each other are deeper than ever before. The security and pleasure we experience together is more than we ever dreamed we would have. Our relationship models the term, "SoulMates." The combination and capitalization of these words is not a mistake. We use this customized term to describe the elevated quality of relationship that is experienced when a couple is willing to work at *building* a SoulMate relationship rather than believing it is a fluke of *fate*.

Looking back, it is frightening to think that we nearly forfeited the rich life we now enjoy.

Our family is also healing. Every time we gather, we celebrate the bonds of love that have been forged. So far, we have welcomed into our circle two fine sons-in-law, a lovely daughter-in-law and six wonderful grandchildren. We are so grateful that our choices led to the sharing of this precious, expanding family.

Looking back, it is frightening to think that we nearly forfeited the rich life we now enjoy.

While we were learning in the laboratory of our own marriage, professional researchers were coming to the same conclusions as we had. Diane Sollee is the director of the Coalition for Marriage, Family and Couples Education, a clearinghouse for all the latest marriage research and education programs. She said, "Marriage is skill-based. Like football. The way we have it set up now a couple gets married, and we send them out there to win based on 'love and commitment.' That's like asking a football team to win on team spirit—'for the Gipper'—but not letting them learn any plays or signals. No skills at all—just win on love. The basis for smart marriage is exciting new research that finds that what is different about the marriages that make it—that go the distance and stay happy—are behaviors or skills. And even more exciting, they are simple skills that any fool can learn." She added, "Love is not an absolute, a truth, or a limited substance—that you're in it or out of it. It's a feeling that ebbs and flows depending on how you treat each other. If you learn new ways to interact, the feelings can come flowing back, often stronger than before."[1]

A national registry of marriage education classes is available at www. smart marriages .com.

If your marriage is in eminent jeopardy, get help. Find a skills-based marriage class in your area and enroll immediately. (A national registry of marriage education classes is available at www.smartmarriages.com. Some classes are held weekly. Others combine learning with a weekend away from home or even a romantic cruise.) Statistically, these classes have been found to be more effective than traditional therapy. The classes provide support and accountability for making the changes needed when a marriage is on the edge. As a bonus, a class with other struggling couples is, for some, less threatening to attend than walking into a therapist's office—a fact that often makes the difference between getting help or waiting until it's too late. If your spouse is not willing to go, then go by yourself. The relationship *changes* even when only one is willing to change.[2]

If you cannot attend a class, interview several therapists. Make it clear that the first appointment is for an interview and you don't expect to pay. Ask these questions: Have you had training specific to working with marriage issues? When? With whom? (Check to see if the organization is registered at www.smartmarriages.com.) Will you tell me something about your own marriage? If I (we) came to see you, what would be your approach? What percentage of your clients are couples? What percentage of your former clients would you estimate were significantly helped and have gone on to experience a great marriage?

These questions will help you sense:

♦ if the therapist has been able to establish a successful marriage of his or her own,

♦ has been interested enough in couple dynamics to take extra training in marriage skills,

♦ is skills-based in approach rather than traditional therapy based on analysis,

♦ whether or not the therapist has confidence in his or her marriage counseling skills.

We suggest that you ask God for help. The act of acknowledging that you need help from a source wiser than yourself opens the door to synchronous and sometimes miraculous aid. And keep on asking. Expect surprises!

In this book, we'll share the four essential elements for building and maintaining not just a tolerable marriage, but one of SoulMate quality. Looking back, Jim and I see these four elements and the skills that express them as the critical pieces that enabled us to pull our marriage back from the brink of divorce. They are the foundation that supports the great marriage we now enjoy. These are:

♦ accept your partner's points of view as valid,

♦ use communication and conflict resolution skills that get the desired result,

♦ always treat yourself and your spouse with respect, and

♦ be fully committed to this partnership for life.

Just as solving a complicated puzzle is easier once the four corners are in place, these four elements and the skills that demonstrate them are the ones you need in place first. One or more chapters are dedicated to each of these corner puzzle pieces and specific skills are taught to infuse these elements into yourself and your marriage.

Completing the rest of the SoulMate puzzle is easy once these four are in place. Even if your marriage is not in jeopardy these corner pieces are still the "frame" of *any* well-functioning marriage and must be consistently demonstrated before a SoulMate marriage can be assured. If your relationship is relatively stable use this book as a checklist to identify anything that could use improvement.

In the next volume, *How to Stay Married & Love It Even More!* we define the other six pieces that complete the puzzle of a SoulMate marriage. Those six elements took our marriage from "communicating, able to successfully resolve conflict, no danger of divorce," to "deeply in love, treasuring emotional and physical intimacy, grateful for each day together—SoulMates."

It isn't that we exclusively worked on the first four puzzle pieces, mastered them, and then moved on to puzzle pieces #6-#10. Life just isn't that neat. Although we were integrating many concepts and skills somewhat simultaneously, the ones we had to work the hardest to establish and that made the biggest difference in the beginning were Puzzle Pieces #1-#4. Also, if we had tried to put all ten pieces into one book it would have been too heavy to enjoy reading in bed, (something I love to do) and too intimidating to take from the bookstore shelf. Therefore, the most essential parts are in this book followed by the balance of the puzzle in the next volume. [3]

The laws that dictate the success or failure of a marriage are no longer invisible. Like gravity, they are now understood, documented, and so clear that anyone can choose from a menu of behaviors that determine what degree of suffering or love one experiences in one's marriage. The pieces are all here. You can solve your own puzzle of How to Stay Married & Love It! by beginning with the four essential corners.

Before you begin, however, take time to read Chapter 2 about what is missing in the old formula for a successful marriage—"What Our Parents Didn't Know..."

Whatever you can do, or dream you can, begin it.
Boldness has genius, power, and magic in it. Begin it now.
~ Goethe[4]

If you want better insight and discernment, and are searching
for them as you would for lost money or hidden treasure,
then wisdom will be given you.
~ Proverbs 2:3-5[5]

ENDNOTES

1   Sollee, Diane, Director of the Coalition for Marriage, Family and Couples Education. Interview by Jon Galuckie during a Coalition conference in Washington, DC in July, 1998. www.smartmarriages.com.

2   Michele Weiner Davis makes a very strong case for the powerful effectiveness of deliberate change by only one partner in her book, *The Divorce Remedy.* New York: Simon & Schuster, 2001.

3   If you would like to be notified of the publication of *How to Stay Married & Love It Even More*! or pre-order a copy refer to the form on the back page of this book or visit us at www.howtostaymarried.com. Available in Fall, 2002.

4   Although this is frequently attributed to Goethe, it is actually a rather free translation of *Faust* by John Anster made in 1808. They're spoken by the Manager in the "Prelude at the Theatre."

5   Except as otherwise noted, all Bible quotes are from *The Living Bible* by Tyndale House available in most bookstores. This book of Proverbs, which appears in the Old Testament, is attributed to King Solomon, who was renowned for his wisdom.

Chapter 2

What Our Parents Didn't Know . . .

All marriages are happy. It's the living together afterward that's rough.
~ Milton Berle

Our wedding day was magical. Because we both were involved in churches with large congregations who loved us, about 700 friends and family members came to share our joy.

While waiting in the Bride's Dressing Room, I watched with wonder as Jim's daughters, Teri and Karen, wound their long hair into top-knots. Wispy, feminine tendrils framed their faces and necks. Every movement—pulling on sheer hose, adjusting undergarments, applying make-up to themselves and each other—was accompanied by constant chatter and giggles. They were enchanting.

Jim: As a minister, I'd married hundreds of couples. I'd always counseled them to relax and enjoy their wedding day. Nancy and I had agreed that we would not let anything spoil the joy of that day. So, 10 minutes before time to start, when 8-year-old Jimmy spilled cola on his tuxedo, I just chuckled while my best man brushed it off. We hung it outside the choir room door, hoping the warm California sun would quickly dry it.

❧

Through the intercom I could hear the beautiful old hymns being played as a prelude. The familiar tunes were a soothing background for all the excitement. Earlier, I'd seen my sons, Steven and Peter, in tuxes. They looked so handsome—young men, no longer boys. I knew they would be thoughtful and dignified as they ushered their grandmothers to the front row.

Suddenly, it was as though someone turned up the volume of the sound system. I heard the stately and comforting hymn "Great Is Thy Faithfulness"[1] above the rustle of petticoats and the clicking of a lipstick cap being replaced. Tears sprang to my eyes. I was sure God was reminding me of how faithful He had been to me and my children for the nearly 13 years since their father's death. I felt rewarded for the many times of loneliness when I had refused to settle for a second-best relationship. Jim was so right for me. I felt blessed and very sure of our happy future together.

❧

Jim: I, too, had the experience of thinking the sound had been turned up as I heard "Great Is Thy Faithfulness" being played. And, like Nancy, I felt full of gratitude for the 14 extra years the children and I had with Dixie after the first diagnosis of her illness. God had also been with me during the long, empty months of grief after her death. And now, the very air of this soft, warm spring day sparkled with celebration. Nancy and I had found each other!

❧

Years later we recalled the strange volume increase that brought the old hymn's tune to our attention and its words to our minds. We realized then, that God had not only been reminding us of His faithfulness to us in the past, but promising his faithfulness to us in the future—an angry, conflict filled future we could not possibly imagine on that most perfect of all wedding days.

We were typical of most couples in love…full of hopeful plans, confident in our future together, sure that we would have a great life. As in many second marriages, we assumed that because we loved each other so much, our children would love each other, also. In spite of the war stories we'd heard, we were sure that the blending of *our* families would happen smoothly and effortlessly.[2] With the benefit of 20-20 hindsight, it's hard to believe how naive we were!

We'd been taught that if a couple loved each other and were committed to each other, a good and lasting marriage would follow. It had worked for our parents' generation. We were bewildered. Even after several years of unrelent-

Love is needed to get a relationship off the ground, but it doesn't provide enough fuel to keep a marriage flying toward success over time…nor does commitment.

ing conflict, we still loved each other. We were still faithful and committed to each other. We wanted the marriage to work more than anything! But some essential piece was missing …

We were stunned to read: "Love is needed to get a relationship off the ground, but it doesn't provide enough fuel to keep a marriage flying toward success over time…nor does commitment. *It's how couples manage conflict that makes the difference. The key to marital success is to teach couples how to talk without fighting*"[3]

Love provides the "blast off" for the relationship…
Full commitment is a necessity…
But managing conflict successfully is the missing ingredient—
the guidance system of the rocket—
that determines the ultimate destination of the relationship.

Conflict is not damaging and can even be a powerful stimulus for personal growth.

Conflict is inevitable, even normal, in any close, caring relationship. Conflict is not damaging and can even be a powerful stimulus for personal growth. It is *unresolved* conflict that drains the energies of both partners, pollutes the quality of their love, and sometimes becomes the main focus of attention, overshadowing the areas of their partnership that otherwise would be rewarding.

In other relationships, conflict can be ignored, sidestepped or patched up with relatively superficial attempts at resolution. If the conflict is severe enough, the relationship can simply be abandoned. One *lives*, however, with one's mate. There are only four ways that I can think of for handling conflict in a marriage:

1. **Endure periodic or frequent arguing.** With this choice, someone may *appear* to win in each encounter, but, in reality, everyone loses.

2. **Arrange the relationship so that conflict is hidden, or avoided at any cost**—a choice that is often temporary, as hidden conflict always extracts a toll in the relationship and sometimes in personal health.

3. **Divorce.** This option is deceptive because the conflict often continues or even escalates after the breakup. Often, the same conflicts resurface with a new partner.

4. **Be open about conflict and learn to resolve it** in ways that are satisfactory to both partners.

Today's couples expect more out of marriage than any previous generation. In the past, our legal structure and culture strongly supported marriage for life, period. Unhappy or conflicted marriages, for the most part, remained intact. It was assumed that love and commitment were all that was necessary for a lasting marriage. Since the passage of no-fault divorce laws, however, our culture no longer demands or even expects that a couple remain married for life "no matter what." Now, when a marriage is unhappy—when there are unresolved conflicts or passive neglect—either partner has the freedom to leave. Now we not only want an arrangement that provides a safe sex partner, financial stability, and a good structure for rearing children, we also want to be happy—to feel intimately known, passionately loved, and the development of our gifts or careers enthusiastically supported. In our current jargon, we want a soul mate!

Recent studies of the long-term effects of divorce[4] are documenting what some of you may have experienced for yourselves. Divorce is not a simple discarding of a garment that just didn't fit well. It is a major emotional upheaval even for unions without children. It leaves lasting scars for adults in addition to devastating disillusionment and damaged self-esteem for most children of divorced parents. In an effort to prevent the emotional and financial devastation of divorce, researchers have been evaluating good marriages and asking, "Can struggling couples learn to duplicate the skills that are demonstrated in a successful marriage?" The answer is, "Yes!"

Divorce is not a simple discarding of a garment that just didn't fit well. It is a major emotional upheaval even for unions without children.

Some of you may have little conflict in your relationship, so you are reading this to make a good marriage even better. Bravo! Some, in spite of the basic stability of your marriage, may have a recurring issue that continues prevent total satisfaction. Some, as we did, may be experiencing the daily, grinding stress of constant conflict and are just hanging on by your fingertips! Although your conflicts may be about different issues than ours were, we offer our own experience as proof that the love you once shared can be recaptured, and more. In the majority of marriages, *it doesn't matter what the conflict is about*. The problem is that many of us never learned *how* to resolve conflict successfully in any relationship, let alone one as vital and intimate as a marriage.

This book will teach you the tried-and-true skills that enabled Jim and me to resolve the elephantine-sized conflict that nearly destroyed our marriage as well as dozens of less threatening ones. These skills do not work their magic for us alone, however. Their power to heal relationships has been repeatedly witnessed in our workshops and in my office.

Before we dump the puzzle pieces out onto the table and begin the process of fitting them together into a SoulMate relationship, it is wise to note the phenomenon of *homeostasis*. For our purposes, homeostasis means that every ongoing relationship has a certain balance. On a conscious level, you may not like some of the things happening in your relationship (its current balance); however, the subconscious mind often has reasons for maintaining a relationship in its current state.

One husband, after attending our workshop, completely changed the way he was treating his wife. She told us later that she couldn't handle it! It was too good! She badgered him until he returned to his disrespectful treatment of her! The former quality of the relationship must, in some way, have reflected what felt normal or what she unconsciously believed she deserved. Peace or closeness may have felt unfamiliar to her, leaving her vulnerable and scared.

As in the previous example, resistance to improvement may come from without—your spouse or even other family members. Other times the resistance is from within. Have changes been requested that you have the power to make and yet you refuse? Why?

Conflicting feelings about achieving a better marriage are common.

(**Tip:** Beating yourself up will not remove the resistance.)

Conflicting feelings about achieving a better marriage are common. For example, one part of you may desire an improved relationship more than anything. That part led you to this book. Another part may feel undeserving of a great marriage, so it resists improvement. A third part may be dedicated to punishing your partner for hurting you in the past, so it sabotages any efforts to change things for the better. There may be a part that doesn't believe a great marriage is possible. In order to prevent a crushing disappointment, that part won't let you try. We have all had the experience of wondering why we did something so diametrically opposed to what we *consciously* wanted to do—eating too many desserts when we're trying to lose weight, for instance.

Our *hidden motivations* are powerful enough to countermand our *conscious choices*.

You may be thinking, "This doesn't apply to me. I really want a SoulMate relationship and will do whatever it takes to make it happen." If so, you will move forward very quickly as you apply the tools you're about to learn.

For those of you who do experience resistance, however, it is helpful to talk about it to a counselor or a trusted friend. In the process of talking it out, an old distorted belief may surface or a fear that at one time was reasonable but now is unfounded. It is sometimes uncomfortable digging around below the surface of consciousness, but without willingness to examine the inner resistance and push through it, the relationship will not improve.

Once you understand why there is resistance, your more conscious self (the part that knows an improved relationship is in your best interest) can choose whether or not to allow the resistant part to limit progress toward a happier marriage. These inner parts often require repeated, firm nudging in order to move into alignment with your goal of a SoulMate marriage. It's important that this be done in a patient, compassionate way, as though one were dealing with a frightened child. Indeed, these defensive parts of ourselves were adopted in response to being hurt, often in childhood.

With many stops and starts, plenty of failures, and in ways far from perfect, Jim and I were willing to overcome our resistance to learning new relationship skills. Our marriage was once at risk, however, because I thought I was pretty good—it was *Jim* who needed to change! Of course, he thought he was just fine as he was. *I* was the one who needed to change! Just in case you may have similar thoughts, the next chapter describes the truth we discovered on our journey toward a great marriage: most SoulMates are *self-made*, rather than accidentally found. Read on…

Courage is resistance to fear, mastery of fear, not absence of fear.
~ Mark Twain

Honey whets the appetite, and so does wisdom! When you enjoy
becoming wise, there is hope for you! A bright future lies ahead!
~ Proverbs 24:13-14

ENDNOTES

1   Words by Thomas O. Chisholm, Music by William M. Runyan, Public Domain.

2   The unique stresses of stepfamilies are addressed in the companion to this book, *How to Stay Married & Love It Even More! Completing the Puzzle of a SoulMate Marriage* by Nancy Landrum with Jim Landrum. Help for stepfamilies can be found at www.steplife.com.

3   Notarius, C. & Markham, H., *We Can Work It Out, Making Sense Out of Marital Conflict* , p. 21. New York: G.P. Putnam & Sons. 1993.

4   See Chapter 18.

Chapter 3

Acres of Diamonds

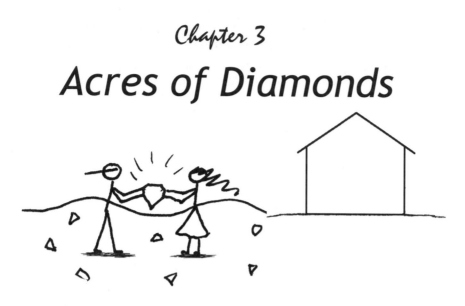

*Unless you understand that marriage doesn't make people happy,
you will spend the rest of your life trading in marital partners
for new ones.
Unless you feel satisfied with your own life, you will not be able to
determine whether your unhappiness stems from personal or
relationship issues.*

~ Michele Weiner Davis[1]

After the deaths of our first mates, we were so grateful to have found each other. The bond we experienced was deep. We were each other's best friend. We were passionate and joyful. We considered ourselves two of the lucky ones. We had each found our soul mate.

Our conflicts, however, would not stay resolved. They kept reappearing like obsessive stalkers. Instead of soul mates, we became hurt mates, anger mates, and fight mates. For several months we lived in separate homes. We both thought we must have been wrong about the sense of destiny and rightness we had felt at the time of our marriage. Neither of us, however, could quite let go of the hope that we were meant for each other and might still live "happily ever after."

As mentioned before, Jim and I sought the advice of a few counselors.[2] We also received tidbits of help from several books, tapes, and marriage seminars. We became learning mates. Saving our marriage was a *huge* puzzle, and we gradually became puzzle-solving mates who were beginning to see the pieces come together.

♥ 16 ♥

In the process of rebuilding our marriage, we slowly began discovering treasures in each other we hadn't even dreamed existed.

In the process of rebuilding our marriage, we slowly began discovering treasures in each other we hadn't even dreamed existed. We became treasure-hunting mates, glorying in the riches we found. The process began to be exciting!

In 1994, Jim suggested we begin sharing with others what had taken us so long to learn and had cost us such agony. We put a rough draft of the material in little folders, and began inviting every one we could think of to come to our workshop entitled, "How to Stay Married & Love It!" After several classes, we polished up the workbook and had a thousand copies printed. We began presenting ourselves to audiences as experts in resolving marital conflict and building emotional intimacy. Because we were willing to do the work of healing our own marriage, we were experiencing not only our own happiness, but the unparalleled joy of giving others the pieces so they could solve the puzzle of *their* marriages. We had become teaching mates!

Largely owing to Jim's encouragement, I celebrated my 50th birthday by applying to the University of Santa Monica. In August 1998, I donned a cap and gown to be awarded a Master's Degree in Spiritual Psychology with an emphasis in Consciousness, Health, and Healing. It was the fulfillment of a 25-year dream.

Another secret dream began to surface. Ever since discovering the magic of reading for myself, I'd wanted to write and be published. Jim kept telling me I could do it. He believed in me. One Sunday morning, we opened *The Orange County Register* to the Home & Garden section to find an article I had written was featured on the front page! Without his encouragement, I might never have known the incredibly delicious pleasure of seeing my words in print. I was reaping the personal benefits of having an encouragement mate and adventure mate.

Russell Herman Conwell, a Baptist minister and founder of Temple University, is best known for his lecture, "Acres of Diamonds." He delivered it more than 6,000 times, devoting the proceeds to the education of more than 10,000 young adults.

He tells the story of a farmer in Africa who was content until he heard how rich he would be if he had diamonds. He sold his farm, left his wife and children with a relative, and went off in search of diamonds. In a few years, after exhausting his grubstake and losing heart, he drowned himself in the sea.

Meanwhile, the man who had bought the little farm, happened on an interesting rock while plowing. He displayed it on the mantle. Some time later a visitor came to his home, picked it up and excitedly declared that a diamond was encapsulated in its center. As they sifted through the dirt in the field, they found others. The first owner of the farm had abandoned acres of diamonds, to die broken and destitute looking for them in some other place.

In the "Acres of Diamonds" speech, Conwell cited many other true examples of persons setting off in search of their fortunes, after unknowingly leaving hidden treasure for someone else to find.

Americans love stories that teach "hard work pays off in the end" or "faithfulness and integrity overcome!" Our universally favorite get-rich stories are about ordinary folks who turn adversity into triumph by mining the treasure found in their own back yards. We envy the computer nerd who started a company in his garage and has made billions (Bill Gates). We admire the housewife whose great tasting cookies led her from one small cookie stall to outlets in every mall in America (Mrs. Fields Cookies). We shake our heads and marvel at a man "too old" to be seriously considered as a candidate for founding a successful business who nevertheless parlayed his home made fried chicken recipe into thousands of Colonel Sanders franchises.

Our universally favorite get-rich stories are about ordinary folks who turn adversity into triumph by mining the treasure found in their own back yards.

There are others, less known, who quietly spend their lives mining for different treasures. My brother-in-law, C.W. Perry, started a church in a living room with just a handful of attendees. Year by year, the numbers grew. Soon a place of worship and a school appeared as housing tracts replaced the orange groves near the site. While he and my sister, Mary, were bringing up their five great kids, they also helped thousands explore their relationships with God in an up-beat, fun atmosphere. When C.W. died recently, 4,000 persons attended his memorial service to celebrate the contribution he had made to their lives. He found and mined a field of diamonds.

My husband, Jim, and his first wife, Dixie, lost one of their daughters at birth. Several years later, Dixie died. Jim knows what it means to suffer loss. He's experienced the long, lonely process of grieving. If he so desired, he could be bitter about the barren field he "owned." Instead, Jim has brought comfort and reassurance to thousands as he sensitively and compassionately ministers to the bereaved. He *shares* his diamonds.

When my sister, Sally's thirty-plus year marriage was deteriorating, she was determined to save it. She was devastated when she realized she had to let it go. The family in which she had invested so much of her life seemed to be in shambles. Her four adult children were hurt, angry and divided. She could have chosen to spend the rest of her life moaning "poor me." Instead, she answered the challenge with this question, "What can I learn from this experience?" Always a seeker, she now sought a path of forgiveness, dignity, and healing. She utilized this time to get her Master's Degree in Spiritual Psychology (she was *my* inspiration!). She says she was on a quest to learn more about how to love...love herself, her children, and *even her ex!* Today it is not unusual to find them all—her children, grandchildren, and at times, her ex-husband—gathered around her table celebrating family events and holidays. The atmosphere is one of genuine love, caring, and gratitude. She kept mining and collecting the diamonds from the yard where she lived.

When life as she knew it fell apart, another sister, Jean, put her son in the car and began driving. She was searching for a community where she and Matt could make a new life. She believed they both would just *know* it when they arrived. They found Red Lodge, Montana, nestled in a little valley below the Bear Tooth Mountains. She took her love of movies, coupled with her bright willing mind, and with a big dose of courage, bought a failing video store on Main Street. Within a short time, the business was booming, she was enthusiastically welcomed into the town's life, and Matt was thriving. (By the time their first winter in Montana had arrived, he *knew* they'd found the right place! If the snow conditions are good, every Friday at noon school is dismissed and the kids are bussed to the nearby ski lift for snowboarding or skiing!) Jean and Matt found the diamonds of healthy change within themselves.

We never tire of stories like these. Every month, *Reader's Digest, Guideposts*, and even *Money Magazine* feature adversity to treasure, "lemons to lemonade" articles because they *sell*. We hunger for heroes.

Yet in the arena of marriage, it seems the most common solution to adversity is divorce.[3]

A few years ago, knowing that Jim and I were very happy with each other, two of my beautiful nieces asked me, "Is he your soul mate?" As we talked, I realized that they had bought into the currently popular myth that each person has only one soul mate. If I believed that to be true, there would be intense pressure to search far and wide for that one person in the world with whom I was destined to be a soul mate. If I were in a relationship that was struggling, it would be natural to conclude I had misunderstood or misjudged. So, determined to settle for nothing less than my highest good, I would leave this "mistake" and begin searching again.

Whatever the reason, marriages are being abandoned in staggering numbers. Several sets of statistics have been published. The numbers vary a little, but, nationwide, roughly 50 percent of first time marriages end in divorce. The failure rate of second and third marriages is significantly higher. Something isn't working here. Could it be that the treasure we seek is not "out there" after all?

Recently, a charming man named Hans called and said, "We need help." (Remember the recommendation in the first chapter to get help? Yea, Hans!)

This was the fourth marriage for him, and the third marriage for Janet, his wife. When they said, "I do," they vowed this was it! They would stay and make it work no matter what! Now, after seven years, they were hurting badly. The love that had brought them together was eroding at a frightening rate. The prospect of another failure was unbearable, but the conflict was devastating. They were tired. Neither of them wanted to look for a solution "out there" *again*, so they signed up for our workshop.

In the first two sessions, Hans and Janet leaned forward on their chairs to be sure they heard every word. They asked questions. They devoured every concept and practiced the exercises. In between weeks two and three, they called me. They were having a huge fight. Would I see them? Together we probed deeply into their pain. We mined for truths they had overlooked. I shared a few concepts with them that they had never heard before. They examined their differing perspectives. They left exhausted but hopeful. By the time weeks three and four had passed, and after one more personal session, their relationship made a gigantic turn around.

Their marriage began functioning much better because both Hans and Janet were willing to assume responsibility for their own contributions to the problems. Hans accepted that he was seeing old ghosts in Janet's face, blaming her for the "stuff" he'd brought with him from his past. She realized she was playing out her own lifelong habits of martyrdom and peacemaking to the detriment of herself and this marriage. He refocused his attention on his attitudes and behaviors. He accepted that it is his choice, moment by moment, how he functions in relationship to Janet. She realized there was no "bad guy" here. Her dysfunctional relationship habits were engaging perfectly with the issues Hans brought to the marriage. She determined to change herself.

A few weeks later, Hans called to say they were paying for some friends of theirs to come to our next workshop! The leader of a marriage support group they attend told us that Hans and Janet were transformed! They were enthusiastically sharing with others the concepts they'd learned that were restoring their love. In Janet's words, "We like each other again!" Their marriage has become a springboard for profound healing and personal growth. They are mining the field of diamonds in their own back yard!

What changed? Hans, as do most men whose marriages become troubled, had been focused on changing his wife. After all, *she* was the problem. Janet, as do most women who are with "hopeless" men, was sure Hans was the one who needed changing. After all, *he* was the problem! (Sound familiar?) If they divorced, however, instead of leaving the "problem" behind, they would each carry with them the same relationship baggage as they had brought into *this*

Their marriage began functioning much better because both Hans and Janet were willing to assume responsibility for their own contributions to the problems.

When Hans changed the focus of his attention from Janet onto his own behaviors and when Janet began to concentrate on changing her own patterns, magic happened.

marriage. When Hans changed the focus of his attention from Janet onto his own behaviors and when Janet began to concentrate on changing her own patterns, magic happened. They are becoming the SoulMates they had hoped for when they married!

The same process is unfolding with Chris and Erica, George and Carmen, Steve and Kathy, Tim and Julie, Steve and Dena, Eric and Debra, and many others. Like Hans and Janet, they are finding, with some surprise, that they married their SoulMates after all!

The magic isn't in my office or in the workshop. I can name others whose attention is still firmly glued to the wrongs being committed by their partners. They remain unhappy. Each one is waiting for the wife or husband to change so that the marriage can be good. Each is still convinced that his or her happiness is at the mercy of the mate. Some got tired of waiting. They have settled for a lifeless arrangement or they divorced. I wonder if they think their *real* soul mate is still waiting for them "out there."

It is time to expose the myth that is stealing the happiness of too many! Be it children's fairytales, deodorant advertising, song lyrics or movies, we are being bombarded with the lie that our happiness depends on finding the perfect mate. The repeated soul mate theme creates a cultural belief system that causes many to question their choice of spouse and others to be even less confident of making the "final" commitment to marriage. But success in marriage does not *primarily* depend on the partner chosen. Although my choice is certainly important, finding my SoulMate is *less* dependent on the person I choose and *more* dependent on who I am in that relationship. There is a greater chance of success when most of the elements are within my own control. *Everyone* is capable of changing himself or herself. *No one* is capable of changing another.

Success in marriage does not primarily depend on the partner chosen.

This means there are many men with whom I could build a successful, SoulMate marriage. There are many women with whom Jim could be blissfully happy. (Well, maybe just happy. I choose to reserve "blissfully" for his relationship with me!) One of the things that causes SoulMate love to thrive, however, is the commitment between one man and one woman for life. When SoulMates are emerging from the fertile soil of *this* marriage, why should I look elsewhere?

Everyone is capable of changing himself or herself. No one is capable of changing another.

You may be thinking, "Why don't you tell me how to change George? (Shirley?)" I'm sorry if you're disappointed, but hear me out. Most embark on a journey to *find* their soul mate in *another person*. Many of us begin marriage believing a soul mate has been found...someone to deliver happiness "'til death do us part."

The persons who have the greatest chance of success, however, are those who begin the journey with *this* understanding: "I am responsible for my own happiness. I will use every event, every encounter, and each hurt as an opportunity to learn about myself. I will be fully responsible for my own feelings and behavior. I am willing to be taught by the circumstances of my life. I will learn from others whose lives demonstrate the success I seek. I will *become* my partner's SoulMate, and in the *becoming*, trust that I will also *discover* my SoulMate in my spouse. The diamond mine in my own back yard will deliver the riches I seek. I choose to mine the treasure for myself, rather than leaving it for someone else to discover." Gay and Kathlyn Hendricks[4] said, "The most creative and evolved people we know are those who use every situation as an opportunity to learn about themselves…with a strong commitment to inquiring into yourself, the universe does not have to use catastrophe to wake you up."

You've no doubt noticed I'm emphasizing the point of personal responsibility quite heavily! The process of *becoming* SoulMates is, first of all, a journey of self-discovery and self-growth. For the journey to SoulMate love to be successful, it is essential that you be fully responsible for yourself, *whether or not* the *marriage* ultimately succeeds. Should the marriage have to end for reasons beyond your control, you'll have much less baggage to carry with you by fully using the opportunity for personal growth. And, the outcome may surprise you!

It's never too late to begin this journey. We wasted years being upset that we hadn't arrived at the destination—a SoulMate relationship—before we had even begun the journey of assuming responsibility for self-change! The conflicts we experienced in the beginning years, however, served as wise messengers, pushing us to find the puzzle pieces that enable *true* SoulMate love to flourish. Over and over again, SoulMates have been miraculously discovered in previously barren or war-zone relationships as one or both partners chose to begin the journey at the starting point: his or her own contribution to the marriage.

Jim and I savor our life together. We consider ourselves wealthy because we have the great privilege of living, working, and loving together. Our prayers were answered. The work paid off. Our home is full of peace. Our *favorite* times are just before we get up in the morning and just before we go to sleep. At those times we spoon. Or Jim gently says, "Come here." (This is his invitation to put my head on his chest with his arm around me.) We talk about our day. We share our feelings. We plan our goals. We support each other's dreams. We make each other laugh. We enjoy sweet, passionate lovemaking. It is rare for us to be even mildly irritated with each other; but when an issue pops up between us, we are confident that it won't last long. We will work it out respectfully, fairly, and

The diamond mine in my own back yard will deliver the riches I seek. I choose to mine the treasure for myself, rather than leaving it for someone else to discover.

The process of becoming *SoulMates is, first of all, a journey of self-discovery and self-growth.*

SoulMates have been discovered in previously barren or war-zone relationships as one or both partners chose to begin the journey at the starting point: his or her own contribution to the marriage.

quickly. We have a low tolerance for *anything* that disturbs the loving intimacy between us. Neither of us would even *consider* doing *anything* that would jeopardize the depth of loving we share. We are truly SoulMates for keeps.

It may seem as though we're asking you to launch out into space, not knowing where the journey might end. André Gide said, "One doesn't discover new lands without consenting to lose sight of the shore for a very long time."[5] If you haven't already, I challenge you to begin the journey. If you are willing to learn, to grow, to replace broken down relationship tools with gleaming new tools, and willing to stop demanding that your partner change and instead assume responsibility for changing yourself, you are about to embark on the diamond mining adventure of your life! Welcome to the growing number of couples who are staying and finding that the completed SoulMate puzzle reveals a romantic photo of the two of them embracing, surrounded by a field of diamonds!

Be willing to stop demanding that your partner change and instead assume responsibility for changing yourself.

A great marriage is not when the "perfect couple" comes together.
It is when an imperfect couple *learns* to enjoy their differences.
(Emphasis mine)

~ Dave Meurer[6]

If you won't plow in the cold, you won't eat at the harvest.
~ Proverbs 20:4

ENDNOTES

1   Davis, Michele Weiner, *The Divorce Remedy*, p. 57. New York: Simon & Schuster. 2001.

2   We are especially grateful to Jackie Barrile, who masterfully balanced individual and couple therapy with us. We hope this book repays her in part for the wealth of relationship "stuff" she taught us.

3   As we said in Chapter 1, there are certainly marriages where the abuse is so severe and the partner so undeniably unwilling to participate in growth, that the only sane option *is* divorce. In that case, the partner willing to do the work of mining will find the treasure buried even in this situation.

4   Hendricks, Gay & Kathlyn, *Conscious Loving*, p. 6. New York: Bantam Books. 1992.

5   Hallmark Cards, Kansas City, MO.

6   Meurer, Dave, *Daze of Our Wives*. New York: Bethany House. 2000.

Puzzle Piece #1:
A SoulMate
Point of View

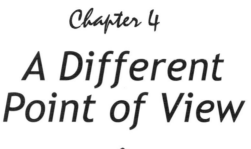

Chapter 4

A Different Point of View

*"Guess what?" exclaimed the white rat upon returning from the
   laboratory. "I've got the doc conditioned!"*
"How's that?" asked his friend.
"Well, every time I run through the maze he gives me something to eat!"

I had several meetings with Carl and Julie[1]. Sometimes they came together and other times they came separately. The adverse results of most of their communication methods were identified (Chapter 6). They heard how to deal with their anger without hurting each other (Chapter 12). We examined their distorted beliefs about men and women. The assignment was given to write out a blueprint of how they wanted their relationship to function.

Nothing helped. They kept rehashing the same complaints. Each insisted on staying focused on what the other one was doing "wrong."

It was all too familiar. Jim and I also used to blame and shame each other. Each of us thought the other's point of view was crazy. Now, Carl and Julie were doing it. Carl was sure he was right! No exceptions! Julie was sure he was wrong! No exceptions! They couldn't move past those opinions!

I thought about this for days. Jim and I had eventually accepted a fundamental truth that Carl and Julie clearly did *not* believe. I concluded that this truth is the foundation of *all* successful communication, the basis of every healthy relationship, especially one between SoulMates: *Each person has a different point of view and each person's point of view is valid.*

I believed this...*except* when it came to Jim! In the intimacy and vulnerability of our marriage, this truth was a tough one to acknowledge! During those early years, the solutions to tough issues were quite clear to me. It seemed impossible to acknowledge that Jim's point of view had any merit whatsoever!

Our points of view begin construction in the womb. The formation continues for the entire length of our lives. Some factors remain fixed, but most go through re-adjustments in response to education, increased maturity, personal experiences, and exposure to new ideas.

Let's look at some primary factors that create our points of view. John Gray wrote a best selling book called *Men are From Mars, Women are From Venus*[2], based on the most primary factor, gender. Although I believe men and women are more alike than different, I also believe that my point of view is enormously influenced by whether I'm male or female.

In my view, the second most influential factor is the family in which I grew up. Did Mom and Dad love each other? Were they glad they had kids? Had me? Did I have siblings? Were extended family members a big part of my life? How did we celebrate birthdays? Holidays? Was education important? Were we poor, middle class, or wealthy? The answers to these questions about my family, plus hundreds more, just *begin* to describe how the factor of my family frames my point of view.

Perhaps the third most influential factor is ethnicity. Caucasian? Oriental? Black? East Indian? American Indian? Mixed? Was my ethnicity accepted in my neighborhood? Was it judged as inferior? Superior? Do my eyes, nose, skin color, body shape, etc., match the ideal for my culture? Or not? Do I live in the country where my ethnicity is native? Or is my race a minority? What are the cultural traditions of my race? Are the women encouraged to be independent? Do men expect to be in charge? What is the traditional family structure?

One of my best friends is an African American woman—a corporate trainer who earns a six-figure salary. She has been stopped while picking up her expensive, sturdy luggage from the airport carousel by a person suspicious that she couldn't possibly be the rightful owner. As a white, middle-class woman, I will never have the same point of view as my friend, because I have not suffered the same experiences.

The fourth factor I consider foundational is my personality type. Am I gregarious? Do I love people and crowds? Am I shy? Prefer quiet? Do I love challenges? Am I competitive? Am I a bookworm? Do I love seeing a project through from beginning to end? Or do I prefer knowing I'm part of a supportive team? Am I happiest when I'm making decisions? Or am I most content following someone else's directions?

In addition to these four major categories are educational level, values, health status, current age, whether or not I have children, political leaning, birth order, geographical locale, experiences in previous relationships of all kinds, marital status, and religious traditions, to name a very few! All of these things influence how I perceive every single event or circumstance in my life.

By itself, having different points of view is not the problem. A variety of perspectives add interest, diversity, and creativity to our lives. It's what I *believe* about my point of view that makes relationships (especially the marriage relationship) easy, hard, or impossible.

If I believe the only reality is my own point of view, I am judging it as "right." If mine is "right," then there has to be a "wrong" point of view. In that case, I am standing so close to the wall constructed of all the factors of my life that I can't see a bigger picture (note illustration). Yet, if I take 10 steps back, or climb a ladder, I can still see through my "window," but I can also see that there are many other views. The moment I look around or over my personal wall, I must acknowledge that there is more to the world than I have seen previously, more truth than I personally know.

From my desk I can look out the window at the house across the street, the hill behind that, and the trees swaying with the wind. The view that I actually *see* is rectangular, framed by the walls around the window; yet I *know* there are other houses on the street. Beyond my street is another, bigger road that is one of the main arteries through my community. Beyond *that* is the freeway, all of Orange County, California, America, the world, and the universe. The parts I have seen personally, I *know* exist based on my experience. The rest I *believe* exist based on the reports of others whom I trust.

Every point of view comes from either personal experience or the report of another. That is why it is so easy for me to judge my point of view as "right." I've *experienced* it or *trusted* someone else's point of view. When circumstances trigger an upset, I've learned to first examine the point of view I've adopted from either my own or another's limited experience.

Even as an adult, I felt pressured to be at my parents' home for every major holiday. Sometimes I enjoyed being with the family, but at other times I resented being there and would act with passive aggressive defiance: "I'm sitting down on the outside, but inside, I'm still standing up!" Even so, I subconsciously adopted the point of view that in order for a holiday to be successful, all family members must be together.

In an effort to be a "good" family, I pressured our teens to attend all family gatherings. In order to escape the guilt trips I dumped on them, they came, but I soon noticed familiar signs. They were resentful, "sitting down on the outside, but standing up on the inside." Finally I told them, "I will always invite you and you are always wanted. When you come to family parties, however, I want to know that you're here because you choose to be, not because I forced you. From now on, your attendance is up to you." I wanted to save myself from the insecurity of wondering whether our children (and later grandchildren) were with us because they wanted to be, or because they felt obligated. As they became adults, we agreed to always be truthful and open about doing what we wanted to do on holidays. As a result, when we *are* together we have a wonderful time because everyone is there by choice.

Until last year, we spent every single Christmas day of our lives with either our parents or our children. Last Christmas, however, the children who live nearest to us wanted to have a leisurely pajama day with *their* children. No one wanted to rush through the morning and drive to someone else's house. This time, they wanted to stay home and just enjoy being individual families rather than an extended family. The only other possibility for being with family was our son and his family, who live about 300 miles away. They had been here for Thanksgiving, though, and were spending Christmas with her family.

Jim and I had a choice. We could have *judged* (based on all the previous Christmases of our lives) "This holiday is ruined! How selfish and rude! They are ungrateful, bad kids!" (If you knew our wonderful children, you'd know those statements are ludicrous!) Instead, we said to each other, "We are so glad that our children feel free to decide what is best for them and their families without fearing our hurt feelings or anger. We honor their choice. We are loved. We are welcome in their homes, but they deserve to have a life apart from us. We will plan something new for ourselves this Christmas."

On Christmas morning, Jim and I dressed in comfortable velour lounging suits. While Jim walked our dog, I put a little table in front of the fireplace and pulled up two stuffed chairs and plumped the pillows. The table was set with beautiful dishes and linens. We ate our favorite omelets, fresh fruit, rolls and coffee. Jim enjoyed the paper and I read a good novel. We talked. We savored the peaceful, unhurried pleasure of opening our presents in private. After the table was cleared and the kitchen cleaned up, we played several games. Puttering around for awhile suited us both. Later we decided to go to a movie, and then finished the day by indulging ourselves at a very nice restaurant. By bedtime, we agreed we'd had a wonderful, stress free day because we were willing to stretch our point of view to include a new possibility.

Have you ever fought over how to celebrate the holiday season? In *her* opinion, it isn't *really* Christmas or Hanukkah unless she goes to Grandma's house the night before and a religious service the next morning. In *his* mind, the night before is spent making Mom's favorite popcorn balls and cuddling by the fire. The next morning is leisurely spent in pajamas, opening gifts and fixing homemade waffles. Each of you has long-standing traditions that mean "this is what the holiday is all about." Is it inconceivable that it could be spent in any other way and still be meaningful? Your respective traditions are firmly entrenched in your points of view. It seems natural to judge yours as "good" and your partner's as "bad."

Holidays can raise difficult issues, but differences in how you believe your child should be reared can truly be explosive! Public or private school? Strictness or leniency? I know a family where the dad believes team sports are good for *every* child. The mom sees the individuality in their daughter and wants to give her dance or gymnastics lessons. There is a conflict over their differing points of view. The desire to do what's best for our children runs so deeply in most of us, it's even more difficult to consider another's point of view.

On a larger scope, a family or an organization may have this perspective: "Our way of being a family is best. Our church is the most perfect. Our view of the world is just the way it really is. Our politics are 'right.' Everyone's priorities should be like ours." This view narrows the field of acceptable friends and associates because the criteria for being peers is so narrow.

The more narrow the view, the more it is defined as prejudice. One of the great poets of our day, Maya Angelou, said, "Prejudice is a burden that confuses the past, threatens the future and renders the present inaccessible."[3] When prejudiced, we see through a very fixed, narrow window. Everything or everyone who doesn't fit a particular definition of "right" will be slapped with a label. This race is generally "smarter." That race is "slow" and "unmotivated." These people are "threatening." Those people are "dominating." That country is "backward." My country is the "best." That man is "evil." This woman is "crazy." His child is "bad."

Recently I discovered that one of the husbands attending our workshop is a rock musician. His group is in negotiations with a publishing company to produce a C.D. I *think* I hid my surprise when he demonstrated a high degree of commitment to building a good and lasting marriage! He was eager to learn good communication tools and interacted very sensitively with his wife! He exposed my judgments of rock musicians. I had separated myself from them by my judgment that "they" don't value committed relationships. By disproving my preconceived ideas, he did me the great favor of expanding my point of view.

Epictetus, the Roman Stoic philosopher, said "Men are disturbed not by things, but by the views they take of them." The trouble comes when I believe that my point of view is "right" or "better" and another's point of view is "wrong," "stupid," unenlightened," "misinformed," or "silly." Inherent in judgment are "better than" and "less than" points of view.

Whenever judgments (labels) are put on one's self, another person, a family, a community, a race, religion, or a country, much of one's view is blocked. A barrier is erected. And we all do it. Judgment can be counted on to create hurt, anger, or, at the very least, suspicion and separation.

Expanding my point of view begins by *noticing* my judgments. Once you know the signs, judgments are easy to spot. The moment I feel upset with someone (including myself) or something, or feel superior or inferior, I am judging. For example, I spent many years feeling uncomfortable because I was judging myself as inferior. That automatically meant that others were superior. Intimidation became a self-imposed source of torture!

The desire to do what's best for our children runs so deeply in most of us, it's even more difficult to consider another's point of view.

Men are disturbed not by things, but by the views they take of them.
~ Epictetus

Expanding my point of view begins by noticing my judgments.

So what is the solution? Am I suggesting there be no standards? No! I am suggesting that we learn to view ourselves and others through evaluation rather than judgment. Evaluation has no emotional "charge." It remains neutral. It says, "This works, this doesn't," or "That may work for him, but this works better for me," or "That choice has consequences I don't want to experience. I believe this choice will result in what I want."

We must learn to view ourselves and others through evaluation rather than judgment.

A client and I have been discussing her tendency to judge herself harshly. She admitted that no matter how severely she judged herself, her unwanted behaviors did not go away. I suggested she begin to experiment with evaluation, rather than judgment. This week she began to sew her niece's wedding dress. After basting the bodice together she noticed that the lining was turned the wrong way. In the past she would have wasted a lot of energy by being upset with herself...even disgusted. Instead, she just looked at it and thought, "I made a mistake." Then she calmly removed the basting and corrected it. We celebrated her step toward greater self-respect as she resisted self-judgment for her imperfection as a seamstress.

I was shocked when my counselor first challenged me to stop thinking in terms of black or white. I thought there were only "right" and "wrong," "bad" and "good." She encouraged me to see that there are often many successful ways to do something, not just one. That concept expanded my view considerably and was one of the primary changes that made it possible for me to begin reconciling my differences with Jim.

Evaluation rather than judgment is the clear choice when it comes to viewing my own behavior. Did my action create an unpleasant result? Then next time I'll do it differently. It may be helpful to think in terms of neutrality rather than judgment when it comes to others. A fundamental belief that makes it possible to be evaluative or neutral with myself and others is: Life is a school that gives the maximum opportunity to learn. Every experience, every choice, every consequence is part of the curriculum. This belief enables me to meet others on a level playing field. I am not better than or worse than anyone. Whatever they have done or not done, whether like me or different from me, they are in their school and I am in mine. No school is better than, or worse than any other.

Life is a school that gives the maximum opportunity to learn. Every experience, every choice, every consequence is part of the curriculum.

Perhaps aloud or just in your thoughts, you are labeling your husband as "dumb" for not understanding that Tommy is too timid and insecure to enjoy competing on the kiddy soccer team. "Why can't he see that Tommy would be miserable?" Identifying judgment is the first step *away* from judgment.

The next step is to change your internal language about the issue. "John must have a good reason for wanting Tommy to play on the team. I trust that his point of view is based on evidence that is valid to him. I want to understand." Now *that* is a *giant* leap toward neutrality.

Then, ask John, without challenge or sarcasm, but with *neutral* sincerity, "Would you please tell me all the reasons why you think this is a good idea? I want to understand your point of view." Chances have just increased astronomically that he will reciprocate with a willingness to hear your point of view. In that environment, a fair exchange of perspectives is more apt to happen. The result could be a decision made together after considering all the factors brought to the table by *both* parties. When that happens, Tommy is a lucky child, indeed, because each parent is willing to combine the rich diversity of viewpoints to arrive at a decision both parents can support.

Suppose you catch yourself thinking your wife is "insensitive" (a label) because she was too tired to respond to your romantic advances. Hurrah! You've caught yourself in judgment!

Next, you shift your view around: "I wonder why she's so tired? I haven't really paid attention to the number of responsibilities she's taken on lately. How can I support her in taking better care of herself?"

How do you imagine your wife would respond if you said to her (without ulterior motives), "I'm concerned about you. You seem very stressed and tired lately. Would you tell me the top three things that weigh you down? Let's see if we can brainstorm ways to take some of the pressure off of you." Chances are she'll fall into your arms in gratitude for noticing and caring.

Let's apply this to a more serious issue. What if your husband beats you, or your wife has an out-of-control spending addiction? What then? Judgment would shout, "He is bad! He is wrong!" or "She is ruining my life!" It may be challenging, but the goal is to simply evaluate that this relationship is not safe as it is now. You may need to protect yourself physically or legally until your partner agrees to get some help. You are not forcing them to change. In fact, his or her behavior doesn't *have* to change at all. To change or not is up to them. It *must* change, however, *if* they want you to participate in a relationship with them. *You* are in charge of what is safe for you. This is evaluation. This is being responsible for *you* rather than judging *him* or *her*.

Judgment comes from a limited point of view. You did not experience all the factors that frame his or her world. It may be that your partner's behavior makes perfect sense and if you could see from his or her point of view, you would understand. That doesn't alter the reality that he or she must live with the consequences of choosing those behaviors—which may include the loss of relationship with you.

It isn't discipline that hurts children or incites their anger. It's the judgment of them that tears apart their self worth.

Judgment creates a lot of pain in parent-child relationships, as well. It isn't discipline that hurts children or incites their anger. It's the judgment of them as "bad" or "a disappointment" or "stupid" that tears apart the fragile fabric of their self worth. Recently I was thrilled to discover the work of Dr. James Jones.[4]

In my opinion, he does an outstanding job of teaching parents how to encourage children to learn self-honoring skills and attitudes without the destructive weapon of judgment. When a system is set up to teach children lessons of responsibility *with neutrality*, the parents are freed to express love lavishly to the children without the pollution of harsh emotions many of us associate with "punishment."

When I was about four years old, the best friend of my older sister was brutally raped and killed. At the time, I was aware only of the dark heaviness that pervaded the atmosphere. Later I learned the full story. The entire community was outraged, deeply hurt and vindictive. With supernatural knowing, the father found the murderer of his 13-year-old and talked him into surrendering to prevent some in our little community from tracking him down and killing him. He was tried, convicted, and eventually executed, but during his incarceration, this bereaved father visited him several times. In the midst of almost unbearable agony, he recognized this event as the school bell calling him to a depth of personal growth that we wouldn't even wish on an enemy. In spite of this dad's very human impulse to judge this man as a monster, he forgave him as a way to liberate himself from bitterness. From a place of evaluation, however, the crime still required that the attacker face a legal consequence. For the remainder of this father's life, hundreds of persons hungry for greater meaning in their lives sought him out as a spiritual mentor.

Fortunately, most of us will never be challenged with a choice that difficult between judgment and evaluation. Are you willing to identify your judgments of your spouse, another person, family or race? What if you then placed the fingers of each hand on the window of your mind and stretched it a little bit more? An expanded view may reveal new possibilities. Each time you go through the process of moving from judgment to evaluation or neutrality, you have contributed to greater peace in your self, marriage, family, community and world.

Corner Puzzle Piece #1:
Accept your partner's point of view as valid.

SoulMate love can only be fostered by this belief:
"We each have a valid point of view.
Neither of us is wrong. We are both right.
I will try to understand the perspective of my partner.
I will share my perspective in a neutral way, understanding that my
viewpoint is limited. I am willing to consider new options.
We will find a win-win solution."

Attachment says we are certain we know what is best.
It does not allow the humility that opens us to something larger.

~ Anodea Judith[5]

Judge not that ye be not judged.

~ Matthew 7:1
King James Version

ENDNOTES

1   The incident is true. The names, of course, are fictitious!
     Identifying distorted beliefs and creating a marriage blueprint are
     covered in *How to Stay Married & Love It Even More! Completing the
     Puzzle of a SoulMate Marriage.*

2   Gray, John, *Men Are From Mars, Women Are From Venus,* New York:
     Harper Collins Publishing. 1992.

3   Angelou, Maya, *All God's Children Need Traveling Shoes*, p. 155.
     New York: Random House. 1997.

4   His tapes, book, and seminar schedule can be found at
     www.familyhood.com or requested by calling 1-800-349-2543. In
     addition to being very instructive, his tapes are hilariously funny!

5   Judith, Anodea, *Sacred Centers Opera Omnia*, p. 11. Ostara Ed:
     Volume 24, Chapter 92. 1991.

Puzzle Piece #2:
SoulMate Communication

Chapter 5

Why Can't We Communicate?

*The simple failure to acknowledge what the other person says
explains much of the friction in our lives.*

~ Michael P. Nichols, Ph.D.[1]

Communication is simple, right? Each word has a meaning. Some words are "nicer" than others, some are more erudite or the meanings more complex. But when you string them together in a sentence, it becomes communication, right? Well, let's take a closer look...

Have you ever had this experience? Your wife is upset about something the teacher said to Suzie. She tells you about it, repeating every word of the exchange and describing how upset Suzie is. Your wife rattles off a list of things she wants to tell Suzie's teacher and her principal. You believe that your wife is over-reacting and, thinking that you are contributing a "rational voice" to the situation, begin explaining to your wife what you think the teacher meant and why Suzie shouldn't be upset. Does she respond with gratitude for your calm and levelheaded assessment? Hardly! You thought you were being helpful and she reacts by assigning you to the enemy's camp. Now she's not just mad at the teacher, but unjustly, upset with you as well.

What happened in this exchange? You care about your wife and child. You contributed something you thought would be helpful to the situation. But your words were interpreted by your wife to mean, "I don't care what you feel. The teacher has a valid reason for what she said. Understanding the situation is more important to me than you and Suzie." So, of course, her response was anger, delivered with words similar to these: "You don't care about Suzie's feelings or mine! The moment I open up to you, you take the other person's side. It will be a long time before I share anything important with you again. Suzie and I will have to work this out alone!"

Or, how about this? You and your husband are looking forward to having friends over Friday for an evening of dinner and cards. On the morning of the occasion, you ask your hubby, "Can you be sure to be home at 5:30 p.m. to help with the kids and other preparations?" He cheerfully replies, "Sure thing!" and walks out the door.

At 5:45 p.m. his car pulls into the garage. You think, "He's late, but I think we can still have everything ready on time. I won't make a big deal out of it." He strolls in, throws his coat over the sofa back and begins asking the kids about their day. You're in the kitchen trying to prepare dinner for children, *and* complete a complicated recipe for the adult meal *and* realizing the dining table has homework assignments spread all over it. Inside these words are beginning to brew, "I *told* him I needed his help tonight. What is he *doing*? He expects me to do it all. He's just another kid." And next thing you know, depending on your reaction of choice, you're either yelling at him and the kids like a boot camp sergeant or sulking like a first-class martyr.

What is obvious to you may not *be obvious to your spouse.*

Why? You *asked* for help. He *agreed*. And yet the brightly anticipated evening was dulled by a film of resentment and hurt. You assumed the message was straightforward enough. You asked, "Would you help?" But what you're *sure* he knew you *meant* was, "While I fix the meal, would you notice what else needs doing and do it? The house will need a last minute pick up. The kids will need directions for what they may and may not do while we have guests. Oh, and, when that's done, check in and see what else you could do to help me." It all seems very obvious to you. You conclude that he *pretends* to be the cooperative and helpful man around the house, but when the chips are down, you just can't depend on him.

Here's what happened from *his* point of view..."I was really looking forward to our evening with friends. I'm always happy to pitch in and help. I think we're a good team. She's a great cook and I'm proud of her and our home. When I walked in the door, everything looked under control to me. I was home, ready to do whatever was needed. I thought catching up with the kids about their day at school was keeping them out of her way. I thought she'd let me know when she needed anything else. I was surprised when she started yelling at all of us. None of us deserve to be treated that way. It sure dampened my enjoyment of the evening. I don't know what she wants from me! I don't want to have friends over anymore if it means she'll get so uptight. It's not worth it."

It took us years, but we eventually began to get the message that there is more to communication than just stringing words together. Most of us have experienced situations similar to these two examples. In fact, there was a time when I was sure that Jim and I were speaking two different languages. In my extreme frustration, I would become sarcastic and condescending, unable to *believe* that he didn't understand what I was saying or what I meant. It was so *obvious*! How *dense* could he be? My eventual conclusion was that he didn't *want* to understand. In fact, I believed that anyone would have to be deliberately *trying* to misunderstand in order to come up with messages that were so distorted from what I intended. And he said things that were so hurtful. No matter how he explained later, I *knew* what he *really* meant.

～

Be sure you are both looking at the same "game plan."

Jim: I was discouraged and driven to the end of my rope by our constant misunderstandings. When Nancy became sarcastic and treated me like a dunce, I either exploded or withdrew in self-righteous martyrdom. We were both trying so hard. It felt like we were trying to put a bicycle together with all the parts on the floor around us, but she was working off of one set of instructions and I had different ones. I *knew* I was in the right, but Nancy was equally sure that *she* was right. At the time, we didn't *know* that we were using two different sets of directions, *neither* of which was accurate or reliable. The set up could be counted on to create disaster.

～

A skit:

Nancy: I'd like to go shopping this afternoon.

Jim: Oh?

Nancy: (To herself) He said that in such a strange tone of voice. The look on his face was suspicion. I'll bet he doesn't trust me with the checkbook! He has *no* reason not to trust me!

Nancy: What's your problem?!!!

Jim: Well, nothing really. I was just afraid you wanted me to go with you, and I hate shopping.

Nancy: (chagrined) Oh.

∽

We each come with a past. In the previous chapter I illustrated how our *beliefs about* our different points of view form the foundation that can either hinder or help the development of a successful SoulMate relationship. Those same thousands and thousands of experiences, cataloged in our memories, also form invisible *filters* between the sender and the receiver through which each communication passes. (Note illustration.) The meaning of a communication being sent is often distorted, and sometimes given a new meaning by the time it travels through the filters of the communication receiver.

Getting the wrong message causes hurt and anger.

In the case presented by the skit:

I was once the head of a small division within a small company. The company's overhead expenses were far more than the president thought they should be. Money was leaking out as if it were going through a sieve. The financial records of my division were kept separately. Although I kept meticulous records and my division was actually *making* money for the company, the president kept insinuating that we were costing him money! I eventually realized that he was a genius at building a business but *not* a bookkeeper. He really didn't understand how to read the financial data he had in front of him. Even so, it hurt badly to be falsely accused, even if only by innuendo. In my mind, my integrity was being questioned. That hurt. It set the stage for me to be hypersensitive in any situation where I might not be trusted to use money reasonably. So when Jim said, "Oh" with a funny look on his face, I immediately jumped to the conclusion that he didn't trust me and I was angry.

∽

Jim: When my first wife said she wanted to go shopping, what she really meant was she wanted me to *take* her shopping. I detest everything about shopping…giving up something else I'd rather be doing, finding a parking place, fighting the crowds, walking, standing, getting the attention of a clerk, etc. Because Dixie loved to shop, a simple 30-minute excursion could turn into a two-hour event. The moment Nancy announced she wanted to go shopping, inwardly I was groaning and bracing myself for an ordeal while trying to think of several good excuses why I couldn't go just then.

～

Neither of us received an accurate message. Before we had received the message, each of us had distorted its meaning because of previous experience filters, so both of us were upset. One simple rule and another simple communication skill avoids these pitfalls.

Rule: *Never assume* you know the meaning of an act, word, tone of voice.

Communication skill: *Perception Check.*

In the situation we described, an appropriate perception check might be, "I notice that you have a strained look on your face and your tone of voice was tentative. I'm wondering if you're nervous about trusting me with the checkbook. Is that what you're thinking?"

～

Jim: And I could have quickly said, "No! Not at all. I trust you. I'm just afraid you want me to go with you? Do you?"

～

And I'd answer, "No! I just wanted you to know my plans."

Whew! Isn't it amazing that we send and receive so many messages every day without incident? It's also easy to understand why so many messages become garbled somewhere between the sender and the receiver.

The first way to perception check is for the *receiver* to repeat in his or her own words the message the receiver heard, and then ask the sender if the meaning received was actually what was meant. This will go over best if done in a neutral, inquiring tone of voice, which conveys your desire to understand. This will probably be your tone of voice and manner *unless* you have *already* jumped to an unfavorable assumption about what was meant. If the message sent sounded hurtful, and, after perception checking, you confirm that it was indeed intended to be hurtful, stay tuned. Help is coming in future chapters.

Some ways of Perception Checking if you're the *receiver* of the message:

"What I just heard was _____. Is that what you meant?"

"I think I was just told _____. Is that accurate?"

"You would like me to _____. What else can you tell me?"

The second way to perception check is done by the *sender* of the message. For instance:

"I'm going shopping but will be home by 5 p.m. I'd appreciate it if you would turn the oven on to 350 degrees at 4:30 p.m. Now, would you repeat back to me what I just said so I can be sure you heard me accurately?"

Some other ways to Perception Check if you're the *sender* of the message:

"Just to be sure I've said this clearly, would you repeat back to me your understanding of my words?"

"It's important to me that we don't suffer through a misunderstanding, so would you please tell me what you just heard me say?"

Suggested exercise:

1. Set an intention, (or write a note to remind you) to notice a minimum of one time each day this week when you are assuming the meaning of a look, a tone of voice, or certain words. When you catch yourself assuming, Perception Check with the sender of the message.

   What was originally said or done?

   What did you assume was meant?

   When you Perception Checked, was your assumption accurate, partially accurate, or totally out of left field?

   What was actually meant?

2. At least one time each day this week, ask the intended receiver of your message to repeat back to you their understanding of the message you sent. Was it received accurately?

Perception Checking is a great place to immediately begin practicing a useful and positive communication skill. It may seem like a minor or even dumb thing to do if you're experiencing extreme stress in your relationship. You might be asking, "How can this lowly little skill help?" The course of a jetliner is changed, however, by adjusting one small degree at a time. Oprah Winfrey

Perception Checking is a great place to immediately begin practicing a useful and positive communication skill.

occasionally featured a strategist on her show who specializes in helping people change their lives.[2] He said the key to making big life changes is to do one thing differently today than you did yesterday. If your relationship needs a lot of work, it could be overwhelming to look at the enormity of the task; but please don't underestimate this common, deceptively simple helper. We predict you will have a great deal of respect for the power of Perception Checking after just a few experiences.

Corner Puzzle Piece #2:
Communicate in ways that get the desired result.

**"I am developing effective communication skills
with the simple practice of Perception Checking."**

Communication has not taken place
until the message received
is identical to the message sent.
~ Jim and Nancy Landrum

Reliable communication permits progress.
~ Proverbs 13:17

ENDNOTES

1   Nichols, Michael P., Ph.D. *The Lost Art of Listening*, p.115. New York: The Guilford Press. 1995.

2   Bill O'Hanlon, *Do One Thing Different,* Morrow, William & Co. 1999.

Chapter 6

Playing Detective

*Nothing is more difficult
than trying to find something wrong with yourself.*

~ Unknown

I love to garden! For me, gardening is a form of meditation, a place to express myself creatively, and a way to connect to the stability, beauty, and support of this Earth. Unfortunately, we live in a place where the soil is predominantly clay. It's very nutrient rich, but when dry, has the consistency of concrete. Let's look at a possible scene, given these conditions.

A beautiful Autumn day arrives. I decide to dig a trench along the 30 feet of weathered wood fence in our back yard. This is where I plant sweet peas every year. They make a spectacularly lavish and fragrant display from March until July. I can hardly wait! I borrow a little plastic hoe from my five-year-old grandson's sandbox toys and begin to *try* to dig up the dirt. The dirt is un-cooperative. The handle of the hoe keeps bending. It hurts when I hack away at the hard soil. I don't like being on my knees so long. The sun is hot and I am tired. After only a few minutes, I'm discouraged and decide to quit.

The next day is also lovely. My energy and enthusiasm are renewed. I am a little put out with the plastic hoe, so I rummage around in the garage and find a large, metal hoe. The handle is missing, but it should work better than the plastic one. I go after the dirt again. It's hard to hold on to the narrow metal neck of the hoe. Every time I raise it up and

♥ 48 ♥

bring it down onto the dirt, the tremor of the metal hitting the hard clay soil travels through my fingers, wrist, elbow and shoulder. It *does* work a little better than the plastic hoe, but my knees are still hurting and my wrist, which has always been weak, is going to be sore tomorrow. So after only an hour, and just a few inches of progress, I again quit.

~

If this scenario were really a true one, you'd have to question the level of my intelligence. In reality, I grab my favorite small shovel…just the right size so the amount of dirt that the shovel brings up is not too heavy for me to lift and turn over. In a couple of hours I have the full 30 feet turned over, mulch mixed in and the seeds planted. A few days later the curly little seedlings begin climbing the fence, preparing to keep us dazzled with their lavish colors. Soon we are stepping out the back door, or looking through the back window, to the visual feast of 30 feet of 8-foot high vines *full* of frilly white, pink, lavender, magenta, and purple flowers. All my friends, family and neighbors love the bouquets I give to share the wealth.

In the physical world, it is easy for us to determine whether a chosen tool is the best one for the job. A large wrench is traded for a smaller one. The screw head requires a Phillips screwdriver rather than a standard one. One key doesn't fit so the other key must be the one to unlock the door. We learn through immediate feedback which tool to use for *this* job, which one is needed for *that* job. The process of trial, feedback and correction is so constant and familiar that, for the most part, we almost *unconsciously* cooperate with course adjustments that enable the job to be accomplished.

In the world of communication, however, most of us haven't learned to evaluate the tools we use according to whether or not they give us the result we want. Was what I said accurately understood? Is the end result of this communication a better relationship or hurt feelings and greater emotional distance? Did the communication tools I used enable us to resolve an issue with mutual satisfaction, or is one of us winning while the other one feels steamrollered?

When Jim continued to do the same things over and over again that deeply hurt me, I just figured *he* was the problem. He was *dense*. He didn't *hear* me. So I said it louder. And with more sarcasm. I moved from the child-sized plastic hoe to the metal hoe with a missing handle. It took *years* and lots of help from a therapist before I finally began to question my communication tools rather than blaming Jim for not "getting it." It didn't occur to me to evaluate the effective-

In the world of communication, most of us haven't learned to evaluate the tools we use according to whether or not they give us the result we want.

ness of yelling and sarcasm. They *never* got the job done. They *always* created more hurt, more distance, and more of an impasse.

❧

Jim: I kept telling Nancy that the louder she yelled, the less I heard her. For months after she quit yelling, however, I continued to react to her using my own defective communication tools. I would communicate my hurt and frustration by withdrawing or by interjecting "hopeless talk" into our attempts to resolve an issue. "Hopeless talk" took the focus of attention *off* resolving the issue and on to poor me. I would say things like, "I can't think on my feet as well as you. You're better at talking than I am. I never win these arguments. Why try?"

Then Nancy would begin propping me up so we could resume our attempts to resolve the issue. She'd say, "You were doing great. You're expressing yourself very well. Please stay in here with me so we can settle this. Please don't leave now." So I would either be pacified by her begging and reassurance, and stay a while longer, or I would get up in a self-righteous huff and go hit a bucket of golf balls. Either way, my communication tools were contributing to the *problem* rather than to a *solution*.

❧

Daniel Goleman in his book, *Emotional Intelligence*,[1] cited the research work of John Gottman, a University of Washington psychologist. In interviews with more than 2,000 couples over a period of 20-plus years, Gottman found that "corrosive conversation takes its toll. Contempt, disgust and personal attack can trigger 'flooding.' Flooded husbands or wives are so overwhelmed by their partner's negativity that they are swamped by dreadful, out-of-control feelings. They can no longer hear without distortion or respond with clear-headedness; they find it hard to organize their thinking, so they fall back on primitive reactions—shouting and screaming."

Gottman goes on to say, "Fighting can be damaging, but fleeing can be more pernicious, particularly when the 'flight' is a retreat into stony silence... Habitual stonewalling is devastating to a relationship because it cuts off all possibility of working out disagreements."

At the end of this chapter, we've compiled a comprehensive list of "defective" communication tools. It's important to remember that *every time* one of these tools is used, you or your partner is attempting to communicate something important, valid and necessary to the development of the

Habitual stonewalling is devastating to a relationship because it cuts off all possibility of working out disagreements.

If defective communication tools continue to be used, the heart of love and intimacy that was once shared will wither and eventually die.

relationship. The problem, however, is that *these* tools do *not* build a relationship, they do *not* resolve issues, they do *not* assist in finding fair compromises. That's why we label them "defective." What they very dependably *do* is increase hurt feelings, defensiveness, humiliation, anger and emotional distance. Given that feedback, each of these defective tools falls somewhere on a scale of relationship abuse. Sarcasm may be a one or a two on the scale of one to ten while physical violence or unfaithfulness rate tens, but they are *all* ineffective and damaging. If these defective communication tools continue to be used, the relationship may be maintained as a practical arrangement if neither of you choose to leave, but the heart of love and intimacy that was once shared will wither and eventually die.

In our workshops, we ask the participants to name the feelings that result when any of the defective communication tools on the list are used against them—when they are addressed with sarcasm, criticized, called by a belittling name, verbally attacked, or their partner retreats in silence. Here are just a few of their answers:

"defensive, hurt, angry, resentful, vindictive, lonely, isolated, abandoned, unimportant, embarrassed, ashamed, hopeless, helpless, less respectful of myself and my partner, and less trusting."

To illustrate the point even further, here is a skit that demonstrates another result of using these tools: issue discussions deteriorate and lose their focus, making resolution impossible. The setting for this skit is in the car on the way to a marriage workshop.

(The skit is fictional, but we used to fight just like this)

She: (Gets a pen out of her purse...looks pointedly over at him) Well, did you bring a pen?

He: No.

She: (With knowing superiority) I knew you wouldn't bring a pen.

He: What's the big deal?

She: (Sarcastically) If you really wanted to learn anything here today, you would have at least brought a pen to take notes.

He: (Defensively) I want to learn! I'm here aren't I?

She: Yeah, you're here about like my father was. Your body's here but you're not really with me.

He: (Louder) Why are you bugging me? You're becoming a real nag, just like your mother. No wonder your dad is so quiet. She's always criticizing him.

She: (Emphatically) I am *not* like my mother and I resent you bringing her into this!

He: (Gathering steam) Just like today, on the way here, telling me how to drive…"slow down," "turn here," "stop!" Like I'm a little kid who doesn't know anything!

She: (With exaggerated patience) You *know* we wouldn't have gotten here on time if I hadn't been reading the map.

He: Oh, yeah! The Great Map Reader! Hah! You're the one that got us lost on the way to the airport for our honeymoon trip. We missed our plane and had to spend the night in the airport, of all places.

She: (Subdued and discouraged) You're never going to forgive me for that, are you?

He: All I know is that Susan would never belittle me the way you do!

(Silence.)

She: Maybe we'd both be better off if you had married *her*!

(Huffy silence, obviously hurt. He reaches out to put his arm around her.)

She: Don't touch me!

(He folds his arms across his chest and slouches. She sniffs and says self-righteously) Let's just try to forget this and go inside and learn something. Lord knows, you need it!

Every time Jim and I perform this skit it *always* provokes *lots* of laughter. Many of us have had the experience of fighting to exhaustion, and, later, not be able to remember what started it. What was so important that we had to verbally beat each other into submission over it? Was anything accomplished? A resounding "YES!" The accomplishment was *more* damage—wounds inflicted on top of previous wounds. Anything resolved? "NO!" In fact, the original issues have been magnified and compounded by the emotional devastation that now surrounds them.

The object of "discussing the issue" is to bring about a satisfactory resolution in such a way that the couple's trust and intimacy are *increased*. Another way to say it is that we want the discussion to rise toward a successful resolution.

This skit illustrates the nosedive that inevitably takes place when defective communication tools are used. The use of each defective tool is followed by the use of the next one until the "discussion" crashes and burns. *No one* wins.

It isn't necessary to do the whole range of defective communication tools before experiencing a loss of intimacy. Every use of even one damages intimacy and reduces the possibility of SoulMate love. The accumulated use of many of these can kill all desire for relationship. In contrast, replacing these defective tools with healthy communication tools will restore intimacy and rebuild SoulMate love. Gary Chapman[2] says, "Screaming is a learned phenomenon and it can be unlearned." So can the use of every other defective communication tool.

In Chapter 15 we take another look at this skit to see exactly what each person was *really* trying to communicate, and *how* it could be communicated differently so that the relationship becomes more intimate, more healing, and more of a refuge for both partners. In the meantime, check off the defective communication tools that you use in your marriage, either habitually or occasionally. You can also check off the ones your partner uses as well. Just for fun, try to identify a minimum of three more defective tools in your column than in your partner's column.

And remember, the point is to do this from a place of evaluation, rather than judgment. Please don't make yourself or your partner bad or wrong for communicating in these destructive ways. You may not have known that other, more effective tools exist. We didn't.

One thousand years ago, one man, using a stone hoe, could work all day from dawn to dusk and only produce a meager crop to barely sustain his family. One hundred years ago, one man, using a mule and a hand-guided plow, could work all day from dawn to dusk and produce enough of a crop to feed his family and sell some to his neighbors. Today, one man, using a tractor with a plow, a disk, an automatic seeder and an irrigation system, putting the same amount of time into the job, can produce enough to feed his own family plus hundreds or even thousands of others. The only difference among these three men is the quality of their tools. Each man was doing the most he could do with the tools he had.

Evaluate your tools. It may be time to trade in some of them.

Both of you have been doing the very best you could do using the tools you have. Now it's time to evaluate your tools. It may be time to trade in some of them. In Chapter 7, we share an explanation for why we communicate in ways that don't work. In Chapter 8, we'll describe the five levels of communication and tell you which levels nourish SoulMate love. We'll also give you two effective and simple communication tools to replace two of the most common defective communication tools: the use of absolutes and the accusatory "you" in a sentence. The two new replacement tools will build on the process begun by

Perception Checking. By the way, have you discovered for yourself the value of Perception Checking? Keep practicing!

Corner Puzzle Piece #2:
Communicate in ways that get the desired result.

"I am taking a giant step toward a SoulMate relationship
as I identify my defective communication tools,
and set the intention to trade them in for new ones."

Insanity: Doing the same thing over and over again
and expecting a different result!

The intelligent man is always open to new ideas.
In fact, he looks for them.

~ Proverbs 18:15

Defective Communication Tools

I do:	Partner does:		I do:	Partner does:	
☐	☐	Use *always* and *never*	☐	☐	Use accusatory *you*
☐	☐	Give unwanted advice	☐	☐	Use the silent treatment
☐	☐	Withdraw with hurt feelings	☐	☐	Use sarcasm
☐	☐	Blame	☐	☐	Make excuses
☐	☐	Heap on shame/guilt	☐	☐	Talk hopeless talk
☐	☐	Run from conflict	☐	☐	Act like a martyr
☐	☐	Condemn in vague generalizations	☐	☐	Slam doors
☐	☐	Sidestep issue (i.e., change subject)	☐	☐	Throw things
☐	☐	Insist on being the leader	☐	☐	Call derogatory names
☐	☐	Insist on being the follower	☐	☐	Bring up old business
☐	☐	Emotionally disconnect	☐	☐	Defend
☐	☐	Compare spouse to another	☐	☐	Use hurtful humor
☐	☐	Jump from issue to issue	☐	☐	Embarrass in public
☐	☐	Use disparaging tone of voice	☐	☐	Yell, scream, rage
☐	☐	Use threats in an attempt to control	☐	☐	Lie
☐	☐	Act condescending/self-righteous	☐	☐	Get others to take sides
☐	☐	Act subservient/passive	☐	☐	Jab with "zingers"
☐	☐	Punish by withholding affection	☐	☐	Use intimidation
☐	☐	Use disparaging physical gestures	☐	☐	Use physical violence
☐	☐	Threaten or flirt with infidelity	☐	☐	Force sex
☐	☐	Be unfaithful	☐	☐	Practice an addiction

1. Do an anatomy of the skit or one of your own recent issue "discussions." Identify the defective communication tools used in the skit or by you. List them.

2. What were your partner's feelings and behaviors in reaction to your defective communication tools? What was the outcome of the "discussion?" Describe.

Directed energy causes change.
To have integrity, we must recognize
that our choices bring consequences,
and that we cannot escape responsibility for the consequences,
not because they are imposed by some external authority,
but because they are inherent in the choices themselves.

~ Starhawk[3]

The fool who provokes his family to anger and resentment will finally have nothing worthwhile left.

~ Proverbs 11:2

ENDNOTES

1   Goleman, Daniel, *Emotional Intelligence*, New York: Bantam Books, a division of Bantam Doubleday Dell. 1995.

2   Gary Chapman is a marriage enrichment speaker and author whose books include *Toward a Growing Marriage* and *The Five Love Languages: How to Express Heartfelt Commitment to Your Mate.* He is quoted here by Art Toalston, *The Baptist Messenger*, "Marriage Works by Communicating, Not Running," October 5, 1995.

3   Starhawk, *Dreaming the Dark,*. New York: Bantam Books. 1997 Second Edition.

Chapter 7

Am I a Duck
or a Chicken?

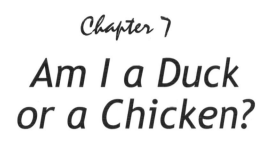

Children are natural mimics who act like their parents...
despite every effort to teach them good manners.

~ **Anonymous**

Do you watch the Discovery Channel? Have you seen a program about a phenomenon called "imprinting?" Some birds, as soon as they hatch, believe they are the progeny of whatever living thing they see moving near them. That image is imprinted on the bird's brain. For example, a duckling may imprint to a mother hen, and forever after, believes itself to be a chicken, trying in all ways to duplicate the behaviors and characteristics of its "mother." This situation precipitates some antics that may look hilarious to us, but must be very baffling to the duckling and, perhaps, annoying to the hen.

Fortunately, in most cases, the image of its own parent is the first one the bird sees, so order is maintained as ducklings learn how to be ducks from their mother duck, and chicks learn how to be chickens from their mother hen.

Most of us experience something similar to imprinting with our parents. Natalie Angier wrote a column for *The New York Times* titled, "Analysis: Parental Influence." She reviewed research verifying that behaviors that duplicate our parents' are very difficult to change. The eternal debate, of course, is whether those behaviors are passed on to us genetically or because, for so many years, we shared the environment with our parents. The researchers indicate it is a combination of both. However it happens, there are thousands of beliefs, behaviors, attitudes, and communication practices picked up in childhood that we bring into adult relationships.

This is usually a mixed blessing. The things we are the *most* determined to do differently from our parents insidiously sneak into our actions and our words. It often seems that the harder we try to do something differently, the more tenaciously we practice the behavior. It's as though we are trying to be ourselves, a duck, but the behavior keeps coming through as a chicken. We are grateful, however, when the imprinting, or training, shows up in ways that benefit us—like balancing the check book regularly, just as Mom did, or cleaning the yard tools before putting them away, just as Dad did.

Angier, in her article, states, "...parents could be masters of so-called phenotypic cloning: *they impress their ways of doing things so firmly on their offspring that the behaviors, or phenotypes, practically look inherited in their strength,*" (emphasis mine) and, "...scientists propose that many animals, including humans, transmit features of themselves from one generation to the next, not simply by passing along their chromosomes, but *by training their offspring to behave as they do.*"[1]

Some deliberate training takes place. If we were fortunate, our parents taught us some of the social niceties that make life more graceful. In Western culture, you have it easier if you know how to eat with a fork, say "please" and "thank you," and bathe frequently.

Most training, however, takes place without conscious deliberation. It really doesn't do any good to say, "Do as I say, not as I do." We can't help but duplicate a large portion of what was both demonstrated or done to us, either useful or dysfunctional!

When I was 16 and had just received my driver's license, I was entrusted to drive my mom's new Chevrolet. I turned left in front of an on-coming car and although no one was hurt, the right front fender of her car took a beating. Our town was small, so a friend saw what happened and called my parents. I was *so* humiliated and sure that I was in *big* trouble.

While waiting for the adults to do whatever needed doing, I looked in the rear view mirror and saw my dad's car pulling up behind me. He walked up to the driver's side, leaned into my open window and quietly asked, "What happened, honey?"

I was braced for anger, but completely undone by his kindness. I burst into tears and poured out my story. His attitude that day told me two essential things: my safety was more important to him than the car and I was still loved when I made a mistake.

The things we were the most determined to do differently from our parents insidiously sneak into our actions and our words.

We can't help but duplicate a large portion of what was both demonstrated or done to us, either useful or dysfunctional!

Years later, my 16-year-old son borrowed my car to attend a school function. Jim and I were also out that evening. When we returned home, the big old station wagon was parked in front with the front bumper dragging on the ground, and one front fender with a gigantic dent in it. My mind immediately went to my experience with my dad. Before we'd even turned off the engine, I said to Jim, "He was able to drive it home, so he must be O.K."

As soon as he heard us arrive, Peter opened the front door and immediately began explaining what happened. His voice, the rigidity of his body posture and the rapidness of his speech telegraphed his anxiety. I couldn't follow what he was saying, but, at that moment, it wasn't important. I put my arms around him and said, "It's O.K. It's just a car. I'm glad you weren't hurt. Take some deep breaths. Calm down and then you can tell us what happened."

Today, Peter has two young children. In the future, if one of them should have a fender-bender, I think I know how Peter will respond.

~

Jim: As Nancy and I began to really examine communication tools, we found many patterns we had clearly cloned from our parents and their relationships to each other. Many worked in our favor, such as our parents' commitment to marriage for life. We both have that very deep commitment to staying married. Our tenacity helped us to hold on until we could find and apply the help we needed to make our marriage work. Now we are reaping abundant benefits because we stayed and worked hard for our marriage.

We practiced other behaviors that didn't work for us, though. I found myself doing something I'd known my dad to do...avoiding conflict rather than facing it and trying to work it out. Consequently the pressure would build, Nancy's frustration would increase, and one of us would finally "blow," doing more damage than if I had just faced the problem when it came up.

Both of us were excellent at using a tactic our parents had employed: diagnosing what the *other* one was doing wrong, and instructing him or her in exactly how to fix it! I'm sure you know from your own experience how grateful we each were for the "help."

~

We observed in ourselves how beneficial *and* dysfunctional ways of confronting conflict were passed on to us. Our most *pressing* motivation for learning different ways of communicating was to find a way out of the excruciating pain we were experiencing; but, in addition, we began to realize that we were, in effect, teaching our children how to "do" marriage. If our married children duplicated our communication skills, their children, and their children's children, would experience the same kind of pain that we had. Since we learned some damaging ways of communicating by living with our parents and absorbing their levels of skill, then there was hope that by making our communication and relationship habits healthier, our children and grandchildren would eventually benefit. The possibility that they would have easier and happier relationships as a result of our work increasingly became another powerful motivator.

We are not into parent bashing. We believe that our parents, indeed *all* parents, ourselves included, do the best job they possibly can with the tools at their disposal. It is helpful, however, to examine the things which we incorporated from our childhood experience and *evaluate*, not *judge*, those that work well for us, and those that don't. We do this not for the purpose of blaming others or excusing ourselves, but *to understand and take full responsibility for change.* Gathering information is an essential first step. It gives us an opportunity to identify the patterns we are playing out. Before we can change something, we must first determine what it is that we want to change. The first step of any journey is knowing where to begin.

Are you uncomfortable evaluating your parents' communication tools? Perhaps there was an invisible rule in your family called, "Children do not question adults" or "You are disloyal and we will not love you if you find fault with us." All families have dozens of spoken and unspoken rules.[2] Perhaps you can identify the "rule" that results in your discomfort with this exercise, and decide now whether it is useful for you to continue obeying that rule.

You may have a belief that if you identify the aspects of your family that you don't want to duplicate, you are being ungrateful for all the benefits you *did* receive from being in that family. Can you be grateful *and* desire to improve at the same time? You may believe that by wanting to do *anything* differently, you are shattering the assumption that *your* family and *your* childhood were perfect. Are the memories of perfection more important to protect than creating the relationships and the life you want *now*? Maybe, as an adult, you can appreciate all that was great about your family and examine and evaluate *in order to move forward.*

If bad communications skills are duplicated by your children, your pain will be experienced by them as well.

Evaluate, not judge your childhood experiences to understand and take full responsibility for changes.

Corner Puzzle Piece #2:
Communicate in ways that get the desired result.

"Examining the source of my defective tools
helps me see the consequences of using them.
Realizing that I, too, am passing on my methods of communication,
motivates me to give my children a healthier communication legacy."

Baby ducks learn to survive by imitating their mothers.
Learning through imitation is fundamental to many species,
including humans.
As we become adults, we have a unique advantage:
we can choose who to imitate.
We can also choose new models to replace the ones we outgrow.

~ Michael Gelb[3]

*Don't worry that children never listen to you;
worry that they are always watching you.*

~ Robert Fulghum[4]

ENDNOTES

1   Article reprinted in the *Orange County Register*, Tuesday, January 3, 1995.

2   Read John Bradshaw's book, *Family Secrets*, for more comprehensive help in identifying and evaluating family rules. New York: Bantam Books. 1995.

3   Gelb, Michael, *How to Think Like Leonardo da Vinci: Seven Steps to Genius Every Day*. New York: Doubleday Publishers. 2000.

4   Fulghum, Robert, *All I Really Need to Know I Learned in Kindergarten: Uncommon Thoughts on Common Things*. New York: Ivy Books. 1986.

Survey of Communication History

We suggest you get a pad and pen and jot down your thoughts as you answer these questions:

1. Who provided the most powerful model for relationships during your childhood?

2. Are your mother and father still married to each other? Or were they married until one died? How would you characterize their relationship histories?

3. What healthy relationship qualities/habits did you observe between or in each of them that you are duplicating?

4. What negative qualities/habits did you observe in them? Can you identify ways that you are duplicating those?

5. Which defective communication tools (page 55) did you see demonstrated in your childhood, either between your parents, or from parent to child?

6. Choose one of those identified defective communication tools, write it in the first blank, and complete this statement: "When my parent(s) _____ I felt _____. I also felt _____ and _____." i.e., "When my parents yelled at each other, I felt anxious. I also felt resentful and torn."

7. Name the person with whom you have or have had the most conflict in your life so far.

8. Identify the defective communication tools you use/used with that person.

9. Are there any similarities between your relationship and the relationship/s experienced by your mom and/or dad?

10. What do you see as the most urgent pattern for you to change in yourself so that you can experience a more satisfying relationship?

11. What small, reasonable step are you willing to take *today* toward that change?

    Note: Doing this exercise is a great first step. Reading further and being willing to try something new would be a promising *next* step. Sharing the results of this survey with your spouse and stating your intention to improve would be fantastic.

Chapter 8

Climbing the Communication Stairs

*Most of our assumptions about why communication breaks down
are about the other guy. We take our own input for granted.*

~ Michael Nichols[1]

Cliches   Casual greetings, neutral conversation

I was on my way to perform a wedding ceremony. As I walked down the sidewalk toward the country club, a man carrying golf clubs was walking toward me. As we passed, he said, "How are you?" and kept on walking. He didn't really want to know how I was. He didn't expect a detailed answer or any answer at all. He wasn't being rude. I just said, "Hi!" and also kept walking. We were both using clichés as a means of greeting a stranger in a neighborly way.

The most elementary level of communication is a cliché. Clichés serve a useful purpose. They smooth out encounters with strangers when we *don't* want a deep conversation but *do* want to be friendly or polite. "Have a nice day," "Good morning," or "How do you do?" are neutral pleasantries that smooth interactions with both strangers and acquaintances.

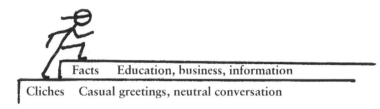

Facts   Education, business, information

Cliches   Casual greetings, neutral conversation

Although a step up from clichés, the fact level is still very basic. A fact is something that is observed as true by everyone present or can be proven. If you were here with me today, we would agree on the fact that the sun is shining and it's a beautiful day. If we looked at a thermometer, we'd be in agreement that the temperature is 74 degrees. You would have to agree that my office walls are a soft yellow and that my desk is (at this moment) a little cluttered. I would agree with you on your hair color, or height because I could see both for myself.

The facts level of communication is generally neutral. Again, we often use this level to converse with strangers. In the supermarket line, the lady ahead of me asks, "Did you notice they have T-bone steaks on sale today?" The sale is a fact. It can be checked out. When Jim asks our grandson Joey, "How many guys did you strike out today?" Joey's answer is a fact because it can be validated by witnesses and the score book. Speaking clichés or facts is not very risky. We don't fight over facts.

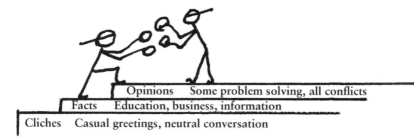

Opinions   Some problem solving, all conflicts
Facts   Education, business, information
Cliches   Casual greetings, neutral conversation

Sometimes an assumption—for example, "The earth is flat"—is believed to be a fact but is shown later to be an opinion. Opinions are the next level on the communication stairs. Opinions are more risky as forms of expression. When most of the people in the known world believed the earth to be flat, imagine how it must have been for Columbus to say, "It may *not* be flat. In fact, it might be spherical. I'm going to sail as far out as I can and see what happens." His loved ones may have fought to keep him on land, afraid for his life. No doubt some of his associates called him crazy. His opinion stirred up controversy and probably triggered fights at the local pub as people took sides on the issue. *All fights take place on the opinion level.* All. Every fight. No exceptions.

Can you discern opinion from fact?

If you think you're fighting over facts, look a little closer. I guarantee that one or both parties are expressing an opinion *as though* it is fact, and judging that opinion as "right." Another way of saying it's "right" is to declare it as "fact," when really it just seems right to me because of my particular point of view (opinion).

Just for fun I dare you to consider a disagreement, either between yourself and someone else, or two other persons. One thinks it's time to leave for the party. The other thinks they have a little more time. Both are expressing an opinion. If they are each "attached" to their opinions, judging them to be "right," they are immediately in conflict. It might be a mild disagreement or escalate into a roaring fight. Either way it was caused by the judgment each one made that his or her opinion was "fact." In the disagreement you observe, see if you can identify the opinion(s). Examine them carefully.

Although they carry some risk of disapproval, or disagreement, opinions are still a very elementary level of communication. Opinions are often discussed with strangers or bare acquaintances but are also appropriate to share with friends, family members, and business associates. Clichés, facts, and opinions work in a wide range of relationships because *they do not create intimacy or closeness, the feeling of being SoulMates.*

The romantic and sexual energy that attracts us to our future mate delivers a *sense* of intimacy that is so powerful it produces the confidence needed to enter the commitment of marriage "til death do us part." With some, that *illusion* or *presumption* of intimacy is supported by communication that *is* indeed intimate, so the relationship sustains its SoulMate quality after the first bloom of wedded bliss fades.

Without intimate communi-cation, a couple's relationship deteriorates into feeling empty or hollow at its core.

Many couples, however, do most or all of their communicating with clichés, facts, or opinions. The more communication takes place on these three levels, the more likely it is that the relationship will eventually cease to *feel* intimate. In fact, it will *not be* intimate. Without intimate communication, a couple's relationship deteriorates into feeling empty or hollow at its core. For some, the relationship becomes pointless. Instead of being partners, they feel like strangers. This happens despite a lifestyle in which they probably share a bathroom, sleep together, share their bodies with each other, rear children and plan a financial future. In many, many ways, both support the life they have under the same roof. This could be what has happened when a couple gives as a reason for divorce, "We just drifted apart."

The use of absolutes is an exagger-ation of an opinion, and an accusatory "you" is an attacking way of stating a fact or an opinion.

All defective communication tools are practiced exclusively on the "fact" and "opinion levels." The habitual use of defective communication tools traps the couple far short of an intimate, SoulMate relationship. Near the top of our list of defective communication tools listed in Chapter 6 are two tools that are practiced by nearly everyone: (1) using absolutes in a negative context, such as "always," "never," "all," "every" and "forever," and (2) using the accusatory "you." The use of absolutes is an exaggeration of an opinion, and an accusatory "you" is an attacking way of stating a fact or an opinion. These are two defective communication tools that we began to change first.

Just as with perception checking, it would be easy to underestimate the importance of eliminating these two habits, habits that may, at first glance, seem insignificant. Changing only these two methods of communicating can reduce negative reactions and produce progress toward SoulMate love. So, along with perception checking, we suggest adding two more tools to your relationship toolbox.

1. **Address your comments to specific times and events.**

    Eliminate the words "always" and "never" or other forms of absolutes from your vocabulary when you are trying to resolve an issue or communicate feelings about a sensitive subject.

    What is your instantaneous response when I say, "You *always* nag"? If you react as most do, you'll immediately remember all the times when you wanted to nag but didn't. "You *never* bring me flowers" may trigger a memory of when you brought home a bouquet for her birthday three years ago. When the discussion is about a "charged" issue or something that could easily stir up hurt, the words "always" and "never" are *guaranteed* to incite defensiveness and provoke or escalate an argument. They *will not* help your partner hear your needs or see your point of view. Those little words will effectively reroute the discussion from the *real* issue to a sidetrack called *rebuttal*, for example, "No, I don't!" or "Remember when…?"

    See if you can catch yourself using "always," "never," or other absolutes in your communication this week. What was the effect? What was said in response? What feelings resulted? Where did the discussion go from there? If you don't catch yourself before the words are out of your mouth, apologize ("I'm sorry. That's not true"). Correct the "always" or "never" gaffe by rewording the statement so that it refers to a specific event, rather than making an absolute generalization. Some examples of specific, qualified statements are:

    ♦ "I was disappointed when you weren't home in time for dinner last night." (rather than, "You never come home for dinner anymore.")

    ♦ Or, "I'm tired of walking the dog. Would you do it this time?" (rather than, "Why do I always have to walk the dog?")

    It's interesting that, even when absolutes are used in a positive, complimentary way—such as "I never have to remind you to take out the trash"—we have an inner voice that argues, "Remember when I forgot to put the trash out after Christmas?" Either silently or audibly that voice often responds to, "You always look so beautiful!" with, "You've got to be kidding. Last Saturday I was a wreck." Even compliments are more easily accepted when given about a *specific action, quality, or event* rather than a broad generalization. It would be more effective to say, "Thank you for remembering to take out the trash today," or, "You look gorgeous tonight! I'm proud to be with you."

Catch yourself using "always," "never," or other absolutes in your communication. What was the effect?

Even compliments are more easily accepted when given about a specific action, quality, or event rather than a broad generalization.

2. In issue discussions, use "I feel..." rather than "You..."!

Blame and accusation are not good tools to use when resolving an issue.

A message containing the accusatory "you" is blaming. Blame and accusation are not good tools to use when resolving an issue. In a "you" message, the attention is focused on the person, rather than the behavior, the issue, or a solution. The one on the receiving end of a "you" message feels verbally attacked. The most frequent reactions to a "you" message are defensiveness, denial, or counterattack.

An accusatory "you" conversation (argument) sounds like this: "You hurt my feelings!" "Well, why did you criticize me at the office party in front of my co-workers?" "I did it because you were acting so obnoxious." "I was just having fun." "Yeah, but you were making a fool of yourself." etc.

Sometimes a truth can be accurately spoken with the accusatory "you" when something has been done that can be proven as fact, but most accusatory "you" messages are just opinion. Either way, accusatory "you" messages never, (here's an absolute that is true) *never* help resolve an issue.

The best antidote for a "you" message is a statement about how you feel.

The best antidote for a "you" message is a statement about how you *feel*. When sharing a feeling, a giant step up has been taken to the fourth level of communication where a SoulMate relationship has the opportunity to develop. The feelings level of communication opens an intimate, vulnerable place. It discloses your heart to your partner, not just your thoughts. Chapter 9 describes a few of the magical things that happen when one or both partners share their feelings rather than their opinions.

Feelings, Intimacy, SoulMate relationship
Opinions   Some problem solving, all conflicts
Facts   Education, business, information
Cliches   Casual greetings, neutral conversation

Often a person's first attempt to avoid the accusatory "you" is to change "You hurt me" to "I feel that you hurt me," or "you made a mistake" to "I feel like you made a mistake." Sorry, but this is still a thinly disguised accusatory "you" message. There are two ways to identify an accusatory "you" message: (1) If the words, "that" or "like" follow immediately after "I feel," and, (2) if you can substitute "think" for "feel" without changing the meaning of the statement.

In both those cases, it isn't a feeling at all, but a judgmental opinion about the other person: "I think that you hurt me," or, "I think that you made a mistake."

Some examples of changing a "you" message into an "I feel…" message are:

♦ "You hurt me" is more truthfully said as, *"I feel hurt."*

♦ "You didn't keep your promise" might be changed into *"I feel disappointed."*

♦ "It is a mistake for you to lend Tommy the car" is more accurate when stated as *"I am uncomfortable with Tommy borrowing the car!"*

When I begin a statement with "I feel…" *and name the feeling or use a feeling verb*, I am telling a truth about *myself* rather than declaring what I know, or think I know, to be true about *you*. Imagine a conversation taking place on a tennis court with the ball (the statements) being hit back and forth over the net. When I tell the truth about myself (my feeling) I stay on my side of the court.[2] Stating my opinion about my partner with a "you" message is playing on my partner's side of the court. Can you see the game? I speak what's true for me (hit the ball from my side of the court) and then try to speak for you (run around to your side of the court to hit the ball for you.) No wonder conversations riddled with "you" messages rarely come to satisfactory conclusions. As with the use of absolutes, "you" messages trigger a defensive response that interferes with the resolution of the issue.

Despite all our emphasis on the negative "you" messages, there are two ways to use "you" that work just great. One is when you use the accusatory "you" in a positive way, such as, "You did a great job on that speech. The outline was clear and everyone's attention was right with you." or "You look so handsome in that suit." Another is when you need to provide a context for a particular feeling, like "When you roll your eyes at me, I feel disrespected" or "Last night, when you forgot to lock the doors downstairs, I felt unprotected." In these cases, the "you" is not an accusation, it is only describing the circumstance in which a particular feeling was experienced.

After practicing for a while, you may find, as we did, that there is a clean integrity to speaking the truth about yourself. Starting statements with "I feel…" keep us clearly on our own side of the court and allow our partner the freedom to play his or her side of the court without interference. By using this great communication tool, the number and severity of defensive reactions is greatly reduced. It is easier, then, to proceed toward a satisfactory resolution.

By the way, judging another's feeling as bad, or inappropriate, or silly, is just another way of stating an opinion in an accusatory way. It *is* just an opinion. There is always a reason for any given feeling. Feelings are the exclusive

Starting statements with "I feel…" keeps the number and severity of defensive reactions greatly reduced.

property of the individual experiencing them. They are not debatable. Judging them, as with all judging, only creates more hurt, distrust and difficulty in resolving the issue successfully.

I hope by now that you've purchased a little notebook or journal to do the recommended exercises so that these truths can be integrated into your relationship more easily. If you haven't, I suggest you find one immediately. Write down the times when you used "always/never," and accusatory "you" messages. Note the response and evaluate it. Did you get a pleasing, helpful response, or did those communications trigger defensiveness? It's hard for some of us to think of a new way of saying things while in the middle of a conversation. The old, habitual way of using "absolutes" and "you" resists change. By writing down the "mistakes," you can take your time figuring out how the communication could have been delivered more effectively. More effectively means creating less defensiveness. Next to the times when you use "always/never," write out a statement that is more qualified and specific (a certain event at a certain time). After writing down a "you" message, write out how it could be said as an "I feel…" statement. When you have written down several revisions, the new way of communicating will start to become familiar. If you have set an intention to step up your communication to the higher SoulMate levels, one day, in the middle of an issue discussion, you'll pause for a moment, sorting the words in your head, and say "I feel…"!

However, beginning to communicate on the feeling level may present another problem: a limited "feeling" vocabulary.

～

Jim: When our counselor first told us to begin changing "you" into "I feel" messages, I was lost! Nancy was very proficient at identifying and stating her feelings, but the only ways I knew to describe my feelings were as "good" or "bad." I *had* feelings, and certainly *felt* them, but I wasn't accustomed to naming them or sharing them verbally.

The counselor gave me the list of feeling words at the end of Chapter 9. Whenever Nancy and I sat down to work on our issues, I would have to find my list of feeling words and have it right in my hand so I could refer to it often. When trying to identify what I was feeling, I'd run down the list. "Do I feel annoyed? No, it's more than that. How about irritated? Not quite it. Angry? That's closer. Enraged! That's what I feel. I feel enraged!" I found that when I ran down the list of feeling words, a little light came on in my head as I found a word that described what I was feeling.

In the beginning, it was quite humiliating to have to get my list before I could join Nancy in an attempt to resolve an issue. I felt outclassed by her verbal dexterity.

My first two children were little girls. I enjoyed the nonstop chatter that filled their younger years. They talked about *everything* and to *anything*. They talked to us, to each other, to their dolls and stuffed animals. They even made up conversations between their toys. How do we guys spend those first few years? With a car in our hand going "Varooom! Varooom!" Some of us never catch up to the verbal skills of women.

Also, our culture encourages women to express feelings, but discourages men from identifying or expressing their feelings verbally. In Chapter One, I briefly touched on the "good ole boy" training I received in the South. But truthfully, all over America, little boys are told to "buck up" and "don't be a cry-baby." We are taught to resolve conflict by force or logic, not with feelings.

I was determined, though, to do whatever it took to save our marriage. I still loved Nancy. For a short while at the beginning of our relationship, we experienced the pleasure of an intimate SoulMate relationship. It was almost like we'd been given a *preview* of what we *could* have *if* we worked at it. I wanted a great SoulMate relationship *all* of the time. So I swallowed my pride and used the list of feeling words. It gradually became satisfying to be able to connect a word to what I was feeling inside. I only needed it for a few months. I don't need it anymore. I'll probably never be as good as Nancy is at identifying and expressing my feelings, but my feeling vocabulary has expanded way beyond "good" or "bad." I can express myself well enough to work through any issues that arise. Nancy gives me a lot of praise for my willingness to learn this foreign language of feelings.

It can be very gratifying to find key words describing how you really feel.

❧

I am so grateful that Jim was willing to learn how to identify his feelings and share them with me using the "I feel…" format. When I sensed that he was angry with me, it helped to hear him say that it was "mild irritation" rather than "seething." Even when he *was* seething, I would rather hear about it as a feeling than experience it in his behavior. In addition, when he said, "I feel angry" I was less defensive. The issue was easier to discuss and resolve.

Many couples have a lot of resistance to communicating in "feeling" language. This level of communication is unfamiliar to most of us, for one thing.

The habit of speaking in "you" messages is deeply entrenched in us; but *if* it were *only* a bad habit, it would be relatively simple to change. The moment we saw that there was a better way to speak that would give us the relationship we wanted, we would begin correcting ourselves. Within a few weeks, the new habit of saying "I feel…" would prevail.

So what stops us?

I frequently said, (or yelled) things like this at Jim; "You are wrong! Can't you see what you are doing? (another form of a "you" message.)" The "you" messages made me feel strong, right, superior, more intelligent, justified for my anger and righteous for defending my position. Metaphorically, my clenched fists were extended, delivering verbal punches…a very aggressive stance. In this mode, I had some illusion of power, control and protection.

In addition, communicating with "you" messages successfully kept my attention focused on *Jim*; what *he* was doing, how *he* acted, *his* tone of voice, the projected consequences of *his* behavior…in short, *his* wrongness. Those *opinions* were very comfortable places on which to focus.

The moment I began to state my *feelings* (humiliated, powerless, hurt, angry or hopeless) I felt vulnerable in the extreme. I felt emotionally naked. To say "I feel hurt," left me without my shield of armor, my righteous cause. It was just me standing there vulnerable to attack. It was terrifying.

I was not only vulnerable to Jim's response, but to my own awareness. When my focus was on Jim, it was easy to ignore my inner knowing that my own conduct was contributing to the ongoing conflict. On the surface, I felt justified in using any method of communicating for the greater good of making Jim see how wrong he was. Underneath, I despised myself for my out-of-control raging and for being such a failure at creating the happy marriage and family for which I had yearned my entire life.

I had a lot invested in my dream of a "happy" family. My first husband died when our marriage was just beginning to work well. When I met Jim, and began loving him, and knew that he loved me, my Cinderella fantasies went wild. Now I realize that I defined myself as a valuable woman only if my husband was happy with me and my children were well behaved and successful. When it became painfully obvious that we were losing our ability to kiss and make up, and our children were acting out the effects of a very conflicted household, my dreams and my world were going up in smoke.

I fought ferociously, trying to force everyone into the shape that I *knew* was best for all of us. I mistakenly viewed my opinion as fact, and judged myself as "right." In truth, I didn't know what was best for any of us. I only knew everyone in the house was in pain. I was just flailing out, trying to latch on to something that would help.

To drop my self-righteous, aggressive posture and simply say "I feel..." felt almost like jumping off a cliff into annihilation. I have watched the same struggle on the faces of dozens of couples. They mirror my initial reluctance, looking as if we've asked them to disrobe in public *and* commit hari kari. It's no wonder that this simple communication tool often meets with so much resistance. Communication on the *feeling* level can make us feel vulnerable and being vulnerable is often scary.

We didn't understand why at the time, but even though we were angry, we felt safer and closer when we expressed ourselves in "I feel..." language. Without knowing it, we were beginning to communicate in ways that encourage SoulMate love to flourish. Being vulnerable by sharing feelings, is *essential* to SoulMate love.

Michael Foal is an American astronaut.[3] He was married, with two small children, when he accepted an assignment in space. He and two Russian astronauts spent four months in the Russian space station, Mir. Through daily e-mails, his wife Rhonda kept him posted about the family activities. She shared *facts* about what she and the children did every day. Around the third month, he began to lose any sense of closeness with his family. He felt closer to his fellow astronauts. He finally told her, "Rhonda, stop telling me news. I want to know how you *feel*."

Communication on the feeling level makes us feel vulnerable and being vulnerable is often scary. But being vulnerable by sharing feelings, is essential to SoulMate love.

Needs	Self-esteem, SoulMate respect and love
Feelings, Intimacy, SoulMate relationship	
Opinions	Some problem solving, all conflicts
Facts	Education, business, information
Cliches	Casual greetings, neutral conversation

The topmost level of communication is the "need level." We often say "need" when what is really meant is "want." A *need* is critical to physical survival or psychological health. My body needs air, food, water, shelter and rest for survival. Fortunately most of us have those things and more. In fact, if you didn't have those needs met, you wouldn't be reading this book. We can focus on higher psychological needs only when our basic needs for physical survival are secure.

Psychological needs are things like having a sense of self-worth, an inner knowing that I deserve to be treated with dignity and respect, being touched affectionately, experiencing some joy and laughter, feeling fulfilled by how I spend my energy, loving and being loved.

I believe that needs are the same for every living soul, but the package through which the need is recognized or met, can be different. I need to feel useful. One way that need is met for me is in teaching and writing. I need to know I am connected to God. One of the ways I feel that connection is by gardening. I need to be treated with respect. Not everyone may treat me with respect, but knowing that I *deserve* to be respected, helps me respond in a self-honoring way when someone is disrespectful to me.

Another person needs may be met by working with children, playing the violin, functioning effectively as an executive or being a good plumber. The vehicles are different. The needs are the same.

❧

Jim: One time, in the middle of a fight, Nancy asked me "What do you need?" I was stunned. No one had ever asked me that before. I didn't know what I needed. All I knew was what I *didn't want*. I'd never thought about what I needed. I needed peace between us. I know now that I needed respect, self-esteem and love. Those needs were intensified by the conflict. As I chose to *face* the conflict and worked at learning new skills for *resolving* the conflict, my needs for self-esteem, respect, and love were gradually met. Now they are abundantly met.

A few years ago, I realized my ministry, as I had practiced it for many years, was changing. Or I was changing. It was no longer a pleasure to direct a choir or lead worship. I didn't ever want to retire, but being a minister in the way I had done it for many years became less and less appealing. I began asking God to send me something to do in my later years that would excite me. I was looking for a new way to serve God and serve people that would fulfill my need of being useful and productive.

As the workshops Nancy and I teach have evolved, I've become increasingly aware that they are the answer to my prayers. I have always loved working with people. It is so gratifying that we can use what we learned to help others who may be struggling. Earning a living is always important, but the real payoff for what I do is seeing understanding dawn in a couple's eyes, hearing them report their communication successes, receiving their gratitude for teaching them skills that are making it possible for them to be SoulMates. It seems ironic (or maybe it's just like God) to make the fulfillment of one need (the happiness of our marriage) pave the way for the fulfillment of another need (to be useful and productive in a way that has meaning for me).

Learning and using the communication tools that are taught in this book probably won't lead to a new profession for you, but these tools *will* enable you to fulfill your need for self-esteem and SoulMate love that comes from sharing your deepest feelings and needs with your spouse. Take the leap. Read on."

Emotional intimacy—the sense of being connected, the heart of a SoulMate relationship—is created and maintained only by communication of your *feelings* and *needs*. Intimate SoulMate love is never found in, or sustained by, communication that is limited to cliché, fact, or opinion.

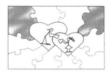

Corner Puzzle Piece #2:
Communicate in ways that get the desired result.

"I am learning the SoulMate skill
of communicating my feelings and needs, because
the quality of relationship I desire evolves from the
feeling and need levels of sharing."

Speaking without thinking is like shooting without aiming.
~ Old Proverb

He who loves wisdom loves his own best interest and will be a success.
~ Proverbs 19:8

ENDNOTES

1   Nichols, Michael P., Ph.D., *The Lost Art of Listening,* p. 132. New York: Guilford Press. 1995.

2   The metaphor of a tennis game representing communication between two persons comes from our good friend, Betty Coble Lawther, who arranged for us to be in the same place at the same time so that we would meet. She is an extraordinary communicator and author.

3   "Space Man of the Year," by Michael Foale, as told to Lisa Sonne, *Life Magazine*, January, 1998, Volume 21, page 90.

Chapter 9
The Looking Glass

Feelings are facts to the person experiencing them.
~ **Michael Nichols**[1]

We were leaving for vacation the next day. One whole week together. I couldn't imagine what we would talk about or do with each other for a week. I was so unhappy. Jim was so withdrawn.

We were through the worst of our marriage problems. I no longer yelled. Jim no longer talked "hopeless talk." I'd given up sarcasm. He no longer needed to march out of the house, slamming the door, going somewhere, doing something until he cooled off.

At the peak of our mess, for a period of about eight months, I spent four days a week in a seaside community in San Diego County about one hour from home. We told everyone I was there to oversee the refurbishing of a severely neglected condominium that we had purchased as an investment. That was true. It was also true that we needed some breathing space. The days we were apart, we gathered our strength so we could pick up the job of saving our marriage on the days we were together. We both had dreamed of living by the beach one day. We loved the area so much that when this first condo sold, we purchased another to fix up and in which we wanted to live permanently. By the time all that had happened, we felt ready to live together again full time.

For the next two years we had fun buying, fixing up and selling condos and homes. Although Jim was still working part time for a church, he earned his real estate license and began working out of an office in Carlsbad. We were so excited. We felt hopeful about our future together, financially and as a couple. I loved working with Jim. He found the properties and did the negotiations and paper work. I decided how to make the best use of our fix-up money, oversaw contractors, shopped for fixtures, cabinets and paint. We were discovering that we worked well together.

Then the bottom dropped out of the California real estate market. We were not experienced enough to know that we should leave ourselves a wide margin of working capital. As prices plummeted, we rushed to complete projects and get them on the market. While waiting for them to sell, the prices dropped some more. We used credit card loans to make mortgage payments in order to protect our credit rating. In the middle of the "crash," we put our own beloved dream condo on the market, sold it at a loss, and rented an apartment. We were worse than broke. By the time we had sold every property, we were thousands of dollars in debt.

We talked about our options. I did *not* want to move back to Orange County. I *loved* living in San Diego County. That's all I knew for sure. Jim kept telling me all his contacts for doing weddings and funerals were in Orange County. I quietly dug my heels in. He quietly went about re-establishing himself with wedding venues and morticians in Orange County. I was devastated. The crushing blow came when we knew we couldn't meet the next month's rent and I called my son to ask if we could rent a room in his little house for awhile.

I was mad at God and at Jim. We had worked so hard to save our marriage. I thought we were going to make a lot of money in real estate and sail through the rest of our lives. After all, didn't we deserve a break?

And now, because I was upset about moving back near the scene of so many painful years, Jim had withdrawn. The vibes I got went like this, "Your attitude stinks. I'm only doing what I have to do in order to start paying off this debt. Your feelings are not my problem. Sooner or later you'll have to straighten up." He never said the words, but I was getting the message. Emotionally, he just wasn't there. It was like he'd climbed into a cave to wait out the storm. I felt so alone. Again.

Our timeshare was already paid for. It was worth virtually nothing on the resale market, or we would have sold it to pay off debts. We decided we might as well use it, so we booked a week at a resort within driving distance since there was no money for air fare or car rentals.

I stopped by my sister Sally's house for some reason and told her how much I did not want to be with Jim for the next week. She mentioned she had picked up a book the week before that looked interesting to her. Maybe I'd like to take it with me. I did.

We drove in silence up Interstate 5 through the heart of California. About 10 p.m., we stopped at a motel for the night. He worked a crossword for a while and then turned over and went to sleep. I dug into the book. It was about resolving relationship struggles. I started in the middle where there was a chapter describing the dynamics of two different couples and how the principles in the book had helped them. One of the couples was just like us.

About midnight I woke Jim up. Crying, I told him I knew now what was wrong. My feelings were not being heard, only judged as wrong. I felt abandoned over the whole issue of moving back to Orange County. It wasn't so much that we *had* to do it. I certainly didn't have a *better* plan. It was that Jim displayed little compassion for how devastating it all was for me. The nonverbal communication I was getting was, "We'll be close again when you straighten out your attitude. Until then, this is your problem, not mine."

Be sure you are listening to each other's feelings about circumstances instead of just criticizing the other's decision.

I told Jim that for 10 years I had carried the lion's share of the burden for the emotional condition of our relationship. I was the one who pursued counseling. If anything seemed out of sorts, I was the one who said, "Do we need to talk? Is anything wrong?" Almost always he was willing to talk, but the *initiative* came from me. I was tired. Completely worn out. Depleted. I could barely carry my own share of the responsibility for our marriage. I didn't have the strength anymore to carry most of Jim's share as well.

I told him I needed the responsibility for our relationship to be equally shared between us. My hurt and disappointment about moving back were my feelings, yes, but the issue affected our relationship. Therefore, how it was handled was, in part, his responsibility also. Did he care? Could he do this?

Bless Jim's heart. He listened. He heard me. He cared. He was willing. He'd been suffering from the distance between us also. He said, "I *want* to carry my share of our relationship, but I'm not sure how to do that. Be specific. What can I do?"

One thing he could do if he sensed any tension between us, was to take the *initiative* to ask, "Is anything wrong?" instead of waiting in an emotional cave for me to pull him out. Another thing might be to read that book with me. I suggested that we take turns initiating a date to read to each other every day. One day I'd make a date with him and read a chapter to him. We'd talk about what we read. The next day, it would be his responsibility to *initiate* a date with me and read a chapter to me. We did that every day of our vacation and continued after we got home. The book had several suggested exercises. There was a notebook available with more extensive exercises. We sent away for it. We did one exercise per week, and on every Wednesday night after dinner, shared what we'd learned.

In addition, Jim tentatively began to break his life long habit of emotionally disappearing whenever there was tension. He began to ask, albeit fearfully, "Is something wrong? Do we need to talk?" By now we had collected some pretty decent communication tools so when he asked, I didn't bite his head off. I was grateful to share the load, so I was very careful to respond to his questions in ways that were emotionally safe for both of us.

Since that night in the motel, nine years ago at this writing, Jim has never again disappeared into that cave. He fully shares the responsibility for keeping our relationship intimately loving and free of interfering issues.

We had already learned that issues are resolved only after feelings are shared and heard.

The book[2] taught a method of taking turns with the sharing of feelings and listening. We had already learned that *issues are resolved only after feelings are shared and heard*. This exercise gave a clear, simple format for doing that more effectively. We practiced. As Jim compassionately heard my hurt feelings about moving, the pain lessened. As he heard how heartbroken I was because we would no longer be working together, he began to understand that I was grieving much more than the loss of money and place.[3] I began to feel comforted.

When we are teaching, Jim introduces this method of communicating by saying we are about to hand them the Crown Jewel of our workshop. I introduce it by quoting Einstein. "The significant problems we face cannot be solved at the same level of thinking we were at when we created them." In the previous chapters I have painted a vivid picture of the defective communication tools individuals use that put relationships into some degree of difficulty. In the chapter about the levels of communication, I told you that a SoulMate relationship is developed and maintained by sharing feelings and needs. As Einstein recommended, sharing feelings and needs is literally the act of moving to a different level of thinking…a level where the feelings can be safely shared and heard, and where issues can successfully be resolved. At this level, intimate loving can thrive and a SoulMate relationship can be experienced. The exercise you're about to learn is the vehicle that makes this level of communication simple to understand and do.

"The most powerful form of nondefensive listening is called mirroring."…

In communication circles, this is called reflective listening, or mirroring. We like "mirroring," hence the title of this chapter. In his book, *Emotional Intelligence*, Daniel Goleman wrote, "The most powerful form of nondefensive listening is called mirroring. When one partner (shares his or her feelings about an issue) the other repeats it in his or her own words, trying to capture not just the thought but also the feelings that go with it. The effect of being mirrored accurately is feeling emotionally attuned and validated."

So this is how to do it:

Step 1: Make the date. It's a good idea to ask, "When can I have your full attention?" If there are unavoidable distractions, choose a time when the phone can be answered automatically, the children are in bed or away, and a giant "Do Not Disturb" sign is on the door. Making a date also sets up an expectation that this is an important event. It is. The intention is to speak, to listen, and then to resolve whatever issue is between you, so that your SoulMate love is unencumbered by any unresolved issue.

Laurie Kehler[4] in an article titled "Fighting Fair" wrote, "Face each other. Look each other in the eye as you discuss problems. This is particularly difficult for those of us who have learned guerrilla warfare—shouting some nasty comment, slamming down the phone or slamming a door—which leave no room for discussion because the other person is absent. Two people can be in the same room, however, and still be absent. If one person has his nose stuck in a newspaper or glued to the TV, he might as well not be there. Set it down or turn it off and come out of hiding."

Reading the paper or watching TV are two ways of avoiding intimate communication, but I've known women who tried to listen to something serious while finishing dinner, or helping a kid with homework. It can't be done. Speaking and listening at the feeling and needs levels is so important and so necessary for SoulMate love that it deserves deliberate preparation and your full attention.

Step 2: Choose roles. Decide which one of you will share your feelings first and which one will listen or "mirror." The one who is the most upset or who has the issue to discuss normally goes first. The partner is the "mirror." For the first several sessions it's best to shelve the hot issues and practice on minor ones. It's very important to talk about *only one issue at a time*! Do not go from one issue to another. Successfully complete one issue, before setting a date for another one. Another idea is to practice by asking your partner to mirror a compliment to him or her.

Especially while learning this, sit down, face each other, knee to knee. Keep open body language; no crossed arms or legs. Do not sit with your body angled away from your partner. As much as you can, maintain eye contact.

Step 3: Speaker: Make a feeling or need statement. The person you have agreed will be first to share makes a simple, short statement beginning with "I feel..." or a feeling verb. Refer to the list at the end of this chapter for help with your feeling vocabulary.

Example*: "I dislike having people over for dinner."*

The listener or mirror may not interrupt, argue, or contradict the speaker. Defending oneself is not allowed. The listener may request that the statement be made with fewer words if it seems too complex to remember. Speaker, this is not an invitation for a verbal marathon. Keep it short and simple.

Step 4: Listener: Mirror the statement. When a clear, simple statement is made, the listener "mirrors" by repeating it back to the speaker exactly as spoken, or in the listener's own words.

Example: *"You dislike having people over to eat dinner. Did I correctly understand what you said and felt?"*

Asking the question after mirroring the statement is important. It conveys a desire to understand and it's asking for feedback to see if you did, in fact, hear accurately.

Step 5: Speaker: Respond to the listener. Example: *"Yes you did"* or alter the communication to make it more accurate, such as, *"Not exactly. What I really mean is I enjoy family coming over because we share the work of cooking and clean up, but I dislike the pressure of entertaining for clients."*

Steps 4 and 5 are repeated until the speaker is satisfied that the listener heard and understands his or her feelings.

Step 6: Reverse roles. Continue process until both partners feel heard. If the mirror has some feelings about this issue, as well, the roles are reversed. Now the mirror becomes the speaker, and the speaker mirrors. *No attempt to find a solution to the problem is made until the feelings of both have been thoroughly shared and heard.*

Step 7: Now, problem solve. Discuss solutions. If possible, agree on one.

Mirroring causes a release of tension that comes from being heard. The change in the atmosphere is almost like hearing the air escape from a tire or releasing your breath after the doctor tells you the tests were negative. To give your partner the gift of compassionately listening to his or her feelings is to meet one of your partner's deepest needs—the need to be validated or emotionally recognized. The atmosphere softens. Where before there may have been the tension of rigidly-held positions on an issue, now there is more flexibility—a willingness to explore options that would not have been considered before.

The first and most obvious solution may just be an apology. When your partner has shared an issue and while you were mirroring you realized that you'd been insensitive, or neglectful, or thoughtless, now's the time to say so! And state your intention to be more loving next time. Only apologize and promise if you mean it.

The first and most obvious solution may just be an apology. If an apology isn't appropriate, go directly to brain-storming solutions.

If an apology isn't appropriate, go directly to brainstorming solutions. Do not judge any idea. From the choices presented, choose one that seems the most agreeable to both of you. It is most effective to make the next step as specific as possible, with a time or date attached. For one couple, the overflowing trash in the kitchen had become an issue. They agreed that he would empty the trash on Mondays, Wednesdays and Fridays whether it needed to be emptied or not. She took the alternate days. Sundays were left open. If one of them doesn't keep their agreement, the other can ask for a mirroring session to express the feeling of disappointment or frustration. If they keep their agreement, trust will be built instead of resentment.

For another couple, excessive spending was an issue. After mirroring, they agreed to budget a set amount of cash that they would each receive every month which could be individually saved or spent as desired. Both agreed to keep all other spending within their budget limits. They decided to go over the totals at the end of every month for the purposes of accountability and encouragement.

A specific plan with accountability attached is *always* better than "I'll try to do better." When the plan is date-, time-, or behavior-specific, the keeping of the agreement builds or rebuilds trust. If the agreement is broken, it is by a specific act or the neglect of a specific act which can be addressed in another mirroring session. With vague promises of "doing better," it is hard to agree whether "better" is being achieved or not. One may *feel* as though he or she is trying harder, but the other may not be able to see concrete proof.

A specific plan with account-ability attached is always better than "I'll try to do better."

There are some issues that can't be resolved by a compromise. The decision must go one way or the other. An example would be the choice between

One partner cannot always be the one to give in without resentment building.

spending your next date sailing or going to Las Vegas. You cannot do both at the same time. In that case, one of you must surrender his or her first choice. The next time a black and white choice comes up, the one who surrendered gets to choose. One partner cannot always be the one to give in without resentment building.

Step 8: Honor each other's limitations. Close the session respectfully.

Make another date. Keep any agreements you made.

Thank each other and praise any successes!

If one has shared all he or she is comfortable sharing and needs to "retreat," the other must learn to appreciate what has been shared and respect the need to recover, not pressing for more at that time. If either person becomes tired or distracted, the only SoulMate thing to do is to tell the truth about no longer being able to give this your best attention. If you don't tell the truth, you might *pretend* to listen. That rudeness is something no one would ever do to a SoulMate. You might just abruptly leave, which will feel like abandonment to your partner—another thing not appropriate for a SoulMate to do. Either of those options will invalidate any good that may have come from communicating on the feeling or need level by mirroring. If one becomes too angry to keep communications respectfully within the mirroring process, call a "time out." Make a date to resume whether it's five minutes from now or 24 hours.

If unable to stay engaged in mirroring any longer, a SoulMate could say something like, "I've heard you. I care about what you are saying. At another time I want to hear more, but I've given you all I have for now. *Can we make another date for Sunday at 4 p.m. to pick this up where we are leaving it now?*" This offer is the key! It communicates that you are not just blowing your partner off. You intend to listen and are suggesting a *specific* time when you will be able to do so. This offer makes it possible for the speaker to postpone being heard. The speaker is reassured that the intention to mirror is still intact, but the energy is low, or the emotions are out of balance. The partner needs time to rest or regain composure. Now, *be certain you honor your commitment and keep the date*. Just as in any other situation or relationship, once a commitment is not honored, trust begins to erode.

By honoring each other's limits and keeping your dates, mirroring becomes a safe place, not another battleground. You are in a process of developing a SoulMate relationship. This is not going to happen in one or two sessions. When we were first married and learning to become sexually attuned to each other, there were times when things just didn't go well. It was always so comforting when Jim said, "We're in this for the long haul. We'll get it right. I don't need to have satisfaction every single time we make love." Jim's attitude made love-making safe for me, not a test to pass. The same attitude is needed when learning to mirror. By honoring each other's limits and keeping dates, mirroring sessions become safe, not an endurance contest.

By honoring each other's limits and keeping your dates, mirroring becomes a safe place, not another battle-ground.

Do your best to understand that postponing the completion of a mirroring session is not rejection. This is a practical, doable skill for being present for one another at the deepest, most intimate levels possible in a relationship. Use positive self-talk if you begin to get hurt feelings, for instance, "My SoulMate has given me all he (she) has. Later, I'll get more of what I need. My partner is not withdrawing love, only attention. For now, I can be here for myself, comfort myself, and reassure myself that telling the truth is the only way to develop a safe, intimate relationship. What can I do right now to provide safety and nurturing for myself?" Then take a warm bath, putter with the car, watch a favorite TV show together or just cuddle for a while. The choice of a soothing activity depends on whether you each need "space" or want to be together.

In the beginning, most of our workshop participants say this exercise feels mechanical and awkward. Also, if it is an issue with your spouse that is being shared, it is surprisingly hard to identify a feeling without using the accusatory "you" messages. How did you feel the first time you tried to ride a bike or roller skate? That felt awkward, too. In fact, you may have taken some spills before mastering the intricate balance necessary for either of those skills. You may take some spills while learning to mirror. Please dust yourself off and set another date to try again. Until you experience it for yourself, take our word for it. This skill will change your marriage and your life!

Carrie[5] was overwhelmed by two very challenging young children. She was constantly nagging at her husband, Bill, to work fewer evenings and be home with them more. He continued to work three and sometimes four evenings a week and occasionally went in to the office on Saturday afternoon as well.

They were sitting in my office, knee to knee, trying to look each other in the eye. She was speaking. He was mirroring. She was trying to tell him how she felt. She kept slipping into "you" messages like, "You're missing the childhoods of your children." I kept coaching her by helping her rephrase the statement into a feeling. He was struggling to mirror her, trying hard to "do it right" but it was obvious he was holding himself aloof from her statements. This went on for several minutes.

All of a sudden, Carrie quietly, and with a lot of sorrow, said, "We miss you." Bill looked stunned. He fumbled for the words and finally mirrored her.

He had tears in his eyes. He never knew he was missed. He'd thought she wanted him home just to give her a break. Within two weeks he volunteered that he would not work more than two nights a week and never on weekends. For this work-driven man, that was a huge step. They are continuing to work on creating more intimacy in their marriage.

Jim and I have experienced that kind of intimate breakthrough that brings with it the desire and energy for healthy change. We've seen the same awesome miracle occur with couple after couple. When that happens, it's as though the couple has stepped through a barrier into a holy place. Such is the power of stepping up to the feeling level of communication.

I've tended to deflect compliments all of my life. When younger, I would deflect them verbally. The last several years I would say "Thank you" to a compliment, but most of the words were heard without my taking them to heart.

A few years after we learned to mirror, our financial condition had improved considerably. We planned a trip to Hawaii. I did all of the work. I spent lots of time on the phone arranging to exchange our timeshare for one in Hawaii. I shopped around and found the cheapest airfare and car rental. I made the reservations. I found a shuttle service that could get us to and from LAX without worrying about friends having to taxi us or leaving the car in a lot. On and on. It took a lot of time and effort.

Jim used to plan youth choir tours. He understands the hassle. He'd hire the bus company, make arrangements for homes for the kids to stay in at various stops, book the concerts, collect permission and emergency medical slips from the parents, write down what the exact limit of luggage was that each kid could bring. On and on. It took a lot of time and effort.

The morning after we arrived in Hawaii, Jim said, "Come here and sit beside me. I've got something to say to you. I want you to mirror me, because it's so important to me that you hear me." I came and sat. We turned toward each other. I could tell by his tone of voice and facial expression that he was not upset. I relaxed. Jim cradled my face in his hands, looked lovingly into my eyes, and began to tell me all the things he appreciated about the way I had organized our trip. He made me mirror back every statement. There were several. He finished by telling me how much he loved me and was looking forward to the time we had together. These compliments were not just physically heard. Because I was mirroring them back to him, they landed squarely inside my heart. I got teary. I felt *soooooo* appreciated and *soooooo* loved!

Jim: Two different men from two different "How to Stay Married & Love It!" classes have commented that mirroring gives everyone a level playing field. The less verbal partner has equal time and opportunity to share his or her feelings and needs with the partner who is more verbal. In typical communication, the more verbal partner dominates the exchange, often "winning" simply because that one is better at expressing him or herself. The less verbal one feels overpowered by the volume of words. That used to be true of me. I felt outclassed by Nancy's ability to express herself verbally. Now I don't. Mirroring not only made a level playing field for us, but over time, taught me how to express myself successfully.

We're not through sharing things about mirroring. There's more to come. In the meantime, begin. Don't put off learning this valuable skill. It truly is a Crown Jewel that elevates your communication to the SoulMate level every time you use it. Begin now.

A "Mirroring Practice Guide" is included as a working outline of the steps of mirroring. You might keep it in front of you to help you stay on track. The last page of this chapter is a list of feeling words. It might be useful to keep it in front of you to help you as you practice changing "you" statements into "I feel…" messages. Passing this chapter of the book back and forth might be awkward. I suggest that you make two photocopies each of the mirroring guide and the list of feeling words. Slip them, back to back, into plastic sleeves. That way they are durable and handy for mirroring sessions. (See the last page of the book to find out how to receive a free laminated copy of the mirroring guide.) Also included is a suggested schedule for practicing this skill.

Corner Puzzle Piece #2:
Communicate in ways that get the desired result.

"I am willing to experience the temporary awkwardness
of learning a new communication skill
in order to build the quality of relationship I desire."

The best and most beautiful things in the world
cannot be seen or even touched,
they must be felt with the heart.

~ Author Unknown

*Communication is basically an act of the will.
It's something we choose to do or not to do.*

~ Gary Chapman[6]

Mirroring Practice Guide

Step 1: Make a date.
The one who has an issue to discuss, or the one whose turn it is, asks one of these questions: "May I have a date with you to practice mirroring at ____ o'clock today?" or "I need to discuss something with you. When is a good time for you to give me your full attention?"

Along with this question, Jim and I both appreciate knowing, "What is this going to be about?" or, "Is this about us or something else?" or "If you're upset with me, on a scale of 1-10 how bad is it?"[7] The answers to these questions help us get ourselves emotionally ready. Mirroring is simple, but it was not an easy thing for us to do in the beginning. We needed to emotionally put on our "mirroring hat." "Full attention" means both of you are doing *nothing* else but mirroring. Turn the TV off, close the book, close the door.

Step 2: Choose who will share and who will mirror. If the session is about an upset, the one who is upset shares first.

Step 3: The speaker makes a simple, short statement beginning with "I feel…" or "When this happens, I feel…" or "I need…" Use the Feeling Word List.

Step 4: The listener mirrors back the speaker's statement exactly as spoken or in his or her own words. Then asks, "Did I understand you correctly?" Other questions are "Can you tell me more?" or "What else are you feeling?" or "Is there anything else?" and finally, "Do you feel heard?" These questions help to draw the speaker out. The expanded information often clarifies and simplifies the issue. Many times the surface upset only camouflages a deeper issue that needs attention.

Step 5: The speaker answers "Yes, you did" or clarifies the communication to make it more accurate, such as "Not exactly. What I really mean is…" Repeat steps 3-5 until the speaker feels heard.

Step 6: Ask the speaker if he or she is ready to be the mirror. A short break may be needed to change mental gears. Reverse roles until both partners' feelings have been heard.

Step 7: Apologize, if appropriate, or problem solve by discussing possible solutions. Make the solution specific with a time, date, or particular behavior agreed upon. If possible, choose a win-win solution or a compromise acceptable to both.

Step 8: Close the session respectfully by: honoring each other's limits, making the next date, keeping any agreements that were made, expressing appreciation for your partner's efforts, and complimenting any success!

Suggested Practice Schedule

Rate issues on a scale of #1 through #10 with #1 being a very minor annoyance, and #10 being an extremely "hot" issue. Suspend any discussion of issues that range from #5 through #10 for a minimum of two weeks while you are gaining proficiency with this skill.

- ♦ For a minimum of 14 days, set dates to practice mirroring. You might agree on every day for 14 days, or every other day for 28 days. I do not recommend letting any more than one day pass without mirroring.

- ♦ Alternate responsibility for setting and keeping the dates. If your partner misses the day for which he or she is responsible, it is not your job to "remind" your partner. Wait until the following day. Make your date, then share how you feel about the partner's forgetting.

♦ In each practice session, after the initiator shares, reverse roles so you each have a turn at both roles.

♦ Keep the Feeling Word List and Mirroring Practice Guides in front of you.

♦ Suggested schedule:

Initiator: Possible Subject:

He: Share a compliment, or an appreciation. Be specific.

She: Share a minor issue, #1-#2 in intensity. Be specific

He: Share compliment or appreciation. Be specific.

She: Share feelings about a favorite shared memory.

He: Share a minor issue, no more than a #3. Be specific.

She: Share a compliment or appreciation. Be specific.

Both: In preparation for the next date, each make a list of favorite activities shared together recently or in the past.

He: Share the feelings you had when you did those things on your list. Set a date to do one of those things together again. Agree how to share responsibility for whatever preparations may be needed for this activity.

She: Share feelings about a moderate issue, no more than #4 on the scale.

He: Share feelings you experienced on your wedding day. If you have them, look at the photos to help you remember.

She: Share feelings about a moderate issue, up to #5 on the scale.

He: Share a feeling about your job.

She: Share a feeling about your marriage.

He: Share a major feeling experienced in your childhood.

She: Share a feeling about the doing of this exercise for the past 13 days. Set a date for sharing your feelings about a "hotter" issue, #6-#8 on the scale, if you have one and if you *both* feel ready. "Hot" issues are not discussed unless both agree.

*****Note:** Occasionally you share a minor annoyance that turns out to be a #10 for your partner. If that should happen, set it aside for now, and agree to tackle it when you both feel more confident of your mirroring skills.

Maybe you won't get through to the other person
as long as you keep approaching him (or her) the same way you always do.
~ Michael P. Nichols, Ph.D.,
The Lost Art of Listening

Men of character like to hear of their faults;
the other class do not like to hear of faults;
they do not wish to be lovely,
but to be loved.
~ Ralph Waldo Emerson[8]

ENDNOTES

1   Nichols, Michael P., Ph.D., *The Lost Art of Listening*, p. 148. New York: Guilford Press. 1995.

2   Hendrix, Harville, *Getting the Love You Want.* New York: Harper & Row. 1988. We highly recommend this jewel.

3   At that time, I couldn't imagine anything else we could ever do that would give us the same experience of being a team, using our complimentary talents, and working toward a common goal that real estate had given us. Little did I know. The workshops that we teach together were just around the corner. How much more rewarding they are to both of us than any property could ever be. I have forgiven Jim *and* God!

4   Kehler, Laurie, Fighting Fair, *Focus on the Family Magazine*, March, 2000.

5   Again, fictitious names.

6   Quoted from "Marriage Works by Communicating, Not Running" by Art Toalston, *The Baptist Messenger*, October 5, 1995.

7   Jim said to tell you he likes to know how much trouble he's in!

8   Emerson, Ralph Waldo, *Emerson Essays: First and Second Series,* p. 269. New York: Random House. 1990.

Feeling Words List

Happy/
Comfortable
airy
blissful
bright
bubbly
buoyant
charmed
cheerful
ecstatic
elated
enchanted
expectant
free
giddy
glad
happy
hilarious
jolly
jovial
joyful
jubilant
light
lighthearted
merry
overjoyed
sparkling
surprised
thrilled
warm

Secure/
Confident
adventurous
at ease
at home
attracted
bold
calm
cherished
comforted
confident
cool
courageous
dashing
determined
easygoing
fearless
free-and-easy
heroic
loose
pleased
poised
relaxed
secure

snug
spontaneous
strong
unbridled
unhindered
unrestrained

Uneasy
awkward
baffled
bruised
embarrassed
fragile
frustrated
nauseated
out-of-sorts
restless
wound up

Unhappy/
Uncomfortable
aching
agonized
ashamed
cheerless
cold
crushed
dejected
depressed
despondent
disconcerted
discouraged
disillusioned
dismal
down-in-the-dumps
down-in-the-mouth
downcast
downhearted
frowny
gloomy
glum
grief-stricken
grieved
heartbroken
heavy
heavyhearted
joyless
lonely
morose
mournful
murky
pained
sad
sullen
unhappy
weepy

whiny
wistful

Afraid
abandoned
alarmed
anxious
apprehensive
betrayed
bewildered
boxed-in
burdened
butterflies-in-stomach
coming unglued
confused
distressed
fragmented
fearful
frightened
guarded
hard-pressed
horrified
horror-stricken
jittery
locked-in
nervous
overwhelmed
panicky
paralyzed
queasy
shaky
shocked
tense
timid
trapped
trembly
uptight
worried

Affectionate
amorous
cozy
cuddly
grateful
loving
moved
passionate
romantic
sensitive
sensuous
sexy
tender
touched
warm

Low Energy
bashful
beat down
bushed
cool
depleted
dull
exhausted
feeble
groggy
listless
pensive
shy
tired
waterlogged
weak

High Energy
alert
alive
attentive
awake
eager
energetic
enthusiastic
excited
exhilarated
fidgety
frisky
peppy
playful
refreshed
rejuvenated
revived
spirited
spry
talkative
vivacious

Angry
abused
annoyed
boiling
cantankerous
demeaned
disrespected
furious
enraged
grouchy
irritated
offended
peeved
provoked
seething
resentful
touchy
victimized

Chapter 10
Feelings Are Scary!

Don't feel that way!
(**Translation:** *Don't upset me with your upset.*)

There are lots of things I've forgotten or never learned or never *will* learn that won't affect my life much one way or the other. I've forgotten all of what I learned of chemistry. I can't remember most of the state capitols. I never could recite the Gettysburg Address. I know very little about Peru, Brazil, Greece or even Canada. I will never know how to split an atom or how to manufacture plastic bags. I expect to go to my grave having never woven fabric from which I made a garment. My life would no doubt be enriched by knowing or experiencing a variety of new things, but if I knew a *million* more facts and had a million more skills, the quality of my life would not be significantly altered.

There is one topic *essential* for a happy life, however, about which I grew up in ignorance. If anyone around me was modeling this skill, I didn't recognize it. I never heard a word about it in any school I ever attended short of graduate school. Unlike my ignorance of chemistry, my ignorance about *this* subject wreaked havoc on my mind, body, and spirit. My lack of knowledge of *this* subject, resulted in enormous pain for myself, my children, and my stepchildren. It nearly cost me my marriage. That subject is feelings: understanding the role of feelings in my life, *acceptance of my feelings,* and the skill of *managing feelings.*

All emotions are available for our benefit. Every emotion simply *delivers information.* That's all. Anger may clue me in that my boundaries are being violated—someone is invading my "space." Anger can also be triggered when

I'm afraid. Fear warns me of danger. If I'm afraid of intimacy, I may push the intimacy away with anger. Resentment may whisper that I've over extended myself and need to cut back on commitments or learn to say "no" to someone to whom I habitually say "yes." Jealousy will let me know if I have needs that I am ignoring or beliefs that need to be examined.

Emotions are the outward manifest-ation of something happening to my inner self or to my body.

More extreme emotions are still just demonstrations of need. Panic attacks and depression are obvious signs that something is amiss, either in my beliefs or the chemistry of my body. Many so-called negative emotions come as the result of faulty beliefs about myself[1]. Rage can be a symptom of a deep emotional wound that has not healed. Even retreat into insanity can be a symptom of extreme stress that can no longer be borne. Emotions are simply the outward manifestation of something happening to my inner self or to my body. All emotions are only neutral feedback.

Fear of the feelings themselves or fear of being hurt as a result of exposing a feeling makes it difficult to mirror.

The Mirroring exercise, by itself, is so easy that any three-year-old can learn it. There are two types of resistance to mirroring, though, that make doing it hard for most of us.[2] One is the *fear of the feelings themselves or fear of being hurt as a result of exposing a feeling*. This is true of both sexes but seems especially true for men.

❧

Jim: I perform a lot of wedding ceremonies. Some of the grooms with whom I have worked had jobs involving great risk: a rodeo bull rider, FBI, ATF, and DEA agents, heads of large corporations, and one race car driver. In spite of the courage needed for their professions, their legs turned to jelly at the wedding ceremony. Some of it was simple stage fright, but I've had many grooms confide in me that they were terrified they would "get emotional" in front of their guests. They were ashamed to be deeply touched by the commitment they were making to the girl of their dreams.

I feel kind of sad for men who would gladly face the town bully or a grizzly bear, but who, when a tear threatens, head for the hills. I admit, however, that even though I feel safe with Nancy, I am sometimes uncomfortable with becoming vulnerable by exposing my feelings.

Nancy and I saw the movie *Billy Elliott* together. It is the story of the son and brother of two tough coal miners in Ireland. He is expected to follow in their footsteps. Instead, he discovers a love for dance, *ballet* in particular, of all things. It has the predictable ending of the brother and dad proudly attending the opening of *Swan Lake* with Billy as the male lead. At the end of the movie, I had tears in my eyes. Nancy didn't.

I felt a little embarrassed. Those beliefs about manhood that have been driven so deeply into our minds are hard to overcome.

When I first began to speak in "I feel…" language, I felt as weird as a three-dollar bill. Nancy says speaking in feeling language was a new skill for her. I had *much* further to go than she did because it threatened my Okie idea of what it meant to be a man. It felt so unnatural.

For a boy in our culture, owning his first car is the closest thing to a rite of passage that we have. That may be true for the transition from childhood to adulthood. The rite of passage, however, from adulthood to SoulMate manhood is learning to accept and openly share feelings.

I didn't want to lose Nancy. The terrible pain I felt when that was a possibility made me willing to try anything, even sharing my feelings!

Now, I love sharing my feelings with Nancy. I feel safe. My manhood is not at stake. In fact, I can't even imagine going back to the old way of our relationship. It would be so shallow and unfulfilling in comparison. Feelings are *not* limited to just the woman's arena. Sharing my feelings opened up a whole new dimension of loving with Nancy and has made me more whole.

It takes real, manly courage to share one's feelings.

Sexual intimacy comes easily to men. We have to really work, though, at becoming emotionally intimate. The emotional intimacy that Nancy and I enjoy now, however, has made our sexual relationship even more pleasurable than it was before. Take my word for it!

The past 50 years have brought a lot of blurring in the formerly rigid dividing lines between men and women. I hope generations of men in the future will believe that *real men share their feelings.* You can begin now, with your wife, to experience the pleasure of a SoulMate relationship by using all your manly courage to share your feelings. There isn't any other way to have a SoulMate relationship.

❧

In spite of the many benefits of communicating on the Feeling Level, there appear to be a variety of reasons that seem to justify *trying* to hide our feelings. It's a bit ludicrous to think we can succeed in hiding our feelings, either from ourselves or from each other. After building up inside, they erupt, letting us know they have been there all along. Some erupt with explosions of anger or jealously. Some unpleasant emotions leak out in devious, underhanded, manipulative ways, like passive-aggressive behavior, sarcasm, and stubbornness. Some are manifested by distance or withdrawal. Some appear in the body as

Emotions will not stay hidden. One way or another, they tell the truth about their presence.

physical ailments. Emotions will not stay hidden. One way or another, they tell the truth about their presence.

I'M ASHAMED!

Admitting the truth, even to myself, is hard. I may believe that some emotions are "bad." I don't want to be *"bad,"* so I won't admit to having any *"bad"* emotions. Emotions like anger, fear, envy, jealousy, hatred, resentment, guilt or shame have gotten a "bad" rap. They are the victims of a huge misunderstanding. We see the *behavior* driven by these emotions and deduce it's the *emotion* that is at fault for all the damage done. In reality, it's *poor management* of how they are *expressed* that damages.[3]

If I believe that some of my feelings are shameful, I'll also hide them from my partner. I'll fear that he or she will judge me, as well as my feelings, as shameful. If my partner believes some feelings are bad, the feeling *will* be judged.

SoulMates do not judge each other's feelings.

I HATE FEELING HELPLESS!

I've had emotions that I tried to hide from myself because once I acknowledged them, a decision needed to be made. It wasn't so much the emotion that frightened me as the helplessness—I didn't know what to do. I was seeing a counselor by myself for almost a year before I could be honest about how angry I was with Jim. It was hard to admit to myself how frightened I felt. The unresolved issues were getting bigger. I liked to think I could handle it all. I hated feeling helpless.

As soon as I admitted feeling helpless about Jim, I realized I also felt helpless about the unhappiness of my boys. One of them was getting into a lot of trouble at school and with the law. He was defiant at home and unmanageable. I was losing him and didn't know what to do. My other son was withdrawn, basically going about his life on his own.

No wonder I wanted to hide! Hiding seemed the only safe thing to do at the time; but the longer I hid, the more healing and solutions were postponed.

Healing of hurts and solutions to issues cannot happen in hiding.

WHAT IF I DO SOMETHING I REGRET?

We laugh, now, about refusing to *seriously* consider divorce. Murder and suicide perhaps, but not divorce!

Joking aside, I had occasional fantasies hoping that Jim would die. That would have been *one* way to end the conflict. Another way might have been suicide. I don't remember being truthful with myself about feeling suicidal until years later, when suicide was no longer an act I would contemplate.

Feeling suicidal, however, is very different than committing the *act* of suicide. *Feeling* murderous is worlds away from committing the *act* of murder. *Feelings* and *behaviors* are very separate entities, totally different categories. I need not fear *any* feeling if I am clear that I am in control of whether or not I choose to act on that feeling. In fact, expressing my feelings in safe, respectful ways prevents them from exploding through out-of-control acts.[4]

I might also keep a feeling submerged, not out of dread of *my* possible actions, but for fear of an unpleasant reaction of hurt or anger from my *spouse*. You may, based on past experience, doubt your partner's ability to control his or her behavior. If you're concerned about your safety, the issue may need to be addressed with a third party present. If physical safety is not the issue, the temporary unpleasantness is a doorway through which a healthier, more satisfying relationship waits.

SoulMates are truthful about feelings and express them respectfully.

Now is a good time to say that our mates don't need to know about every pesky irritation experienced with him or her. It may be a small pettiness that will pass after a good night's sleep or giving myself a little "talking to."

One day I noticed Jim missed some lint when he vacuumed the carpet for me. My initial reaction was, "I wish he'd look more carefully. Why didn't he see that?" The little talk I gave myself was something like this, "He *vacuumed* for me, after all. Give the man a break! It's not like *I* never missed a little lint! The carpet is much cleaner than before he vacuumed. Clean *enough*. He deserves nothing but my appreciation for doing that nasty chore. Besides, if I criticize him he'll be much less willing to vacuum for me next week."

I saw the little irritation in perspective with the huge task that was now complete. So I let go of it. Jim didn't need to know. All he needed to hear was my thanks. The inner process I completed and the release of the fleeting irritation was respectful to myself and to Jim.

SoulMates discharge minor annoyances responsibly.

I DON'T THINK WE CAN DEAL WITH THIS!

Another reason we hid some things from each other was that we lacked confidence in our ability to work out the conflict that the exposure would trigger.

I knew there would be a big upset if I told Jim "When you reverse our decision about the discipline of our children without consulting me, I feel angry." At that time we didn't know how to resolve upsets very well, so I would stifle my anger. The next time the same thing happened, I made some snide, sarcastic remark. This is an example of feelings sneaking out in devious or manipulative ways. Then we'd really go at it! Once more, the strategy of hiding didn't work.

❧

Jim: When Nancy spoke harshly to one of the children, I didn't want to start another fight, so I would let it pass. The next time it happened, though, I would explode saying, "That *will not* happen again!" Because I had hidden my first reaction, the second or third time it came out harshly toward Nancy. I ended up doing the same thing to her that I was angry about.

❧

If you practice mirroring compliments and smaller issues, you will gradually gain confidence in the technique.

The reason we assigned the Suggested Practice Schedule for Mirroring is to address this issue. If you practice mirroring compliments and smaller issues, you will gradually gain confidence in the technique *and* that you can do it.

After we'd been mirroring for a while and had some successes under our belts, Jim would say, "I have an issue I need for you to mirror, but before we start, I want you to know that I am confident we will work this out." I would take a deep breath and relax. Now I could listen and mirror better because he'd reminded me that we'd done this many times before with great results.

I DON'T WANT TO HURT HIM! (HER!)

Don't let feelings build up— express them thoughtfully before they explode.

We had a mistaken idea that it's *always* a loving act to protect my loved one from *every* hurt.

We fought over the big things. But, for years, I didn't tell him that I resented his going off to bed, leaving me with dishes to clean up, for instance. I believed he would be embarrassed, hurt or offended if I told him, so I continued to "spare" him while the resentment piled up in me. Truthfully, I prided myself on being so capable. In those days it was hard for me to ask for help.

One night we had entertained. He helped pick up a little and then went to bed. I was in the kitchen fuming. My inner talk went something like, "I'm tired, too! He'll probably want me to make love with him after leaving me to clean up this mess. He's back there working a crossword puzzle or reading *The Readers Digest*. How dare he! This is not the first time this has happened. He is so inconsiderate. I can't stand it any more!"

This came to a head after I'd had learned some better communication skills, so I *quietly* told him how I felt. He was surprised. He had no idea. He didn't blame me for feeling resentful. He admitted he had been influenced by his Southern upbringing where male and female jobs were strictly assigned. He wouldn't mind helping me at all. He doesn't always notice the things I think need doing, so he graciously began developing a habit of asking me, "Is there anything else I can do to help you before I go to bed?" Simple solution. I am *very* grateful.

Other times it didn't turn out as well or wasn't resolved as quickly. One of us would be hurt. The other would feel bad and apologize. The problem would continue. Next time there would be more resentfulness and more hurt. We finally agreed we would rather be temporarily hurt and go on to work out a permanent solution, rather than *pretend* there was no hurt. The pretending created *more* resentment and *more* distance between us that would eventually erupt anyway.

It's a form of disrespect to act as though my partner is so fragile that he or she can't work his or her way through a hurt in order to come to a better place in the relationship. It's the very working through a hurt or an issue that provides the opportunity to rid myself of pettiness, exposes a belief that needs changing or challenges me to grow. When I "protect" my partner from that opportunity, I am depriving him or her of one of the *primary* benefits of a SoulMate relationship. SoulMate intimacy *does* expose areas in each of us that need attention. The quality of relationship that we craved could not be built on hiding of any kind.

SoulMates do not pretend. Mirroring provides SoulMates with a safe format to express feelings truthfully and respectfully.

I'M AFRAID OF BEING HURT!

This is the biggy! Human beings cannot reach adulthood without some experiences of being hurt or deeply wounded. In various encounters at home, or at school, in friendships, or in other romantic relationships, we have been the object of scorn, anger, teasing, rejection, disapproval or disinterest. Our natural defense is to protect ourselves from further hurt.

One of the ways I attempted to protect myself from being hurt was by aggressive, controlling behavior. I tried to be in charge of everything, tried to control everyone. I hoped that, by making my outer world conform to my standard of "right," I could minimize the pain I was experiencing. Of course it didn't work. In fact, it backfired, creating more resentment and pain. The members of my family didn't appreciate my efforts and wouldn't cooperate.

Aggressiveness came out toward Jim as attacking communications such as sarcasm, "you" accusations, yelling, etc. It was far more comfortable to yell, "Can't you see what you're doing? I'm so angry with you!" than to be vulnerable and say, "I love you so much and I'm afraid I'm losing you." I felt more protected saying, "You're wrong," than admitting "I'm devastated," or "confused," or "sick-at-heart." Metaphorically, I assumed a very aggressive stance—my arms were out in front of me with my fists clenched, delivering punches (see Figure A).

Figure A

⁓

Jim: I tried to avoid more pain by avoiding conflict or withdrawing. My way didn't work either. When avoided, the conflicts grew. When I withdrew from Nancy, she was *more* angry.

I also avoided pain by blaming Nancy for almost everything. I was glad when she decided to see a counselor without me because, after all, she was the one who needed to change. Two and one-half years later, when it began to be obvious that I might lose Nancy, I finally joined her in counseling. I did a huge amount of personal work, but it was several years after the worst of our stuff was behind us before I could bear to assume my fair share of responsibility for what we had gone through.

⁓'

As you learned from the mirroring explanation, saying "I feel..." keeps you on your side of the court. It also keeps you honest about your feelings and often the vulnerability of that honesty is terrifying. What if you open up your heart and get it stomped on? What if your feelings are laughed at? What if your pain is unimportant to your mate? What if you share your deepest feeling and it's ignored?

These are the fears that make it so incredibly hard to speak in "I feel..." language. In the moment of conflict, it feels far more comfortable to keep your emotional guard up. It feels much safer to protect yourself with aggressive communications on the Opinion Level, even though you know they have never resolved conflict before.

Yet, going from "You…" to "I feel…" is *exactly the point* at which the guard comes down and the mirroring process begins to work. *That* is the precise place where the power to resolve issues begins appearing. It is when you say, "I feel…" that a softness begins to invade the space between you, encouraging you both to let go of your defended positions. It is at *this point* that the giant leap is made from the Opinion Level to the Feeling Level of Communication where SoulMate love is born and nurtured.

At the point you risk letting your guard down, the mirroring process begins to work.

When both persons are keeping their guard up—maintaining the resentment and separation—the conflict is maintained. When even just one person in the partnership is willing to take the leap of vulnerability—surrendering the aggressive stance, and say simply "I feel…" and listen to what the partner is saying, (more about listening in Chapter 11)—the dynamic shifts. The partner is

Figure B

disarmed by the fact that there is no longer an opponent supporting his or her aggression by returning verbal blow for blow. Inevitably, the conflict subsides. When practiced consistently, the partner is often lured to the Feeling Level as well. At the very least, there is no support for continuing the conflict (see Figure B).

Virtually everyone arrives at adulthood surrounded by some degree of defensiveness. As children, those layers of defensiveness were all we could grab to protect ourselves from hurt. We didn't know any better. Those old defenses never really worked very well to begin with and now it's time to replace them. We've given you the tool—speaking in "I feel…" language. It's up to you to use it, experiment with it, even play with it. It doesn't have to be a heavy job. Work up to the bigger issues slowly. Experience for yourself the magic that occurs when your partner is given the privilege of seeing into your heart by hearing your true feelings.

We are still learning that feelings are good—that they can be trusted. We now choose to never again feel shame about any feeling. We have learned that acknowledging an uncomfortable feeling does not mean we are a helpless victim of it. We have learned that just because we *have* a feeling, doesn't mean we have to *act* on it. A *feeling* is completely separate from an *act*. We know now to look for and find help when we have feelings that we don't know how to manage. We are accepting our feelings as the good friends they were designed to be.

We no longer fear sharing our feelings with each other. It is interesting that something that started out like a dangerous jump into the unknown—feeling totally defenseless and vulnerable—has instead become a place of safety. There is power in simply speaking the truth about how we feel. Instead of feeling more exposed to hurt, we feel less afraid because we know the outcome will be resolution of conflicts and a healthier SoulMate relationship.

Very, very slowly, I have let down the defenses that I'd built up to ward off the fear of pain. More and more, I feel loved. I certainly love myself more than I used to. And I am able to let Jim's love in to a much deeper, more tender, less defended place inside of my heart. Now I really *hear* him when he tells me how much he loves me. I *feel* more deeply loving toward *him*.

As far as we know, all issues, resentments, and fears that could be walls separating us are gone. We understand the process of personal growth, however, and the valuable role SoulMate love plays by exposing areas in each of us that need attention. We know there will be more "stuff." *Whenever* we need it, mirroring is there for us, a well-worn and trusted communication tool for growing SoulMate love.

Keep practicing…

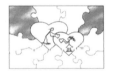

**Corner Puzzle Piece #2:
Communicate in ways that get the desired result.**

**"I will be honest with myself
and truthful with my partner even when it requires great courage.
I want the payoff of a SoulMate relationship."**

Growth demands a temporary surrender of security.
~ Gail Sheehy[5]

*Stop lying to each other;
when we lie to each other we are hurting ourselves.*
~ Ephesians 4:25

~

A VERY SPECIAL POSTSCRIPT:

This is only for those of you who like God stories. You are perfectly free to skip this. I won't be hurt. Neither will God.

For me, the most intimate relationship I am capable of having is with God. When my first husband died, I tried so hard to trust God—to believe that He had my best interests at heart. I said the "churchy" words, but deep inside, where I didn't allow myself to look, I was deeply wounded and had a giant cauldron of rage brewing. In those days, though, I believed anger was a bad emotion. And to be angry with God was unthinkable!

About three years after my husband's death—after three years of just putting one foot in front of the other, after three years of being aware *every* night when 5:30 p.m. came because that's when he used to come home, after three years of my older son's nightmares, after three years of diapers and tantrums and tedium without the support of a husband and daddy, after three years of loneliness and sexual abstinence, after three years of pretending I was "good" and "spiritual" and "trusting God," I marched down the hall and threw myself on my bed. I had no conscious awareness of what was about to happen. I pounded my fists on the bed and screamed at God, "'I *hate* you! I *hate* you! Why did you *do* this to me? I think you're a *coward* because you don't have a body. If you had a body and were standing here I'd *beat* on you! I'd hurt *you* as bad as you've hurt *me!*"

By that time, I woke up to what I was saying and was horrified. I literally lay there, breathing hard, heart pounding, waiting for God to strike me dead. He didn't. (Smile.) After a moment, I had the sensation of a warm, deeply comforting blanket being placed over my body. It was the most loving Presence I'd ever experienced. I somehow knew that I'd been asking the wrong question. Instead of "Why did you do this to me?" what I *really* wanted to know was, "Do you still love me?" I was afraid that I'd done something wrong and God was punishing me. God *already knew* I was angry. My anger didn't offend or intimidate Him in the least. In fact, once the hidden anger had blown out, the love that He'd been sending me was finally free to get through.

It was not the anger itself, but *the hiding of the anger* that kept me unaware of how *very, very much* I was loved.

As I write down this precious memory, it still brings tears to my eyes.

ENDNOTES

1   Beliefs and their consequences will be thoroughly covered in the second book of this set, *How to Stay Married & Love It Even More: Completing the Puzzle of a SoulMate Marriage*, available Fall, 2002 at www.howtostaymarried.com.

2   The second resistance to mirroring will be covered in the next chapter, "Learning to Listen."

3   The healthy management of feelings is covered in Chapters 12-17.

4   See Chapters 12 and 14 for choosing safe methods of acting out strong feelings.

5   Sheehy, Gail, *Passages*, p. 353. Boston, MA: Dutton & Co. Publishing. 1977.

Chapter 11

Learning to Listen

If we want the truth from our partners,
we must make it safe for them to tell it.
~ **Michael P. Nichols, Ph.D.**[1]

Most of us have had instruction in spelling, sentence construction and composition. Many of us have had speech classes. Some of us have even been taught debate. Only a very small minority (usually communication majors in college courses) report receiving some instruction in listening, even though listening is, at the very least, 50 percent of communication. It's impossible to even fathom how different this world would be if we all were taught how to communicate our feelings appropriately (Chapter 9) *and* how to listen.

Gary Chapman said, "The average person will listen to his or her spouse 17 seconds before interrupting."[2] I don't know whether that statistic was derived from a formal experiment or just based on his experience as a marriage counselor. It doesn't really matter because all of us have had the experience of being interrupted before we finish speaking. Just last night one of my clients said, "If I could just finish what I want to say (when he and his wife are fighting), I think I would calm down."

"Next to physical survival," wrote Stephen Covey, "the greatest need of a human being is psychological survival—to be understood, to be affirmed, to be validated, to be appreciated. When you listen you give that person psychological air."[3]

"The average person will listen to his or her spouse 17 seconds before interrupting."[2]

♥ 104 ♥

Jim: Can you imagine how frantic you would be if all the air in your room were suddenly gone? *Nothing* would be more important to you than getting air. Just as our bodies need air, one of our greatest emotional needs is to be heard. Have you ever noticed how the best friends are the ones who listen? Or the meeting was good if your opinion was heard? Or how the answer to your problem came as someone just listened to you talk about it? Some spiritual ministries, as well as some psychological therapies, are based solely on listening. Just to be heard is healing and therapeutic. Not any kind of listening will do, however. As with communication, there are five levels of listening.

Ignoring, Rudeness

This level is not the phenomenon of blocking out extraneous noise in order to focus our full attention on a task at hand. What is meant by "ignoring" is when we are aware that someone is speaking to us, or needs our attention, and we simply refuse to respond.

I took my car in to be washed the other day. I was there at 8 a.m., and though the sign said they were open, no one was by the vacuums. I could see someone at the other end of the car wash doing something with a washing machine. I waited. No one came. At least one person knew I was waiting for service, but he didn't call to fellow employees to let them know. I finally went into the office. The girl said that, yes, they were open. If I wanted to, I could go find someone to help me.

Even though the girl spoke to me, in essence she was also ignoring me. I was a customer waiting for service and my need was being ignored. I felt frustrated and unimportant.

Feeling frustrated and un-important are two primary results of being ignored.

Feeling frustrated and unimportant are two primary results of being ignored. If children are ignored enough, they begin to wonder if they are real. Without someone to affirm their realness by being attentive to them, they feel like an empty shell, unsure that there is anything of value within them. It is impossible to over-emphasize the importance that being heard means to our emotional health.

Pretending to Listen, Dishonest and Disrespectful

Ignoring, Rudeness

I was with a friend recently and was eagerly telling her about our workshops. When her eyes darted away to another part of the room several times, and her responses were lethargic, I knew she wasn't interested and was only pretending to listen. I felt unimportant to her. I felt disrespected. My desire for her friendship lessened.

Sometimes when I'm excited and want to tell Jim something that's happened, he'll say, "I want to listen, but I'm distracted right now. Can you give me five minutes to make this phone call? Then I'll be able to give you my full attention." Yes! I'm glad to give him the time he needs, because then I can be sure to be fully heard.

Selective Listening, Classrooms, Newscasts, or Arguments

Pretending to Listen, Dishonest and Disrespectful

Ignoring, Rudeness

❧

Jim: When my chatty girls were little and playing in the room near me, I'd tune in on their conversation once in awhile just for the fun of hearing what they were saying, or to be one step ahead of them if mischief was brewing.

Selective listening can be a useful skill if you are filtering out noncritical stuff from information you need to know, or listening for a particular event on the evening news.

❧

When arguing, the "listener is often pretending to listen while planning his or her rebuttal."

When two people are arguing, Pretending or Selective are usually the levels of listening being used. While one is speaking, the other is putting together his or her rebuttal (Pretending to Listen) or selecting one phrase of the other's to which to react, discarding the rest of what was said (Selective Listening). In all arguments, only a fraction of what is said is actually being heard. Ruth Brown facetiously wrote in the *National Enquirer*, "The only person who listens to both sides of an argument is the fellow in the next apartment!"

In observing many couples while mirroring, we've noticed that the "mirror" often misses part of what is said. He or she hears and mirrors, "I appreciate it when you take out the trash," but completely miss the next statement which is more intimate, "I feel very loved." One may hear the message delivered about an issue, but totally ignore the message about how much one is respected or loved.

We've heard that it takes 12 positive messages or compliments to cancel out one criticism. We human beings seem to have a very selective ear when it comes to negative words. We hear negative words more clearly, while intimate, caring words pass by our ears unheard.

It takes 12 positive messages or compliments to cancel out one criticism.

When I enrolled in my Master's Degree program, I concurrently completed

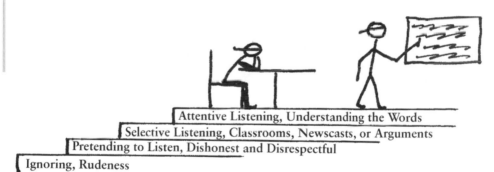

Attentive Listening, Understanding the Words
Selective Listening, Classrooms, Newscasts, or Arguments
Pretending to Listen, Dishonest and Disrespectful
Ignoring, Rudeness

the balance of my Bachelor's Degree requirements by taking equivalency exams rather than sitting in classrooms. I would buy a study guide for the next test I was taking. Then I'd read the questions and the correct answers onto cassette tapes. I listened attentively to those tapes—trying hard to commit to memory every fact. I listened only to understand the content of the words.

If all we need to understand are facts or opinions, listening attentively is appropriate. This is how we study texts, hear classroom lectures, or understand directions.

In relationships, however, there is so much more to be heard. When there is an emotional component to the relationship, only 10 percent of the communication received comes from the words. The tone of voice conveys approximately 30 percent of the meaning behind the words, and body language delivers the remaining 60 percent.

In Chapter 4, we explored the fact that each of us has a different point of

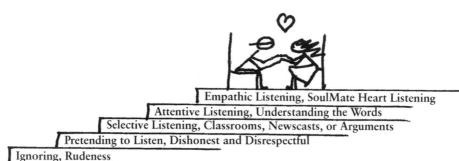

Empathic Listening, SoulMate Heart Listening
Attentive Listening, Understanding the Words
Selective Listening, Classrooms, Newscasts, or Arguments
Pretending to Listen, Dishonest and Disrespectful
Ignoring, Rudeness

The tone of voice conveys approximately 30 percent of the meaning behind the words, and body language delivers the remaining 60 percent.

view. When an issue arises between you and your spouse, it's because you each have differing perspectives. It's as though you are standing back to back taking turns describing what you see. She says, "I see a big picture window with a gorgeous view" while he says, "No. That's not right. I see a blank wall with a doorway leading to a kitchen. There is no picture window."

Understand that both points of view are valid.

When conducted on the Opinion Level, the argument often escalates because there is no acknowledgment that different views are being described *and* that both views are valid. Empathic Listening takes place when one (metaphorically) moves from one's position, turns around, and looks at the issue from the other's point of view. This means listening, not just to the words, but to the tone of voice, the body language, the eyes—listening from the heart. I recently read that the Chinese character for listening includes characters for eyes, ears, intention (to understand), and compassion. *That* is Empathic Listening.

❦

Jim: I'll never forget the first time I was able to see the primary issue between Nancy and me from her point of view. I wept when I realized what I had done to her. Up until then I had only heard her words selectively or attentively. I had understood them mentally. That time, however, I emotionally put myself in her place and saw what had happened through her eyes. It touched my heart and motivated me to change the destructive pattern I had been using against her.

❦

The Story of Us is a movie starring Bruce Willis and Michelle Pfeiffer about a marriage viewed over several years. If you can wade through the conflicts and trials of a decade condensed into 90 minutes, you'll see that there are two magical moments in the movie; one when Bruce's character sees himself through his wife's eyes, another when Michelle's character sees herself through his eyes. A gigantic shift in perspective takes place, transforming each of them and their marriage.

When the mirror steps up to the Empathic Listening level, the relationship moves into SoulMate territory.

Moving from the lower levels of listening to the Empathic Level is often magical, bringing about the same softening of positions that the Feeling and Need Levels bring on the speaking side of the communication. When the mirror steps up to the Empathic Listening level, the relationship moves into SoulMate territory.

As described in Chapter 10, the first resistance to the mirroring process comes from the *speaking* side, the fear of exposing vulnerable feelings. The second resistance to mirroring comes from the mirroring or *listening* side. It is threatening to get up from my position long enough to mentally and emotionally look over my partner's shoulder in order to see the issue from his or her point of view. I must be willing to take a big risk—a risk that is terrifying for most of us. I risk having my view or opinion about the issue changed. That is the primary reason Empathic Listening is so hard at times. In the charged atmosphere of an issue, it really is incredible how tenaciously I insist on my "right" point of view. It is a dead giveaway of my priorities. At that moment, it's more important for my insecure, willful ego to insist on being "right" than it is to resolve the issue between my partner and me.

I was really into being "right." I was sure I had a corner on that market! In order to listen empathically, I had to come up with this visual aid: I imagine that I'm taking my opinion, my feelings, or my needs, and temporarily setting them up on a shelf in my mind where they'll be out of my way. I remind myself that my turn is coming. I will get my chance at being heard, but for now, it's Jim's turn. I reassure myself that I'm not necessarily agreeing with Jim, I'm not throwing out my point of view, or surrendering it as unimportant. I'm just setting it aside *temporarily* so that I am free to see the issue from Jim's point of view. This was the only way I could enable myself to let go of my position long enough to listen at the Empathic Level.

Mentally and emotionally looking over my partner's shoulder to understand his or her point of view doesn't mean I always end up agreeing with it. The goal is simply to understand, on the feeling or need levels, why my partner has this particular point of view.

Another factor that makes listening hard, whether it's empathic or not, is that I am impatiently waiting until it is my turn to speak. This impatience is because I am not accustomed to being heard. Since I'm not sure it's really going to happen, I can barely wait until it's my turn to talk. In the old way of fighting, I was afraid of being interrupted before I was heard. Even if I got to speak the whole message, there was not always the sense of really being understood. We found that after we had experienced several successful mirroring sessions, it was easier to stay with the process patiently because we each knew we would get a turn. Each of us would be heard.

I resist communicating on the Feeling or Need Levels in order to avoid vulnerability and the possibility of being hurt. I resist listening on the Empathic Level in order to defend my "right" position. The distance and pain the conflict causes in the relationship is perpetuated by both of these defensive tactics. The very thing I crave most—a SoulMate relationship—is impossible as long as I am operating with those defenses. I cannot continue to avoid vulnerability and stubbornly hold on to my position and ever expect to have the closeness and harmony I want in this marriage.

You must be willing to surrender the security of self-protection and demanding ego to move to an elevated SoulMate relationship.

Perhaps I have a mistaken assumption of what it takes to be happy. I believe that if I make sure I am not vulnerable to being hurt, and make sure I get "my way," my needs will be met and I will be happy. The truth is I must be willing to surrender the security of self-protection and demanding ego in order to move up to an elevated SoulMate relationship. If this were easy to do, there would be many, many more blissfully happy couples. But, to succeed requires taking the risk of being hurt and the risk of changing my mind, which, for many of us, is a frightening leap.

I am reminded of the paradoxes described in St. Francis of Assisi's prayer:

> *It is in giving that we receive,*
> *It is in pardoning that we are pardoned,*
> *It is in dying that we are born to Eternal Life.*

A SoulMate relationship is not for the faint-of-heart. It takes great courage and heart to move up to the higher level of maturity necessary for the skills of communicating on the Feeling or Need Levels and listening on the Empathic Level. Just as in the prayer, it's in the surrender of what I think I must have that opens the door to the possibility of getting what I most desire: the diamond treasure of a SoulMate.

Nothing facilitates the process of building a SoulMate marriage more than mirroring.

It is my belief that in each of us there is an Authentic Self whose life purpose is to freely give and receive love. Because of whatever hurtful experiences we've had in life, or the emotional patterns that were modeled for us, the warm, open,

Authentic Self may have been camouflaged by defenses and habits that block the easy flow of giving and receiving love. For some, the Authentic Self may be so deeply hidden as to be invisible, and the adopted methods of coping with life very hard and crusty.

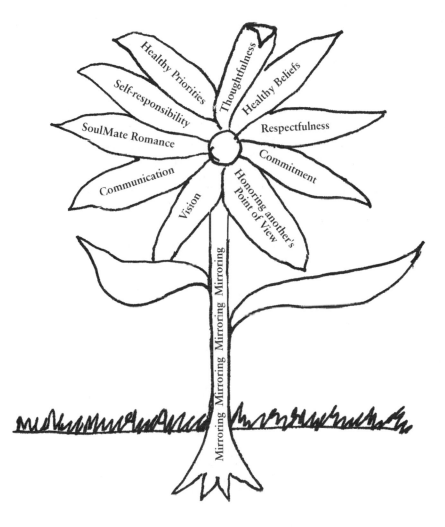

Authentic, Loving Self

The ten qualities that are presented in these two books as necessary for a SoulMate relationship are developed as one learns to love more generously and receive love more graciously. Nothing in this book facilitates that process more than the process of mirroring—communicating feelings and needs and listening empathically. It's as though that process reaches down into the essential soil of who we are, taps into the Authentic Loving Self, and lifts that loving up through roots and stem to nurture the flowering of those ten qualities and skills.

In Latin, intimate means "coming from the most internal place." Becoming intimate is getting to know each other in the deepest, most real way possible. In our most "internal place," we see each other beyond the defenses, the pretenses, the falseness. At that level, we are all lovable and deserving of compassion. Sharing our feelings and needs and listening with our hearts are the vehicles that carry us to true intimacy.

In Latin, intimate means "coming from the most internal place."

In the process of developing a SoulMate relationship, Jim and I have found that many of our defenses—those false selves adopted for self-protection—are dropping away, leaving us more free to give and receive love. This positive, healing effect does not show up just in *our* relationship, however. It is permanently changing for the better the qualities we bring to *every* relationship. In that sense, the quest for a SoulMate relationship is the laboratory in which I am able to experience more of the truth of who I really am—an imperfect human being who is willing to view life (including marriage to this particular person) as a school with a perfectly designed curriculum for self-healing, learning, growing and loving.

Corner Puzzle Piece #2:
Communicate in ways that get the desired result.

"I am learning not only to listen,
but to truly hear my loved one's feelings and needs.
As I validate my partner's point of view,
clearly communicate my own feelings and needs,
and empathically listen,
I am laying a firm foundation for the SoulMate marriage I desire."

One true self speaks to another, using the language of the heart,
and in that bond a person is healed.
~ Deepak Chopra[4]

The wise man learns by listening.

~ **Proverbs 21:11**

ENDNOTES

1   Nichols, Michael P., Ph.D., *The Lost Art of Listening*, pg. 193. New York:
    Guilford Press, 1995.

2   Author of *Toward a Growing Marriage* and *The Five Love Languages*.
    Quoted from "Marriage Works by Communicating, Not Running" by Art
    Toalston, *The Baptist Messenger*, October 5, 1995.

3   Covey, Stephen R., *7 Habits of Highly Effective People*, New York, NY:
    Simon & Schuster, Fireside. 1989.

4   Chopra, Deepak, M.D., *Unconditional Life: Mastering the Forces that
    Shape Personal Reality*, p. 168. New York: Bantam Books. 1991.

Puzzle Piece #3:
SoulMate Respect

Chapter 12

Find the Treasure
in Anger

I married her for her looks but not the ones she's been giving me lately.
~ Milton Berle

Without knowledge of horses and the learned skill of riding, that 2,000-pound animal can be very frightening. My sister, Jean, is a horse lover. When we were in our teens, she had a half-Arabian mare named Nugget. That horse was beautiful and Jean made riding her look like a piece of cake. Horses weren't my thing but, one day after school, I asked her if I could ride.

Jean's eyebrows shot up in surprise. With a shrug and a little smirk she answered, "Sure."

I barely settled in the saddle when I sensed this was a mistake. Nugget *knew* I lacked the knowledge or confidence to control her. She *loved* to run, so she just bolted. We circled the orange grove surrounding our house at a gallop, the loose reins whipping around us, and one stirrup flopping against Nugget's flank. I would have screamed, but all my strength was focused on trying to keep my body on Nugget's back and my head below the tree branches. As the corridor between rows of trees funneled us toward the corral, the pounding of Nugget's hooves and the roaring in my ears blocked the sound of Jean's laughter. At the last possible moment, Nugget skidded to a stop just short of Jean who wasn't even flinching. I dropped off of Nugget and handed the reins over with relief. I was so humiliated. I took one shaky step after another into the house, trying in vain to regain my dignity.

Strong emotions—like envy, jealousy, fear, grief and anger—can be like Nugget. They can run away with us if we don't know how to manage them. Unrestrained words and actions propelled by these emotions can be temporarily exhilarating, but it's never fun and sometimes impossible to clean up the mess left in the dust of an emotional stampede. No wonder these feelings are scary!

Letting emotions run amok, like an unrestrained Nugget, is one extreme. Locking them up because they scare us is the other. In the movie, "The Horse Whisperer,"[1] a severely traumatized horse-gone-wild was kept in a locked, dark stall for months. Everyone was afraid of him. The stall was never cleaned, so the horse and the stall became filthy. The story might have ended with the gradual death of the animal. Instead, the owner heard about a man who had a reputation for helping troubled horses. He could often find and recover the safe, manageable horse that was locked inside the outlaw. He had learned how to communicate with them. He knew how to give them what they needed. He had a healthy respect for the power of the animal but was not afraid because he understood how to manage it. Of course, in the movie, the horse is redeemed amid subplots of romance and the emotional healing of the teen owner, as well. It's an inspiring story!

For many of us, powerful emotions either run out of control—damaging the relationship—or remain locked inside—befouling the host. When we were thoroughly tired of those two options, we became serious about learning a third way of handling the strong emotion of anger—harnessing its energy to facilitate healing.

How we manage the strong emotions stirred up by conflict determines the outcome of the marriage. Relationship scientists[2] John Gottman, Robert Levenson, Howard Markman, Richard Notarius, and Scott Stanley (to name a few), are able to predict with more than 90 percent accuracy whether a particular marriage will live or die, based on only a short interview and a careful analysis of how the partners fight. In every example of what these scientists called "corrosive" fighting, the couples were using one or more of the Defective Communication Tools listed in Chapter 6.

How we manage the strong emotions stirred up by conflict determines the outcome of the marriage.

Marriage partners seem to fall into two major categories in their use of corrosive methods of expressing anger. The first is The Tiger, who uses such aggressive tools as verbal attacking, yelling, physical intimidation and throwing things. This expression of anger, if not curbed, increases in intensity over time. The second type is The Turtle. This one favors the more subtle tactics, such as withdrawal, pouting, martyrdom and other passive aggressive behaviors. "Fighting can be damaging, but fleeing can be more pernicious, particularly when the 'flight' is a retreat into stony silence. Habitual stonewalling is devastating to a relationship because it cuts off all possibility of working out disagreements."[3]

It's possible to begin an argument as a Tiger and resort to being a Turtle when you are either frightened by the intensity of the anger, or believe resolving the issue to be hopeless. Withdrawing may be the only way you know to halt the escalation of out-of-control anger.

Statistically, men are more prone to Turtle tactics than women. In general, women consider themselves relationship fixers, and tend to stay engaged in dialogue until the issue is resolved. Men are more prone to "flooding," a condition of being overwhelmed by the anger, causing a rush of adrenaline and accelerated heart rate. The return of a normal adrenaline level and a normal heart rate generally takes longer for a man than for a woman. The experts believe this "fight or flight" response has to do with man's early role of provider and defender.

Elevated levels of adrenaline and heart rate are very uncomfortable, often prompting men to withdraw from an argument sooner than a woman would.

The elevated levels of adrenaline and heart rate are very uncomfortable, often prompting men to withdraw from an argument sooner than a woman would. Once a man withdraws, or "stonewalls," his heartbeat immediately begins to drop, which gives him some relief. At the same time, however, his partner's heart rate often shoots up to high distress levels. Women consider withdrawal to be abandonment. In reality, the man is withdrawing in order to prevent his behavior from becoming even more out of control. A wise wife could use this scientific information as motivation to stay within the safe boundaries provided by mirroring so that her husband is less apt to become "flooded." He is then more prone to stay with the process until the issue is resolved.

Women consider withdrawal to be abandonment.

The experts all agree that the answer to both Tiger and Turtle expressions of anger is a pre-arranged structure for talking about issues (fighting). The structure provides safe ground that prevents the argument from escalating to the level that spawns corrosive communications, "flooding," and withdrawal. The structures recommended vary a little, but all of them have components identical or similar to the pattern for mirroring mapped out for you in Chapter 9: set a date to talk (the most upset one goes first using non-attacking language like "I feel…"), mirroring until the feelings have been heard, problem solving, then keeping your agreements.

In a recent workshop, after going through the mirroring routine, one husband said, "This is great, but let's get real. What if I'm too angry to mirror?" That's the glitch. Although this chapter will deal primarily with anger, the concepts and methods can be used with any strong emotion: jealousy, envy, grief, sadness, fear, etc.

If anger is not addressed as it occurs, event after event will add pressure, build up steam, and eventually "blow" like the lid of a pressure cooker with its steam vent blocked.

A frantic young wife, Lisa, called me about a year ago. She had been married to Sean[4] for four years. In that time her husband had never expressed any unhappiness, and certainly never any anger toward her; but a few days before, he had simply walked out, intending never to return.

Lisa was devastated and bewildered. She came to see me several times and diligently did an enormous amount of personal work. Fortunately, Sean was willing to come and see me, as well. For one hour a week for several weeks, Sean sat in my office telling me all the reasons why he was so angry. Sean had left his anger locked inside until it poisoned his love for Lisa. He thought he couldn't possibly ever love her again. Even her touch was repulsive to him. I mostly listened and validated his anger. Each week, sometime during the session, I also suggested that leaving her was only *one* option. *Another* option would be to learn how to tell her what he was feeling and what he needed so that the anger wouldn't build up to explosive levels.

After a couple of months, Lisa called and said Sean had tentatively moved back home. A few weeks later, she reported that they were experiencing a second honeymoon! Recently they followed up that intense period of personal counseling by attending a workshop. When we had the participants check off the Defective Communication Tools that they use, Sean and Lisa were encouraged to note that they no longer practiced many of the ones they had previously been using. There were only a few defective tools left to eliminate.

The expression of powerful emotions is called venting. Webster defines the verb, "vent," as "to expose to the air, to give expression to, to relieve pressure." Repressed, bottled-up anger poisons the host, literally altering the chemistry on the cellular level. If left unresolved, anger can sometimes express itself as illness.[5]

There are many unhealthy, unsafe ways to vent anger. Sean vented his anger first by stuffing it, then by leaving Lisa, then by pouring it out in my office. I used to express anger by yelling. Jim alternately withdrew and yelled. Many addictions—such as compulsive use of alcohol, drugs, sex, and shopping—have buried anger as the fuel that drives them. Verbal and physical abuses are vents for anger. Some drivers vent by driving recklessly.

When I am too angry to stay engaged in a mirroring session, I can stuff it, as Sean did, and wait for the explosion that must come; I can emotionally or physically withdraw, as Jim did; or I can spew verbal or physical abuse. Anger vented at my partner is corrosive and abusive. For those of you who have

If anger is not addressed as it occurs, event after event will add pressure.

If left unresolved, anger can sometimes express itself as illness.[5]

Out-of-control or repressed anger can only damage the person and the relationship.

children, just being in the presence of that kind of anger is abusive to them as well, not to mention venting it *toward* them. Out-of-control or repressed anger can *only* damage the person and the relationship. Instead, it's time to vent that anger *away from your partner.*

There *are* healthy ways to vent anger. But, before we discuss these, allow me to make something very clear. No one *makes* me angry. If that were true, then the things that trigger my anger would also trigger the anger of everyone else. I feel anger (actually, mild annoyance) when Jim leaves clutter on the kitchen table. Many women would not even notice that, yet would be irritated by his leaving his shoes on the floor outside of the closet, which doesn't bother me at all. Therefore, the act is not causing the anger. My anger is triggered by certain things, and other things trigger yours. It is *my* anger. My anger and what I do with it is always, *always* my sole responsibility. No one ever *makes* me act any particular way, even when I'm angry. If it were true that he or she *makes* me react a certain way, I would hopelessly be a victim, subject to the whim of my partner.

Your anger and what you do with is your responsibility.

Every incident that triggers anger has three components: the stimulus (whatever triggers the anger), the choice, and the chosen reaction or response—(see illustration).

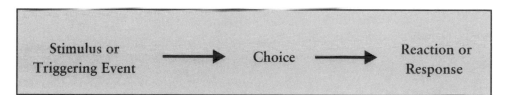

When I first heard this I couldn't believe it! The stimulus and my reaction happened in only a split second. I was sure my anger was Jim's fault. There was *no time* for a choice. Gradually, I learned to slow the process down. My anger would be triggered. I would hold my breath for a few seconds, or walk down the hall and back, giving myself time to recognize that I was in control of the next move. I *did* have a choice. As I learned new ways to manage anger, the choice became very clear. I could react with my old tools—tongue lashings, sarcasm, etc.—or I could choose to use a more respectful, safer way of expressing my anger.

Mild or even moderate anger can be expressed within the safe structure of mirroring.

Mild or even moderate anger can be expressed within the safe structure of mirroring. When the anger is too strong—when you can't keep yourself within the controlled boundaries of mirroring—then it is time to choose a healthy method of venting anger *away from your partner.*

When venting away from the partner, there are a few rules:

1. Do not direct the anger at another person or animal, such as

   a. Taking anger for your spouse out on your child, or

   b. Kicking the dog.

   c. Exception: venting anger with a counselor, as Sean did. In his case. It was not vented *at me*, just in my (consenting) presence.

2. Do not vent explosive anger in the presence of a child, because

   a. It's inappropriate for a child to hear out-of-control anger toward your spouse. Your partner is also the child's parent.

   b. It's frightening for a child to hear out-of-control anger. It amounts to emotional abuse.

3. Do not endanger yourself by taking foolish risks.

4. Do not endanger others (by driving recklessly, for example).

5. Do not damage valuable property, by

   a. Breaking a valuable item, particularly if it isn't yours, or

   b. Punching a hole in the wall, for instance.

What *can* you do? When by yourself, you may:

1. Physically hit an inanimate object (such as a pillow or mattress) while yelling anything you want at it, pretending it's your spouse.

2. Scream in the car with all the windows up, or into a pillow.

3. Keep a journal to write out your anger.

4. Throw valueless objects in a safe place (such as a ball against a block wall).

5. Beat the sofa with a plastic bat.

6. Weed, walk, or do some other vigorously physical activity.

7. Sculpt something ugly, or paint your feeling on canvas.

8. Attack a dirty job with a vengeance (clean the stove, the garage, the house, the car).

9. Tell your partner off into a tape recorder, then erase the tape.

10. Tear up that old pile of newspapers.

11. Write a nasty letter to your spouse, then burn it.

12. King David often vented his anger in prayers to God.[6]

13. Be creative and find a new, safe way for yourself.

Piero Ferrucci,[7] wrote about safe venting: "Such methods work equally well with current hurts as with accumulated resentments, and they should become part of our habits as a culture. They enable us to eliminate emotional debris which would otherwise impede the free flow of our functioning. Unfortunately, people who most need to use these methods often rationalize their fear of adopting them, by calling them ridiculous, useless, or undignified."

Yes, these safe methods feel stupid at first; but, would you rather tear apart your spouse and your marriage? Or, damage your health? The anger must go someplace. Vent it in a place where it benefits you by letting off the steam, yet does no harm to anyone or anything.

⟡

Jim: My late wife and I lived in a housing tract. A psychologist lived across the street and down a few doors. One summer afternoon, when everyone had their windows open, I heard a lot of yelling going on. Like everyone else, I stuck my head out the front door to see if someone needed help. About that time I saw the psychologist burst through his front door. His face was red. His fists were clenching and unclenching. He was breathing hard and looking frantically around his porch as though he'd lost something. He spied a tubular aluminum chaise, grabbed it and began beating the concrete porch with it and bending it over his knee. He kept at it until it was torn up into a dozen pieces. Then he quietly picked them all up, dumped them in the trash barrel, and went back in to his wife.

I thought it was hilarious! An angry person's antics can look pretty funny when they're not directed at me! I now understand that he was venting out-of-control anger at a relatively valueless object rather than destructively directing it at his wife. After he went back into the house, I didn't hear any more yelling. I assume they quietly worked out whatever had triggered the storm.

When I was first told to call a time out whenever I was about to lose it and go somewhere else to safely vent anger, I'd just get up and leave, slamming the door. After a few times of this, Nancy told me that even though I was leaving to safely vent, she felt frightened and abandoned. My abruptly walking out brought up some of the devastating feelings connected with her husband leaving and never coming home. With our counselor's help, we formulated a solution that worked for us. When I knew my anger was building to the point that I was in danger of losing control, I'd say to Nancy, "I love you. I'm not going to leave you. I just need to vent. I'll be back by ___." She would be reassured and I was free to leave without unnecessarily adding more grief to the situation.

At first, I wasn't sure how I could safely vent. Writing in a journal didn't do it for me, and I felt too inhibited by my position as a minister to be seen tearing a chair to pieces. Occasionally, I'd go hit a bucket of golf balls, pretending Nancy's face was on every ball. Eventually, I bought a micro-cassette recorder. I kept it in my car with some blank cassettes. When I was too angry to mirror, I'd reassure Nancy. Then I'd drive to a nearby park and, with the windows rolled up, yell into the tape recorder as though I were yelling at Nancy. I'd really tell her off! I'd say everything I wanted to say in person and use any Defective Communication Tool I chose. I'd play back what I'd said and say to myself, "Yeah, that's right! That's exactly right! And here's more!" Then I'd add some more choice sentences to the tape.

I'd yell, play back, listen, and yell some more until it finally began to sound funny or ridiculous to me. When I got to that stage, I knew the worst of the anger was over. At that point I could begin to plan how I would talk to Nancy about this issue within the mirroring format.

These things may sound either crazy or violent to some of you, but think about it. Isn't it better that the anger be taken out on a cheap chair, a tape, or a golf ball rather than stored in my body or used to attack the person I love? By the time I heard about *safely* venting anger, I'd had enough of seeing Nancy's shattered face when I threw verbal garbage at her. Our marriage had come very close to being one of those statistics. I was ready to try something different, even something that felt foolish at first.

❧

My primary venting method of choice was journaling. In my journal, I did *not* have to be nice. I could say anything I wanted, any way I wanted. Over the four-year period that was the most intensely angry time of our marriage, I filled four three-inch thick notebooks with typed pages full of my feelings. I had a battery-operated typewriter that I used for journaling, because I couldn't write fast enough to get all my racing thoughts down on paper. I know many therapists prefer that journals be written by hand because there is more of a direct connection between the anger in your body and the paper on which you write. That's great for many; but for me, typing worked best.

When I couldn't find a secluded place at home, I would take my typewriter to the park. Today, a laptop would work. Be sure your journal file is either accessed by a code that only you know, or delete the entry when you're through.

It's imperative that any record of venting be treated as respected, private property never to be read or heard without permission. Jim and I had a deal—I'd never listen to his tapes and he'd never read my journal. Why would we want to, anyway? I was just glad that toxic waste was going onto a tape rather than toward me and grateful when I learned that my anger could be funneled onto a page rather than attacking Jim.

It may feel strange the first few times you try venting in one of these safe ways. When you vent in these ways, you may be breaking family and cultural traditions. Only a lucky few of you had models for safe anger management in your homes when you were growing up. Remember: Insanity is doing the same thing over and over but expecting a different result. It is insane and cruel to continue letting anger corrode our bodies, our loved ones and our relationships. It is sane and humane to practice safe venting of anger.

This is a good time to practice being evaluative rather than judgmental. This concept may challenge a belief that anger is bad. It's not anger that is harmful. It's how that anger is expressed. It's not safe venting that is ridiculous—it's using our anger in ways that absolutely prevent a SoulMate relationship from evolving. Be kind and gentle with yourself if you are ready to change this pattern in your life. Pat yourself on the back for any progress you make. This is a big shift for most of us to make.

There is a part of you that is capable of remaining detached—an observer. The observer part can be rational while another part of you is angry. The observer says, "You're about to be out-of-control. Call a time out. It is not in your best interests to let this anger loose. Chances are you'll just get it thrown back at you, and you know how that hurts. Go vent. Venting is safe. It's not bad to be angry, it just needs safe expression. Later you can come back to resume the mirroring."

When are you through venting? When you are calm enough to plan a sane strategy for using respectful communication methods like mirroring to share your feelings about an issue with your partner. *If you leave a mirroring session to vent, you are responsible for making a date to resume mirroring the issue.*

One afternoon, Jim was about to leave for a few hours. Before he left, he said something that didn't really register until later. When it finally sank in, I was enraged. In my perception, he had taken the credit for something that had been my dream and I'd worked very hard to bring about.

It's impera-tive that any record of venting be treated as respected, private property never to be read or heard without permission.

It's not bad to be angry, it just needs safe expression.

Fortunately, the house was empty, because I was too angry to journal quietly. I stomped around the house, looking for a safe way to let this volcano blow. Finally, I marched back to our bedroom, threw myself on the bed, and began pounding the bed with my fists and feet, all the time yelling at the top of my lungs. I called Jim every dirty word I'd ever heard. I screamed until I was hoarse. I pounded until my muscles gave out in exhaustion. Eventually the anger was spent.

While quietly lying there, I remembered a series of questions my counselor recommended I ask myself after venting:

1. Is the degree of anger appropriate for the situation?
   I had to answer, "No. It's way out of proportion to the offense."
   If it seems out of proportion to the offense, then

2. When have I felt this feeling in the past?

3. What was the circumstance?

4. Who was the person involved?

5. What is the degree of anger toward my partner and what degree is due to a past offense or offenses?

You, too, can mine the treasure of healing from the safe explosion of buried anger.

As I asked myself these questions, a flood of memories hit me. As a quiet, meek, compliant child, I remembered many times when my parents said, "Thank you" to someone's compliment to me. It seemed to me that they were taking credit for my accomplishments. I particularly remembered my senior high pipe organ recital...

The instrument was a Swiss organ with four manuals (keyboards), a two-octave foot pedal, and multiple stops (choices of various sounds). There were two twelve-foot square rooms behind the balcony of the auditorium that housed hundreds of pipes. Playing the organ was a skill that my parents valued highly. The teacher gave me the first and last pieces of the recital, both places of honor. I worked so hard to prepare. For this timid teen—who spent most of her energy trying to be invisible—rattling the windows with bold, earth-rumbling sound was quite brave and very exciting. My mother attended. That day, for the first time, I made it through both magnificent pieces without a mistake. Afterwards, I introduced my teacher to my mother and heard Mom say, as usual, "Thank you" when my teacher praised *me*. I barely noticed that but hoped that I had finally done something big enough to warrant a word of praise from my mom. Some part of me was paused and waiting as my mother and I left the auditorium that day. We were halfway to the car when I realized there would be only silence. I was heartbroken. I never played the organ for pleasure again.

As the pain of these memories surfaced that day, I sobbed with grief. I realized that, for all of my life, I had not known how to stand up for my need to be acknowledged for an accomplishment. With every loss, another bit of pain had been shoved deeply inside me, creating an increasing amount of pressure. When Jim made his remark, it was as though he tripped a hidden land mine. He was lucky, and I was grateful, that he wasn't home when it exploded. He would have taken a lot of flak that didn't rightfully belong to him.

As I quieted, I began to plan how to talk with Jim about this issue. When he got home several hours later, I was subdued but friendly. I asked if he had time to talk about an issue. He did.

I quietly told him all of it. I told him what I'd realized about my past. I told him only about five percent of the anger was really with him. The other 95 percent was old stuff that I'd never acknowledged or vented. He was interested in the process I'd gone through, and very, very sorry for what he had (innocently) done.

Since that time, Jim has bent over backwards to make sure I get credit for anything I do. His understanding and support continue to heal that wounded place. I am so amazed by the awesome power of anger and the healing that can take place when it is safely vented. On that day I began to mine the treasure of healing from the safe explosion of buried anger.[8]

We all have buried "land mines." The persons closest to us seem to have been given the assignment of tripping the wires for us. It's been our experience that most land mines have roots that go down to what we call "The Pit." Each person's "pit" is a murky, mucky, mass of unresolved pain revolving around a few core issues: fear of abandonment, unworthiness, a belief that you have to do it all alone, despair of ever being loved, or fear of betrayal. In other words, many different issues may "trip" my anger, but most of my anger is probably rooted in one or two core issues. When the land mines explode, however, we're given a perfect opportunity to let out the poison. When the old wound is deep and large, it may take many occasions of venting before all the poison is drained; but the treasure to be found is healing.

My most devastating "pits" were "I am unlovable" and "I am unworthy of receiving what I want." Jim's primary "pit" was "I am stupid. I will never do it right." By venting anger responsibly and using mirroring to be respectfully truthful about our hurts and irritations, we have considerably reduced the size of our pits. They used to be the size of a good-sized swamp, but now are comparable to a mud puddle. The painful feelings are still there, but are not triggered as often and we recover our balance far more quickly than in the past. Those devastating beliefs are slowly losing their power to sabotage our lives.

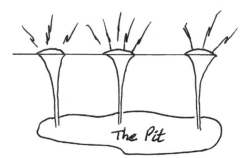

The Pit

"Land mines" are events that trigger explosive anger that is out of all proportion to the event. Almost every major event of anger has roots that can be traced back to "The Pit," a subconscious repository of core issues such as:

- ♦ "I am unlovable," or
- ♦ "I am unworthy of a good life," or
- ♦ "I can't do anything right," or
- ♦ "If I really love someone, I'll be betrayed," or
- ♦ "I'm all alone. I must do everything myself."

Almost every major event of anger has roots that can be traced back to "The Pit."

The combination of mirroring and safe, responsible venting is what brought our marriage back from the brink. When we think back to those years, the memories almost feel like watching a movie of other desperate, hurting people. It's only been in the past few years that we could talk about that time without crying.

The researchers cited at the beginning of this chapter say that healthy couples have at least a 5:1 ratio of positive exchanges to negative ones. We are way ahead of that! In the past year we may have had five or six minor irritations, and maybe one or two that were big enough to require a few minutes of mirroring before they were settled. Our days are full of loving expressions: appreciation, laughter, loving touches, creative planning, cooperative working, practical jokes, the doing of favors, frequent kisses and kind words scattered throughout the responsibilities of normal living. Our marriage is light years ahead of anything either of us was capable of imagining.

Safe venting is the vehicle through which anger can be used creatively and powerfully for healing. That treasure is worth every effort it takes to find it.

In summary:

1. Mirror. Agree at the outset to call a time out if needed.
2. If your anger approaches the out-of-control stage, call a time out.
3. Respectfully excuse yourself, and safely vent.
4. When the storm has passed, ask these questions:
   - ♦ When have I felt this feeling in the past?

- ◆ What was the circumstance?

- ◆ Who was the person involved?

- ◆ What degree of anger is really toward my partner and what degree of anger is about past events?

- ◆ From what "pit" (deep negative belief) do the roots of this upset come?

5. Plan how to share your feelings about this issue with your spouse.

6. Reschedule mirroring.

7. Share appreciation with each other for getting through a hot issue in a way that is healing and respectful for you both.

8. Do something soothing, either together or apart.

Corner Puzzle Piece #3:
Always treat yourself and your partner with respect.

"I assume full responsibility for my anger.
I choose to use the energy and power of anger to help me heal
by using safe methods of venting when I am too angry
to respectfully participate in mirroring."

There is something beautiful and profoundly vital
about aggressive energy.
While aggressive energy at its most primitive levels
can become destructive,
In its more evolved form it becomes creative power.
~ Piero Ferruci[9]

It is better to be slow-tempered than famous;
it is better to have self-control than to control an army.
~ Proverbs 16:32

ENDNOTES

1   Robert Redford's part in the movie was modeled after Monty Roberts, who wrote the book (with Lawrence Scanlan), *The Man Who Listens to Horses*. New York: Random House. 1998. Mr. Roberts could gentle wild, unbroken horses without any of the brutal tactics so often associated with training. He was the official trainer of all the horses in Queen Elizabeth's stable.

2   "New Secrets Any Couple Can Use to Keep the Flame Burning" by Anthony Schmitz, *HEALTH Magazine*, 1995.

3   "Why Husbands Tune Out," condensed from *Emotional Intelligence* by Daniel Goleman, *Readers Digest Magazine*, December, 1995.

4   Fictitious names.

5   Millenson, J.R., Ph.D, M.R.H., *Mind Matters*, p. 53-57. Seattle, WA: Eastland Press. 1995.

6   In the Bible, many of The Psalms that were written by King David begin with venting and end with gratitude or faith in God.

7   Piero Ferrucci is the founder of a method of therapy called "psychosynthesis." This quote is taken from his book, *What We May Be*, p. 88, New York: G.P. Putnam's Sons. 1982.

8   When I learned that being angry did not make me a bad person, I found my anger erupting almost constantly and at everyone. Although (most of the time) I restrained myself from acting out that anger inappropriately, I would seethe with impatience even if a store clerk were a little slow. I knew that a lifetime of buried anger had finally been given permission to escape. This period of time lasted about 18 months and then tapered off. Although I still am quite capable of being angry, it doesn't happen very often.

9   Perruci, Piero, *What We May Be,* p. 88, New York: G.P. Putnam's Sons. 1982.

Chapter 13

A Watershed Decision

*It makes a lot of difference in life whether you
live and learn...or just live.*

~ **Unknown**

There is a line running along the crest of the Rocky Mountains called a watershed. The line itself is very narrow, even insignificant. It isn't painted in white like a baseline on a baseball diamond or the 50-yard line on a football field. Without surveying tools, it probably can't be precisely identified; yet it's the line that results in two very different journeys, two very different destinations.

Several times every year a great drama is begun when mammoth clouds ball up against the mountains. Sizzling forks of lightening look like giant flaming arrows attacking the granite peaks. Explosions of thunder follow close behind, announcing the beginning of those two journeys. When the clouds disgorge their cargo along the crest, the raindrops that fall on one side of that watershed begin their trip toward the Gulf of Mexico a thousand or more miles away. The raindrops that fall on the other side of that line head toward the Pacific Ocean.

On the day we crossed the watershed line in our relationship, we didn't even recognize it. That day was a lot like all the recent days had been; we were fighting. We were struggling to learn some new communication tools: using "I feel..." messages rather than "You..."; referring to one specific event rather than bringing up the past; saying "When this happened..." rather than "You always..."; and, sticking to one issue at a time. We were sitting on a small sofa in our bedroom, angry, using the old defective tools and, without much grace, telling each other to rephrase whatever had just been said with one of the new tools. With several jerky stops and starts, our brains were grinding their way through the unfamiliar territory of "I feel…" when we suddenly stepped into that place where magic happens—we heard each other. And in the hearing, some little pieces of our respective defenses dropped away. Our hearts softened and without knowing it, we stepped over the line toward the ultimate healing of our marriage and rebirth of SoulMate love.

Just as along the crest of a mountain range, there was no marker delineating that watershed. All we knew was that the new tools we were awkwardly using had created a different outcome than we had experienced before. It felt good. That particular encounter ended with tears of relief and hugs. Before we got up off of that sofa, Jim put a name on what we were experiencing—respect. Each of us felt respected by the other.

We made a pact. From that moment on, we each agreed to do our very best to communicate in respectful ways. Use respectful tools. Treat each other with respect.

Before we left our room that day, we added some more conditions to the pact. We agreed that each could ask for a respectful method of communication whenever the other "forgot" and resorted to one of the disrespectful (defective) tools. Jim could ask me to lower my voice if my tone of voice began to climb into a zone that felt threatening to him. I could ask him to rephrase a "you…" message into an "I…" message before I responded to it. If he picked up a twist of sarcasm in my voice, he had my permission to ask for a restatement without the sarcastic tone of voice. If he resorted to "hopeless talk," I had his permission to say, "I feel frustrated that our discussion has been derailed by hopeless talk."

Agree to ask for respectful methods of communication.

It was rough going for the next few months. We were constantly calling each other back to the terms of our pact. It wasn't fun. I felt as though I were tied up in a straight-jacket, limited as I now was to just a few "respectful" methods of communicating. I missed my old, ugly, broken-down tools. I missed the thrill of popping off with a very clever, cutting, sarcastic remark.

It seemed to me that Jim's definition of respectful communicating was too narrow. I wanted more leeway. I thought he was deriving sadistic satisfaction from enforcing our pact on me. *Every time* he asked me to rephrase my statement in a lower tone of voice or without sarcasm, I felt an additional spurt of anger erupt within me. I'd frequently have to take a deep breath and hold it for a moment to avoid snapping back at him.

Not only that, it was my perception that I was restricting myself to "respectful" methods of communicating for *Jim's* benefit. To keep *him* from being hurt. To satisfy *his* definition of respectful. There were times I was so angry with him that I didn't *want* to treat him respectfully. I wanted to *hurt* him!

However, I didn't want to sabotage the improved ways *he* was speaking to *me*. I would bite my tongue, struggle through the maze of words to find the "right" ones and the "correct" way of putting them together that would pass the "respectful" limit we had placed on ourselves. *Each time* I had to tell myself, "I gave him permission to do this. Remember, I gave him *permission* to correct me."

As we refined the details of our pact, we decided that the only person qualified to determine whether the communication was respectful or not was the one on the receiving end. If the receiver felt threatened or disrespected, the speaker agreed to "tone it down." This narrowed the field even more.

Determining respectful communication should come from the "receiving end."

Very, very gradually, however, like a little rivulet of rainwater beginning its journey toward the ocean, we began to gain proficiency in using more respectful language. We made it through several "issue discussions" without yelling, hopeless talk, sarcasm or door-slamming exits. A number of times, we were both satisfied with the exchange and actually worked out a few solutions to some of the more minor issues.

I began to notice something else. A surprise. Although I thought I was restricting my communication to respectful methods for *Jim's* benefit, I noticed that I was feeling more *self*-respect. I was starting to like myself more than I did when I was yelling and cleverly tossing out sarcastic remarks. The little rivulet grew to a fairly good-sized stream when I began to choose respectful ways of communicating because I wanted *more* of the feeling of liking *myself* for a change. It was no longer just for Jim. The change was one I wanted for my *own* benefit.

There is a difference between choosing behaviors and communication methods that are respect*ful* and having *respect* for an individual. *This* piece of the puzzle is about being respect*ful*. I need not feel respect for a person in order to behave respectfully. It's interesting, however, that after several months of treating each other respectfully, Jim and I began to feel genuine respect for each other. We were working hard to incorporate new attitudes and behaviors into our relationship. Our efforts—and increasingly frequent successes—were not only building respect*ful* communication habits but were producing mutual *respect* as well.

We *feel* respect for those who demonstrate qualities that are valued by us. I do my best to be respect*ful* toward everyone with whom I interact, however, even though I may not understand or condone their behavior. This is because I like myself better when I am respectful and I believe every individual deserves to be treated respectfully. We are all human beings with struggles and lessons to learn while on earth. We each do that in the best way we know.

It was only after traveling for three or four months on the far side of the line that we looked back and realized we'd crossed the watershed at the crest of our own Rocky Mountains. Today, after approximately 15 years, we are certain that the day we made our pact was the day when we began traveling toward the destination of SoulMate love rather than a bitterly painful divorce.

The watershed in our relationship divided respectful from disrespectful behaviors. There is an identical watershed line in every relationship: husband and wife, boyfriend and girlfriend, father and child, mother and child, adult child and aging parent, friend to friend, employer and employee.

On one side of the watershed is disrespect. When communication methods on the List of Defective Communication Tools are used, the relationship is flowing down the disrespectful side of the mountain. On that side of the mountain, but still near the line, are minor cuts and bruises and occasional squalls. Further down the disrespectful side of the mountain are gorges of deep hurt, tumultuous falls of loneliness and despair, and raging rivers of anger and disillusionment. For a marriage, the downward journey on this side of the watershed leads to one of two destinations: the stagnant backwater of a lifeless arrangement or divorce.

On the other side of the watershed is respect. When respectful methods are practiced—such as venting anger safely, mirroring, "I feel…" messages, sticking to one issue at a time, setting dates for working things out, honoring of each other's limits, and appreciation for each other's efforts—the relationship gradually begins flowing in wider, more peaceful streams toward the verdant valley where SoulMates dwell.

The more time we spent on the respectful side of the watershed, the more distinct the line between respectful and disrespectful communications became. As we enjoyed the benefits on the respectful side of the mountain, stepping back over the line to disrespect became less appealing, so we ventured there less often. The lush richness of the relationship we now share is so treasured, that the occasional slips on the other side of the line are rare and quickly corrected.

It's easy to tell which side of the watershed you are on. Before you communicate with your loved one, ask yourself questions similar to these: "Do I feel good about the way I am planning to speak? Is this communication method on the defective tools list? Does my behavior fall within the boundaries taught by those who are further along than I? What has been the result when I've done this before? Even if what I'm about to say may temporarily hurt my loved one, am I stating my feelings and/or my needs in a reasonable, respectful manner? Or am I feeling smug because I'm about to get him? (or her?) Do I feel vindictive? Do I truthfully want this issue resolved in a way that is good for both of us? And don't forget this important one: Am I willing to empathically listen to his or her side of this issue as well?

What side of the watershed are you on?

We would be remiss if we didn't give you the opportunity to make the same pact with your partner as the one that was the dividing line between failure and success in our own relationship. It certainly was ideal that Jim and I reached the same point at the same time and were willing to make the pact mutual on the same day. We sincerely hope you have the same privilege, but being able to do this at the same time isn't necessary. First of all, the pact to only communicate in respectful ways is an individual decision and of benefit to *you*. This is a choice for which only you can be responsible. This pact will clear out what hinders a SoulMate marriage from *your* side of the relationship and leads to greater self-respect. *You* are in control of how *you* communicate. This does not require your partner's cooperation. The changes you make can't help but influence the way your partner responds and will positively affect the quality of your relationship. Not only that, calling yourself forward to a respectful standard will benefit every relationship in your life.

Whether you take this step alone or with your partner, what follows at the end of this chapter is a nicer, cleaned-up version of the awkward words we spoke on our watershed day. We encourage you to sign the pact. Make a few copies of it and keep it where it will remind you of your intention.

By the way, an intention determines the ultimate direction of the journey. It does not require perfection. We know of no one who has been able to keep to the respectful side of the watershed without some forays over the line. Don't judge yourself as a failure and give up just because you aren't doing it perfectly. As long as respectful communication is your intention, and you keep catching yourself, apologizing, and then pulling yourself back across the line, you will experience the reward of growing self-respect and improved relationships.

Old habits create deep grooves in the brain. When we begin a new practice, it's as though we have to climb out of the deep, old groove and thrash our way through a virgin forest to find a new path. For the first several weeks or months, it is still easy to slip into the old, well-established groove. It takes time for the new path to become well marked, familiar and easy to follow.

There are good reasons why it is hard to change old habits. As we said in Chapter 7, we patterned some of our relationship habits in childhood. Like ours, your marriage may have been flowing on the disrespect side of the watershed for some time, so those patterns of behavior are deeply entrenched. Perhaps your communications may be mostly respectful, with just a few defective tools to replace. Either way, it takes time and patience to establish new habits. Be kind to yourself. Be evaluative rather than judgmental. Be generous with mercy for yourself and your partner.

The course of your communication cannot help but eventually follow the direction of your intention. This sample pact may serve as an early step to formalize your intention.

It is my intention to communicate only in ways that give you the respect you deserve and that allow me to gain more self-respect. I give you permission to quietly call it to my attention any time I choose a disrespectful method of communicating my needs or feelings to you (or to our children). I will do my very best to respond with appreciation to your efforts to support me as I change bad habits into habits that will nurture SoulMate love. It is my intention (if this is a mutual pact) to remind you gently when you forget and use a communication tool that is disrespectful to me (or to our children). I intend to be patient, not expecting perfection, but appreciating and celebrating every step either of us take on our journey toward SoulMate love.

Signed _____ Date _____
Signed _____ Date _____

Of course this can be signed in secret and your intentions kept private. But the intention is greatly reinforced if it is openly shared with your partner (and your children if there are children in your home). We highly recommend enlisting the support of everyone in the home to help you change as quickly as possible whatever disrespectful habits you currently have into respectful ones. The next few weeks may require intense focus. If your partner is not ready to participate in this effort with you, ask for encouragement from an understanding friend or counselor.

Jim and I send our love and support to each of you reading this chapter and setting your intention to live on the respectful side of the watershed. Bless you.

Corner Puzzle Piece #3:
Always treat yourself and your partner with respect.

"I will live on the respectful side of the watershed.
If behave disrespectfully,
(notice it in myself or have it called to my attention by someone I love)
I will immediately apologize and choose a respectful method to
communicate my feelings and needs."

Learning to do things differently
requires practice, persistence, and patience.
~ Jim and Nancy Landrum

Your own soul is nourished when you are kind;
It is destroyed when you are cruel.
~ Proverbs 11:17

Chapter 14
Me? A Two-Year Old?

Title of a newspaper article:
"Couple Shoot Each Other in Counseling Session."
~ From Associated Press

I was visiting our son, Peter, his wife, Shelley, and their two children, Katie and Nicholas. Because of the distance between our homes, I had not been present for Katie's previous birthdays and was determined that I would not miss this one. Mid-morning, while Daddy was at work, and Mommy was enjoying some much needed time shopping all alone, Katie and I baked our family's favorite "Green Cake" (a pistachio nut cake). After it cooled, and while two-year-old Nick was taking a nap, Katie and I spread chocolate frosting between the bottom and top layers. I left it sitting on the kitchen counter, ready to add the final frosting.[1]

After Nick woke up, Katie and I were reading a story. Nick was impatient with sitting, so he was puttering around and entertaining himself. When I finished reading the book, I realized I hadn't heard anything from Nick for quite a few minutes. I went looking for him. You guessed it! From Katie's work table in the family room, he had dragged a little chair into the kitchen. He climbed up on the chair which put him at the perfect height to stick his chubby little fingers into the chocolate frosting. There were several finger-sized gouges in the frosting and plenty of evidence all over Nick's face and hands. He looked quite pleased with himself!

Two-year olds have many, many wonderful qualities. As proven by Nicholas, they are determined, imaginative, creative and resourceful. They are insatiably curious and take in and integrate an astounding number of facts about their world. At the same time, their improving coordination enables them to navigate amazingly well. To top it all off, they are learning the extremely complex skills required to master a language. If children are reared in a bilingual home, they master two separate languages at once.

We all know what happens, however, when a two-year-old's will is thwarted. The darling becomes a raging, self-centered tyrant, demanding that he or she be obeyed. At these times, unappealing willfulness, physical violence and irrationality are common characteristics. Everyone within hearing distance will suffer through this child's loud protestations.

All of us have a two-year old within. It's the two-year old in us who loves parties, plays practical jokes and sees the humor in a ridiculous situation. It's the two-year old within who dares to be creative when decorating the downstairs bathroom, or is curious about what new system might work better at the office, or designs a better mouse trap. The two-year old within is the one who won't take "no" for an answer when there is something needed that is vital to his or her well-being. We would be boring robots without our internal two-year old.

Two-year olds living in adult bodies destroy a lot of marriages.

It's that same two-year old, however, who loves to express anger without restraint and dishes out the silent treatment for days at a time. It's the two-year old within us who willfully uses the old defective communication tools, even though newer, safer, more respectful ones are at hand. The internal two-year old wants immediate gratification and does not want to consider consequences—not great qualities for building a SoulMate relationship. Two-year olds living in adult bodies destroy a lot of marriages.

Jim and I were sitting in the food court of a shopping center. At the center of this ground floor area was a large, circular, concrete fountain. The core was about five feet high, and the outer rim was an 18-inch wall topped by about a six-inch flat lip. The whole thing was large—at least eight feet in diameter. We finished dinner and were playing a game at our table when I noticed a young boy who looked as though he had just recently learned to walk. His dad must have lifted him up on the narrow lip, because the boy was now walking precariously around the edge of the fountain with the dad holding his hand. Every few feet, the child tried to pull his little hand free of Daddy's, wanting to navigate all by himself. Dad never got impatient, never scolded, hardly even responded to the boy's attempts at freedom. But dad would not let go of his hand.

The dad knew something the little boy didn't. The child didn't have the coordination necessary to walk around that narrow lip without either falling in the water on the one side, or falling on the concrete floor on the other side. Dad was letting him have the adventuresome, harmless fun of "walking the line" without risking the harmful consequences of doing it without a safe tether. He was providing what was needed to keep the child safe.

There are two things that make parenting a two-year old a bit easier. The first is safe, consistent boundaries. One of my clients was struggling with a very intelligent, willful young child. The child was frustrating and exhausting the mom, who felt as if she was not capable of meeting the creative challenges this child continually posed. She chose a few rules that were absolutely necessary both for the child's safety or her own sanity. I suggested a few simple consequences to be consistently and immediately delivered if the child "broke" one of the rules. The client decided in favor of zero tolerance for broken rules (for instance, no repeated warnings). Within a couple of short weeks, the household was peaceful. Mom was happy. The child was content. A lot more of mom's energy was now free to cuddle, love, and positively reinforce the behaviors she desired for her child.

Set up safe, consistant, self-imposed boundaries for the two-year old within.

My two-year old within needs simple, safe, strong boundaries that are lovingly enforced. I decided on a few self-imposed boundaries for my own behavior when I was so angry with Jim that I wanted to forget everything I'd learned, forget being "good," and have the immediate, childish satisfaction of hurting him. When I wasn't able to control my enraged child out of concern for *Jim*, I used something every two-year old would understand—*selfishness*. I would remind my soon-to-be out-of-control child that if she went ahead with her tantrum, she would have to apologize later, and would still have to deal the original issue on top of whatever damage she had added to the mess. I also reminded her that she would feel sorry and ashamed of her behavior once the heat of the moment had passed. Is that what she wanted?

In the early months of the respect-pact between Jim and me (Chapter 13: A Watershed Decision), my willful child would sometimes answer, "It's worth it!" There were a few more tantrums when she had to clean up the hurtful consequences of her behavior. Since my two-year old has never liked cleaning up messes, she increasingly cooperated with my intention to use respectful methods of communication. The result was progress toward resolutions for our conflicts and greater self-respect. As the contrast between a tantrum and respectful methods of communication became more vivid, she began to answer with a resigned "No!" to the impulse of unrestrained behavior. She became a healthy kind of selfish, showing concern about the consequences of her behavior to herself, if not to someone else.

These are the safe boundaries I made for my two-year old within:

♦ I will choose respectful communication techniques at all times.

♦ I will call a time out if I'm about to lose control.

- I will vent uncontrollable anger away from anyone whom I might hurt.
- I will leave the discussion if my partner is out of control, rather than retaliate.
- If I slip, I will humbly apologize as quickly as possible.

Create a clear vision for yourself and what you desire from your marriage.

The second thing to make parenting a two-year old easier is a clear vision of what you want for that child. A healthy parent wants plenty of safe opportunities for a child to explore, invent, be curious, be creative and learn new skills. A healthy parent also wants a child to have spirit, but learn to respect age-appropriate boundaries. The vision is a child who is self-confident, reasonably polite, and usually pleasant to be around. In this environment, most children would thrive, reaching their greatest potential for intelligence, creativity, and happiness.

The vision I had for myself was the same one that had been there since I was a young child. I saw myself in a loving relationship where there was mutual trust, respect, abundant affection, cooperation, support and romance. I knew that this kind of relationship was one in which I could thrive. As Jim and I began to use better communication skills, my hope for this vision revived. It motivated me to operate within my self-imposed boundaries.

Another motivation: I could see some of the healthy generational patterns I was successfully modeling for our children. I also regretfully recognized the dysfunctional patterns I was repeating. To begin with, I didn't know the "healthy" patterns to replace the ones I hoped to eliminate. I'd been trying to get good results with bad tools (doing the same thing over and over, but expecting a different result). As Jim and I found and used better tools, I envisioned Jim and myself changing the course of our family's history. We were weeding out patterns that wouldn't serve our children very well and instead offering, by example, some patterns that had delivered better results in our own relationship.

These boundaries and this vision are very self-serving in the best sense of the word. This marriage provided me the most exquisite training opportunity. Fortunately, I chose to use it to develop the qualities I needed in order to participate in the kind of loving relationship of which I had dreamed since childhood. Marrying Jim was not a mistake, but, in my opinion, a gift given by a loving God who knew exactly what I needed in order, ultimately, to thrive.

There is a theory about falling in love that makes sense to us. It does not belong exclusively to Harville Hendrix, but he does a superb job of describing it for ordinary folks in his book, *Getting the Love You Want.*[2] The theory suggests that the chemistry that attracts us to one particular person but not to another comes from our subconscious. In that deep place, a knowing, instinctual intelligence draws us to the mate who will trigger unresolved childhood issues for the purpose of healing. The book is rich with exercises that, by the time we completed them, gave us profound appreciation for the inner wisdom that brought us together.

It is *so* true that it is a universal married-person joke—every marriage is faced with unpleasant surprises after the "I do's." As the initial honeymoon wanes, the issues triggered by the relationship give us a tailor made opportunity to resolve old wounds.

Because both Jim and I perform wedding ceremonies, we have met many couples who have lived together, some of them for years, before formalizing their relationship with marriage vows. Even with those couples, some undesirable behaviors surface after the partnership becomes "legal." It's as though the subconscious knows that with full commitment comes full readiness to face unresolved issues so all the stops are pulled in an effort to heal old wounds.

One of the highest purposes of intimate relationship is helping to heal old wounds from our past.

This is not a sadistic joke. It is one of the highest purposes of intimate relationship. We serve each other by triggering these issues for healing *so that we can move on to greater wholeness of being.*

This would explain, for example, why a woman who might repeatedly get involved with abusive men finally resolves *that* issue by deciding to believe in her own worthiness of respectful treatment. Once that issue is resolved, the spouse will either adjust to her new belief and treat her with respect, or she will leave the relationship. Either way, the subconscious agenda for that relationship was successfully completed.

A young couple was in my office recently. Mary was telling me that even when she asks very nicely for a favor, Tom accuses her of nagging. Other times, she admits, she *does* nag. I asked Tom who had nagged him in his past. He started to say "No one" but then his eyes widened. His Mom was always after him for something, and his Dad, even though Tom is now an adult and married, had called him several times the previous week to remind him to take care of his car insurance.

Tom and Mary now have a choice. Tom could leave in a shallow, self-righteous huff, convinced that Mary had hidden that unpleasant behavior until after the vows were spoken. Or he can use this opportunity to assert his ability to be responsible for himself, and learn respectful, non-reactive ways to speak to Mary when she nags (and to his mother and father, for that matter). Because he is choosing to stay in the relationship, he is assuming responsibility for the times he accuses her of nagging when it was a kindly spoken request.

That hypersensitivity to being told *anything* is simply evidence of the internal bruising Tom has after years of being nagged.

Mary was sure that Tom had deceived *her* about himself as well. She had no idea he had a bad temper or could be so unreasonable. She was ready to call it quits. Instead, she is learning to respectfully tell Tom how she feels when she takes care to ask a request politely and he still reacts with anger. She is also recognizing that she learned nagging from a master (her mother), and she is responsible for changing that unappealing habit.

In the process of saving and rebuilding our love, many of my childhood wounds that have been exposed are healing. I now know that I am lovable and loved. I have broken through many artificial barriers to reach the place of believing that this book will help others, and that I'm the best person to write it. I am happy. I feel fulfilled in the work that I do. My gifts are being encouraged and my weaknesses are less dominant.

Jim is no longer terrified by the prospect of someone being angry with him or disapproving of him. His self-esteem has increased by quantum leaps! He has stood up for himself in situations that, in the past, would have intimidated him. He is not as apt to run from conflict. He is content.

Occasionally, Jim and I shudder when we think of what we would have missed had we given up on our marriage. We would not only have gone through the agony and humiliation of a divorce for ourselves but, by our example, made it easier for our children and grandchildren to choose that option. Instead, we hung on. If we had left and eventually found new partners, we *may* have beat the statistical odds and learned what we needed in order to mine the diamonds in *those* relationships, but we would have forever missed the diamonds waiting for us in *this* marriage.

Look for the richest of diamond fields in your current partnership.

The main purpose of sharing our story, first through the workshops, and now through this book, is to encourage couples to do the work and find the richest of diamond fields in your current partnership. When learning to use new, unfamiliar tools seems too hard; when your partner isn't doing what you consider his or her share; when you're so discouraged or so angry that you want to indulge yourself in some nasty, disrespectful communication, use the motivation of your own self interests to keep you on the SoulMate side of the watershed. When the internal two-year old begins to wrench control of your behavior away from your adult self, take this two-year old aside and review the boundaries and the consequences for violating them. Refresh your vision. Has this rampaging two-year old ever effected a better relationship in the past? Will the unbridled child be able to give you what you want from this relationship?

The diamonds are waiting for you on the respectful side of the watershed. Happy mining!

Corner Puzzle Piece #3:
Always treat yourself and your partner with respect.

"I will enforce safe boundaries
and hold onto a clear vision of a SoulMate marriage
rather than allow my two-year old within to wreak havoc with anger."

Be a healthy kind of selfish!

~ Nancy Landrum

Watch your step. Stick to the path and be safe.
Don't sidetrack; pull back your foot from danger.

~ Proverbs 4:26, 27

ENDNOTES

1   The recipe is at the end of this chapter.

2   Hendrix, Harville, *Getting the Love You Want.* New York: Harper & Row, Publishers, Inc. 1988.

The "Green" Cake
(Pistachio Nut Cake)

Mix together until fluffy:

> 1 boxed white cake
>
> 1 box instant pistachio nut pudding
>
> 1 c. water or soda water
>
> ½ c. non fat yogurt or vegetable oil
>
> ½ c. chopped nuts
>
> 3 eggs

Divide batter between two greased and floured layer-cake pans and bake at 350 degrees, 30-35 minutes. Let cool for five minutes, remove from pans to wire racks to finish cooling.

Use 1 can pre-mixed chocolate frosting in between the two layers. Finish frosting outer cake with this recipe:

> 1 pkg. Pistachio nut instant pudding
>
> 1 pkg. Dream Whip
>
> 1 ½ c. cold milk

Whip on high speed until soft peaks form. Frost cake. Top cake with shaved chocolate if desired. Because of the whipped topping, this cake must be refrigerated.

Chapter 15

The "Mother Lode"

When feelings of not being understood come out as anger,
hearing them, not shutting your ears and fighting back,
is the key to calming things down.

~ Michael P. Nichols, Ph.D.[1]

There is no question that it's ideal to ask for a mirroring date when experiencing an upset. You would be following our directions if you asked for a time out and vented your out-of-control anger away from your partner. You would be lucky, indeed, if your partner happened to be out of the vicinity when your volcano erupted. But what do you do when a land mine goes off without warning? When before you are aware of what is happening, you're in the middle of a nasty fight? What then?

Chapter 12, "Finding the Treasure in Anger," introduced the radical thought that there is personal treasure to be found in anger. It described the *individual* exploration of one's anger for the purpose of healing issues that otherwise remain buried, like a land mine, just below the surface, waiting for an unsuspecting foot to "trip" the explosion. This chapter will describe the awkward and difficult, but incredibly beautiful *couple*-process that, often, unearths the "mother lode" of all treasure in a SoulMate marriage.

Let's reenact the skit from Chapter 6 and see what happens when one of the partners grabs the runaway two-year old and switches, mid-stream, from childish knee-jerk reactions to the conscious use of some new communication tools. Again, this skit is fictitious, although Jim and I have had similar experiences countless times.

She: (Gets a pen out of her purse...looks pointedly over at him) Well, did you bring a pen?

He: No.

She: (With knowing superiority) I knew you wouldn't bring a pen!

He: What's the big deal?

She: (Sarcastically) If you really wanted to learn anything here today you would have at least brought a pen to take notes.

He: (Defensively) I want to learn! I'm here aren't I?

She: Yeah, you're here about like my father was. Your body's here but you're not really with me.

He: (Louder) Why are you bugging me? You're becoming a real nag, just like your mother. No wonder your dad is so quiet. She's always criticizing him!

She: (Emphatically) I am *not* like my mother and I resent you bringing her into this.

He: (Gathering steam) Just like today, on the way here, telling me how to drive..."slow down," "turn here," "stop!" Like I'm a little kid who doesn't know anything!

She: (With exaggerated patience) You *know* we wouldn't have gotten here on time if I hadn't been reading the map!

He: (Pause. Sigh. He thinks, Boy, would I like to "zing" her now! I could say, "The Great Map Reader!" and remind her of how she got us lost on our honeymoon and made us miss the plane...but would that get me what I really want? I want peace and harmony. I don't like where this is currently heading. I know the result. We've gone there before and recovering from the hurt feelings isn't fun.)

He: (Quietly) You know, you're right. We wouldn't have gotten here on time if you hadn't been reading the map. (Pause...)

She: Well, thank you for that. (Pause...) We really got off track, didn't we?

He: Yeah. What happened?

She: Oh, I was upset about the pen.

He: Was it really the pen, or was there something else?

She: (After thought) I guess I'm feeling pretty nervous about attending this marriage seminar with you.

He: You're feeling anxious about our attending this seminar together?

She: Yes. I'm afraid that you really don't want to be here—that you only came to avoid another fight.

He: So you think I don't want to be here?

She: Yes. The men in my family don't show much interest in developing good relationships. Their attitude is that relationship stuff is for women. I guess I have a belief that all men feel the same way. Is that true?

He: It's not true about *me*. I came tonight because I *want* our relationship to be better. I *love* the times when we are close. I want that to be true about us all the time, not just occasionally.

She: Wow! It feels so good to me to hear you say that...Do you mind if I ask you a question?

He: Ask away!

She: (A little timidly) Why didn't you bring a pen?

He: (Sigh) I intended to bring a pad and a pen to take notes, but we overslept. By the time I put the garbage barrels out for the trash pick-up and shaved, we were late and I forgot. When you asked me, I was embarrassed and gave you a smart-mouth answer that you didn't deserve. I'm sorry.

She: I accept your apology. I know that the first time I asked about the pen, I asked in a challenging tone of voice. I'd already made up my mind that you were going to disappoint me. Would you forgive me?

He: You got it!

Both: (Big sighs...)

She: We made it through that one really well. I am so grateful that you paused and changed the direction we were heading. It was getting nasty.

He: Well, I'm proud of the way you got in touch with what was really going on—your fear that I didn't want to be here.

She: I need a hug...

He: Me, too!

XOXOXO

Don't make the mistake of reacting without listening!

If you're human, you've no doubt had the experience of a fight starting up the way this one did. Many of us have had fights that consist of one nasty comment after another until neither person can remember what started the fight in the first place. These "discussions" are really two concurrent monologues in which each person talks and reacts, but doesn't listen.

Finding something about which you can agree is a great way to interrupt the downward spiral of a heated "discussion." The transformation began, however, when the husband stopped to evaluate whether his reaction was going to get him what he really wanted. His two-year old wanted to defend himself, fight back, and retaliate against his wife. Instead he wrested control away from his inner two-year old and chose a response in alignment with his (adult) long-term goal—a saner, closer relationship with his wife. *Either partner can interrupt the crash-and-burn direction of a fight at any point during the fight. Every exchange provides another opportunity to change course.* Since Jim particularly hates conflict, it has often been he who finds something with which he can agree or begins to mirror my feelings—pulling us back from the brink of disaster and exposing the treasure of greater healing and intimacy in our relationship. But not always…

We were in Arizona on a vacation. We decided to spend the morning exploring a beautiful new museum outside of Scottsdale. We walked up from the parking lot into a large inner courtyard with a wide portico that enticingly pulled visitors into the gift shops. We wandered into the first shop. The merchandise was displayed along the walls; the sales counter formed an island in the center of the room. I browsed around the periphery.

Three-fourths of the way around, I glanced up to see where Jim was. I couldn't see him. I felt a little tightening in my stomach as I walked a full circle around the shop and still didn't find him. I stepped outside the door and glanced down the wide covered sidewalk to my left. No Jim. I stopped breathing. I looked to my right. There were at least a hundred people on the walkway. I couldn't see him. I launched into the crowd, dodging strollers and ladies with big shopping bags. I looked in shop windows as I passed, in case he'd gone into another store.

Finally, I spotted his glorious white hair above the crowd. My anxiety instantly turned to anger. I marched up to him and hissed, "Why did you go off and leave me?"

His warm welcome immediately turned to outrage. "I'm not a little boy! I don't have to be kept on a leash! What? Did you think I was going to drive off and leave you here?"

We glared at each other for a moment and then one of us said, "Let's go to the car."

Each wrapped in our own blanket of self-righteous indignation, we silently stomped to the car. The moment we closed the doors, Jim said, "I'm too angry to talk. I'm going to take a walk and try to cool off."

Taking a "time out" was a good strategy. We were both very angry. I knew we would eventually talk (mirror) and the upset would be settled—we'd been through enough of these that there was no doubt about the eventual resolution, even though it had been a long time since we'd set each other off *this* badly. But I decided to try to take a short cut. I mentally set my issue up on a shelf, and mirrored Jim, "You are very angry."

Either partner can interrupt the crash-and-burn direction of a fight at any point during the fight.

Jim: I knew what Nancy was doing. She was mirroring me in an effort to settle this erupting volcano faster. I thought, "Oh, shoot! I don't want to mirror. I just want to be mad." I wrestled with my choices. Going for a walk would not have been a bad thing. I would calm down and *then* we would mirror. I had nothing to lose by trying now, however, so eventually I responded, "Yes, I'm *very* angry!"

Nancy: You are *very* angry!

Jim: (His voice lowering a little) When you were angry with me for leaving the store I felt like a little boy tied to his mother's apron strings.

Nancy: So, you felt like a child being yanked on a leash. Is that right?

Jim: (His voice even more calm) Yes. I wasn't going to leave you here. I only walked a few feet down the sidewalk. I thought you would know that I had just walked a little ahead. I don't deserve to be attacked like I was.

Nancy: You assumed I would know that you just walked ahead.

Jim: Yes. That assumption seemed reasonable to me.

Nancy: Do you feel that I've heard you?

Jim: Yes.

Nancy: Are you in a place where you can mirror me?

Jim: I'm still pretty upset, but I'll try. If I can't, I'll go for a walk.

Nancy: O.K. First of all, I apologize. You're right. You didn't deserve the angry reaction you got from me. Would you forgive me?

Jim: Yes. And thank you for your apology.

Nancy: When I looked and didn't see you, I panicked inside.

Jim: You panicked when you couldn't see me near you.

Nancy: Yes. I know it wasn't logical. I know you wouldn't drive off and leave me.

Jim: Your reaction of panic wasn't a logical reaction.

Nancy: No. My panic was out of all proportion to the real situation. If I had been able to think, I might have calmed down, but, for those few minutes, I couldn't think! In the past eighteen months three close family members have died. In addition, I've already had the very real experience of my husband walking out the door one evening to play in a softball game and dropping dead and never coming home. When I looked around and couldn't see you, I thought you were dead!

(Jim knew how traumatic each of these losses had been. The most recent had been the previous week with the death of my first mother-in-law with whom I was very close. By the time I finished speaking we were both crying.)

Jim: Can I hold you?

We held each other while we dried our tears. The "mother lode" that came out of this experience was the awareness of my deep fear of another loss. Jim was so sorry that he hadn't been more sensitive to my feelings. We needed a plan for keeping track of each other in public places. Since that day, Jim has been conscientious about letting me know when he's had enough window shopping and telling me where he will be. When we separate to use public restrooms, for example, we agree on a meeting place. He no longer sees these acts as being on a short leash. He kindly cooperates as an act of love and concern for me. Although I will forever live with the reality that any of us can die at any time, his thoughtfulness has helped to reduce the irrational, mindless fear of eminent, catastrophic loss.

~

A couple in my office recently had a similar breakthrough resulting in powerful healing. Stan and Diana are newlyweds who attended our beginning and advanced workshops and then scheduled periodic appointments with me to help them implement the skills they learned. A few weeks ago they walked into my office, and laughing, said, "We had a big fight about money this week."

We talked about the particulars. Stan tends to be controlling with their money. Diana feels she has little say in their decisions. Stan wanted to pay off debts before beginning to save. Diana would feel more secure if they had a growing savings account. She wanted to plan for travel. He felt pressured to make more money. None of the points, in themselves, were huge. Compromises could have been worked out but, instead, this had been one of those land mines that exploded into a nasty fight.

I asked, "After you fought, did you have a mirroring session about this?"

They looked sheepish, admitting, "No."

I suggested that they have one now. Stan rolled his eyes and said, "O.K. But I don't know what good it will do. It's just a difference of opinion."

Diana shared her feelings first. With every statement Stan mirrored, he became more uptight. After about the sixth exchange, he muttered under his breath, "This is going to blow!" Since he was smiling, I missed the significance of his remark, and was surprised when he *did* blow. He stopped mirroring Diana and began defending himself and attacking her. At that point I began to mirror Stan, taking the heat off Diana.

I mirrored his feelings of resentfulness, of being unappreciated for how hard he works. We heard his feelings of helplessness when he was a child and his father had to declare bankruptcy. He shared his agony over leaving his home, moving to a different state and the fear of attending a new school. Stan told of his lack of security when it happened again before his parents finally achieved some financial stability. He attended college and chose the major of aeronautical engineering, certain of a lucrative career, only to have the aerospace industry collapse just before he graduated. He shared his humiliation when he couldn't find a job, and had to declare bankruptcy.

By this time, his head was bowed and his hands were vainly trying to cover the tears streaming down his face. I said, "You need Diana to understand how hard you have been trying to make *sure* that nothing like that ever happens to you or your family *ever again,* is that right?"

He nodded his head.

I asked Diana, "Did you know all this?"

She answered, "*I knew the facts; I didn't know the feelings.*" She put her arms around him. They held each other for several minutes.

As long as their discussions were limited to opinions, Stan and Diana were polarized into opposing camps. The intensity of Stan's anger was a giant clue that there was a deep wound that needed healing. By elevating the communication to the feeling level, Stan's pain was exposed so healing could begin. Diana now has the information she needed, and the desire, to participate willingly in the process of his emotional healing. The experience of having his

Elevate communication to the feeling level to expose ancient wounds that need healing.

agony empathically heard opened a door of cooperation within Stan. His wall of resistance melted and, with Diana's understanding, came an eagerness to work together to find ways of handling their finances that will meet his need to get out of debt and her need to plan for the future. They are learning to be financial partners, a goal that can be met now that they are sympathetic to each other's needs. Without this understanding, they, like many couples, may have made their finances a battleground—something that separated them—rather than a vehicle for healing and growth.

In this case, I mirrored Stan's feelings while he was too out-of-control to phrase his statements very respectfully. With a little more experience, and possessing increased confidence in the power of mirroring, Diana could have done the same thing on her own. It only takes one person to pick up the tools of respectful communication and change the course of a fight in order to find the "mother lode" buried beneath the partner's anger. At the very least, meeting anger with compassionate mirroring reduces the intensity of anger so that the issue can be discussed and resolved successfully.

Anger presents an opportunity to participate in the process of healing.

Anger (conflict) presents an opportunity. When expressed impulsively or vented unthinkingly, it leaves a broad swath of barren landscape similar to the devastation left by strip mining. When channeled through the safe boundaries of communicating feelings respectfully and mirroring with empathy, anger becomes a gateway—a mineshaft, if you will—into the wounded soul, allowing the one who cares the most to participate in the process of healing. To know each other's pain—to play an intimate and vital part in the healing of each other's wounds—to discover the "mother lode" in anger—these experiences forge the treasure of a SoulMate bond into steel.

Corner Puzzle Piece #3:
Always treat yourself and your partner with respect.

"I have the power to change the direction of
any argument from hurt to healing.
Because I can, I will."

(Energy) floods through us when our partners understand
what we are thinking and feeling.
We feel better about ourselves; we feel closer to them.
A longer-lasting and more important consequence of the
Mirroring exercise
is that it begins to heal the many splits (wounds) of our childhood.
When our partners (hear us), our entire being is validated.
We no longer feel that we have to cut off parts of ourselves
to be loved and accepted.
~ Harville Hendrix[2]

Love (the person who is acting like) your enemy,
Do good to him (her).
Lend (your compassion) to him (her),
Do for others as you would like them to do for you.
~ Luke 6:35.31

Postscript:

Mirroring is amazingly effective in any relationship. The acting unit chief of the FBI's Crisis Negotiation Unit, Stephen Romano, says about negotiating with a hostage-taker, "They love to have their emotions fed back at them, and they open up more if the negotiator can really demonstrate that he or she is listening. This is accomplished by paraphrasing or repeating the hostage-takers' thoughts or words."[3]

The incredible power of mirroring on an international level was demonstrated by President Jimmy Carter at Camp David in September 1978. He and Rosalyn hosted Egypt's President Sadat and Israel's Prime Minister Begin in a setting where each had the opportunity to freely speak his mind. Carter believed that a resolution to the Mideast conflict was possible if the leaders could be in a private, informal environment long enough to simply hear each other. When tempers flared and communication broke down, President Carter acted as a mirror. Although he occasionally became impatient and directive, for the most part, Carter carefully listened to Sadat and, without editorializing, delivered the message to Begin. He listened to Begin's response, and simply, nonjudgmentally, delivered it to Sadat. When all hope for a favorable outcome seemed lost, Begin went to Sadat's cabin on his own and they agreed on the language of the Knesset vote. There were many factors that supported the positive outcome of the Camp David meetings, some of which were serendipitous, but there's no doubt that President Carter's strong desire for a peaceful resolution and his ability to act as a neutral mirror facilitated the successful outcome.[4] As long as there is *any* desire for peaceful resolution, mirroring works, even between warring nations.

ENDNOTES

1   Nichols, Michael, Ph.D., *The Lost Art of Listening*, p. 154. New York: The Guilford Press. 1995.

2   Hendrix, Harville, Ph.D., *Getting the Love You Want*, p. 147-148. New York. Perennial Library Edition, Harper & Row, Publishers. 1988.

3   Liu, Lynda, *Biography Magazine*, p. 58. A & E Television Network Publication. June, 2001.

4   Rogers, Carl R., Ph.D. and Ryback, David, Ph.D., "One Alternative to Nuclear Planetary Suicide," an unpublished manuscript documenting group processes between historical enemies that facilitate open, non-judgmental listening as a method of resolving international conflicts. 1984.

Chapter 16

I'm Only Trying to Help!

Sharing problems makes people feel better.
Listening is how we help them soothe themselves
and how we build closer relationships.
~ Michael P. Nichols, Ph.D.[1]

A few years ago, our daughter, Teri, took a bad fall while skiing with her sons, Joey and Christian. When they got home, she discovered she had locked her keys in the house. The only way into the house was through a bathroom window. Teri climbed through it, but before she had her balance, she fell, again landing hard. A few months after that, her car was rear-ended and she suffered a severe whiplash injury to her neck. For the next year she was in and out of the doctor's office with pain in her hip and down her leg as well as pain in her right shoulder and arm. The pain in her hip slowly got worse, not better.

Eventually she decided to consult another doctor. When an orthopedic surgeon saw her MRI, he scheduled immediate surgery. She had five herniated discs. The three in her lower back were pinching nerves in her hip and down her leg. The two in her neck were threatening to paralyze her permanently!

The surgeries were grueling, the recovery both long and discouraging. She suffered permanent nerve damage in her right hand and right foot. The physical damage and recovery was one part. The emotional toll was another. The processing of all the feelings have taken a long time and a great deal of energy.

I helped her make the rounds of several medical appointments shortly before the surgeries. Jim and I were with her on the days of the surgeries. In the months before surgery, Greg, Teri's husband, had taken over house cleaning and many other chores. He continued as she recovered. For the most part, we were able to give her only our love and willingness to listening. There was no doubt about the fact that we could not "fix" it for her. We couldn't do anything to make the pain go away. We couldn't give her back the nerves that were dead. We could not operate more brilliantly than the surgeon. We were not inclined to beat up the negligent doctor, and it would not help if we did. We had nothing to offer the legal process. The most we could give her was our willingness to listen with compassion when she needed to talk. According to Teri, those of us who listened compassionately played an essential role in helping her get through those years.

Clearly, jumping in to "help" is not always welcome.

If there is *any* hope of "fixing" something for someone we love, our instinct is to try. In the past, Jim would hesitate to tell me about some frustration, because I would immediately jump in with my advice describing what he should do about it. When he tried to "fix" my complaints with his advice, I felt emotionally abandoned. Clearly, jumping in to "help" is not always welcome.

Jim: When I'm upset about anything other than with my wife, there is no one with whom I'd rather talk than my best friend, Nancy. But I don't want her to solve the problem *for* me. I feel insulted when, by giving her advice, she implies that she is smarter than me. I just want to be given a safe place to "let off steam." And I don't want her to "take up my cause" or "go to bat" for me if she thinks someone has wronged me.

In our workshops, we get a lot of feedback about this section, mostly from the women. When they are hurt or upset, we guys seem to think we are morally responsible to come to their rescue. More often than not, our jumping in to "fix it" results in their anger or frustration being turned on us! Evidently he-man responses are not always what women want.

In chapter 12, some principles are described for venting anger when it is anger with your spouse—vent out-of-control anger away from the person with whom you're angry, and vent in a way that is safe for you, others and valued property.

Now, how can we be helpful when a loved one is venting a feeling about someone or something else? There is a principle that, when we learned it, changed frustrating exchanges into successes; there is such a huge chasm between a *"feeling"* conversation and a *"problem solving"* conversation, they should *never* be mixed!

Stated plainly, this is how it works:

1. When I vent, I do *not* want your judgment, logic, solutions, or rescue.

2. When I vent, I *do* want your undivided attention, comfort and, perhaps, help with clarification.

3. When you have ideas for a solution, I *do* want the respect of being asked if I want them, or I'll ask for your help if I need it.

Judgment: Feelings are just feelings—neither good nor bad. None of us has the right to judge another's feelings as "wrong," but how many of us have been told, "You shouldn't feel that way"? What is your inner response? Eagerness to change your feeling? Outrage? Self-doubt? Withdrawal? If we used the evaluation of the result to determine whether a particular response works or not, *judgment* of feelings would be a failure 100 percent of the time!

Logic: When you walk in the door from work—exhausted because you've had a hard day, the boss was on your case and you had a flat tire on the way home—do you yearn to hear the words, "Well, that's just life! Some days are like that"? Do those logical, technically correct statements help? Feel comforting? Are they what you need? When pigs fly!

Solutions: When you discover that your best friend told her other friend something that you had shared with her in confidence, do you want to hear, "Dump her!" or "Call her up right now and tell her exactly how wrong she's been!"? Is someone else's solution to the problem really what you need in that moment? Probably not. *When unsought advice is given, it communicates doubt that you have the ability to find your own answers.*

On the *receiving* side, it's easy to know that *I* don't need advice. I'll eventually come up with a solution. But when it's *someone else* who is upset, I am quick to *give* advice when it hasn't been requested. The answer is so obvious to me. This person needs help, and I'm only trying to help. From the giving side, it's harder to recognize the insult of offering advice for which my friend, spouse or child has not asked.

We do not have the right to judge another's feelings as wrong.

When unsought advice is given, it communicates doubt that you have the ability to find your own answers.

Rescue: When someone at work is undermining your position by lying about you, do you want your spouse to call up your boss and be an advocate for you? When a friend is condescending with you, do you want your spouse to call that friend and read him or her the riot act about treating you in a demeaning way? Usually not.

There are times and ways when some of these responses may be welcome, but never without permission, and never until after the feelings triggered by those circumstances have been thoroughly heard.

It feels powerful to be the solution finder or the rescuer.

In spite of repeated experiences proving that these four responses to venting are not satisfying when we're on the receiving end of them, some of us continue to dish them out to others. The reason may be that it feels powerful to be the judge, the one who has a cool head, the solution finder or the rescuer. It gives us the mistaken feeling that we're actually doing something to help someone for whom we care. We want to take away his or her hurt, anger, frustration, even their grief. We come up with something that makes *us* feel useful, even if the needs of the one we care for are not met by our reactions.

Grief is an emotion with which many people are especially uncomfortable. Here are some common attempts to make grief go away that are particularly brutal:

♦ "You're young. You'll marry again!"
(Is that supposed to comfort me? So I shouldn't grieve?)

♦ "God must have something special in mind for you to make you go through this tragedy."
(So this is God's fault? Then I wish God would be *special* to someone else!)

♦ "At least she's not suffering anymore."
(Obviously, but what about me?)

♦ "Time heals all wounds."
(Maybe so, how do I get through today?)

♦ "Children are supposed to outlive their parents!"
(So he didn't do what he was *supposed* to do! How do *I* go on?)

♦ "You'll have other children"
(Does that mean this child was unimportant? Replaceable, as though she were a broken vase?)

In all fairness, people say whatever they say because they're *trying* to be helpful and comforting. If they have not had personal experience with deep grief, they have no way of knowing how hurtful those comments are. A deeper explanation for many awkward, unthinking responses to grief is the great cultural discomfort with any feelings that can't be quickly and easily "fixed" and our culture's extreme discomfort with death.

In the days after my first husband's death, I saw or heard from hundreds of persons. As the pain was so raw and the prospect of surviving his loss so daunting, responses like those I've described felt like salt rubbed in an open wound. Two days after he died, my sister was with me. We sat down at my table to have a bit of lunch. Our tradition is to say a blessing. I bowed my head and began to softly cry. I didn't think I could pray and wasn't sure I could eat. When I finally raised my head, I saw that Sally was quietly crying *with me*. I still remember that as the most profoundly comforting act that anyone, before or since, has done for me. She made no attempt to stop my tears. She didn't try to say anything comforting when there was nothing that could be said. Sally validated the enormity of my pain by just letting me hurt and hurting with me.

There were others: another sister, Mary, my parents, and one or two close friends who, for the first several years, welcomed my two active babies and me to hang out with them. They patiently gave me time and a place to go when I couldn't bear to be at home. Those gifts were comfort delivered in very practical ways.

So what *do* we need when we talk about our grief, anger, frustration, depression, or other upsets?

Undivided Attention: When I am upset about something, I know that when I tell Jim I need to talk, he will put down whatever he's doing, turn off the T.V. and give me his undivided attention. I never feel more loved than in those moments when he tells me. by every gesture and look, that nothing is more important to him, at that moment, than hearing me. This, in itself, is comforting. It shortens the time I need because I'm not attempting to be heard in competition with something else.

When Teri and Karen's children were small, there were times they demanded constant attention. This is what they both discovered: when Mommy would stop what she was doing and give that child her full attention, it was usually only minutes until the little one was satisfied and ready to move on to something else. If Mommy was busy, impatient, or anything other than totally focused on the child, the nagging whininess would often escalate to a tantrum or crying jag.

We never outgrow our need to be given undivided attention.

We never outgrow our need to be given undivided attention. It is not childish. It is not weak. It is simply comforting and healing to have our importance validated by the unconditional love and undivided attention of our spouse or friend.

Just plain comforting meets a valid need.

I recently spoke with a woman from a large church in Texas who was trained to minister by just listening—giving undivided, compassionate attention to those in need. So much healing of heart aches, loneliness and confusion often takes place within the warm circle of undivided, caring attention.

Comfort: A client's husband is under tremendous stress at his job as an engineer. One Saturday, when he'd gone in to work to try to catch up, he called her twice during the day. All he said was, "I'm feeling so overwhelmed. I don't see how I can get all of this done." My client said he sounded like he was about to cry. She didn't know what he wanted her to do about it—she would come in to help if she could, but she's not an engineer. She wondered why he was wasting time calling her when he could have been using the same time to make progress with the work.

When our habit is ignoring our own needs, we are very likely to not recognize, and to minimize or ignore the needs of others, as well.

He was asking for comfort but didn't know how to verbalize what he needed. Because he's a man, he was ineligible for comfort in her mind. She wasn't being cruel and he wasn't being stupid. It simply didn't occur to either of them that comforting was a valid need in this situation.

Comforting sometimes doesn't come naturally. If we did not receive comfort as a child, we may have unconsciously decided that we either weren't supposed to need it or were not deserving of it. We may even have a deeply buried belief that life is hard and we each must get through it alone; receiving comfort from another is, somehow, unacceptable or weakening. Without experiencing comfort, we may have a highly developed ability to deny emotional or physical pain or a tendency to ignore our own needs. When our habit is ignoring our *own* needs, we are very likely to not recognize, and to minimize or ignore the needs of others, as well.

Male or female, we need and deserve comforting words and acts when we are experiencing physical or emotional pain, stress, depression, anger, frustration or grief. The words of comfort may feel strange or silly if comforting is not familiar to you. Jim and I both had to practice using comforting words before they felt natural.

Try to use phrases similar to these:

- ♦ "I'm so sorry." (In this context "sorry" does not mean you are assuming responsibility or apologizing for anything.)

- ♦ "I'm sorry that you're hurting (or that you're upset, that you're going through this, or that this has happened to you).

- ♦ "This is so unfair (awful, stressful, intolerable, painful) for you, isn't it?"

- ♦ "Cry as long as you need to. I don't mind tears."

Without jumping in to fix anything, it can be helpful to mirror the statement or feelings, matching the emotions in your tone of voice, such as:

- ♦ "He's being such a jerk!"
  (response) "What a jerk!"

- ♦ "I just don't know how I'm going to get through this."
  (response) "Right now this seems impossible to get through."

- ♦ "I feel so angry!"
  (response) "Of course you are angry!"

- ♦ "I am so sad."
  (response) "This *is* so sad for you."

Sometimes, physical acts can add to the comfort if your spouse, friend, or child wants it:

- ♦ "Would it feel good if I held you?"

- ♦ "How would you like me to massage your feet while you talk?"

- ♦ "Would you like me to get your favorite afghan?"

- ♦ "Would you like me fix us a cup of tea while you're talking?"

and, my personal favorite from Jim,

- ♦ "Let's go upstairs and lie down so I can hold you while you talk."

When a client curled up on the floor, grieving the probable loss of her marriage, I got down on the floor with her and invited her to put her head on my thigh. While she cried, I just stroked her hair and back while saying comforting words. Although several friends had sympathized with her when her husband moved out, "No one has comforted me!" she said.

Appropriate comforting brings us back to our coping resources much more quickly.

Appropriate comforting brings us back to our coping resources much more quickly. Denying or postponing comfort keeps the feelings stuck, creating a bottle-neck through which our natural abilities to cope cannot emerge—our ability to move forward with our lives is slowed down when we deny our need for comfort.

We are not dependent solely on another's presence or compassion for comfort. It's a great mental health skill to learn to comfort one's self. I can place my arms around myself, rock myself, and say comforting words to myself. I can wrap myself up in a favorite quilt, play soothing music, or allow myself the old standby, a bubble bath. I can do some puttering task that is quieting for me. Soft foods are comforting to me—a bowl of oatmeal or a soft scrambled egg.

You can learn how to comfort yourself.

Four-year-old Katie had been happily playing with me, but now she was crabby. Nothing pleased her. I turned to pay attention to Nick, and when I turned back, she was gone. After ten minutes or so, I walked down the hall toward her room. Through her closed door, I could hear her singing and talking to her animals and dolls. I asked her mom about it. Shelley told me that sometimes Katie would announce, "I need to be alone!" and march back to her room, and that after half an hour or so, she comes out happy again. Sure enough, about 20 minutes later she returned to play with Nick and me. Already, she has the skill of knowing when she needs the comfort of solitude and her own private space to restore her to balance. She's a lucky girl. It took me 40 years to learn that skill.

Clarification: Sometimes questions like these assist in the venting process:

◆ "Are you the most upset about _____ or _____?"

◆ "Do you have other feelings about this?"

◆ "Is there anything else you need to add?"

◆ "Might you also be feeling _____?"

◆ "Is that everything or is there more?"

Many of us have had the experience of gaining an insight or reaching a conclusion about our next step after talking about it with someone who cares.

Just like soaking in warm Epsom salts helps to draw poison from a wound, caring, patient questions like these sometimes help to draw all feelings about the issue out into the open. Many of us have had the experience of gaining an insight or reaching a conclusion about our next step after talking about it with someone who cares. In a SoulMate relationship, there is no one better suited to the role of listener than our spouse.

However, it's important to tell your SoulMate what you need. He or she is not capable of reading your mind. If you need to vent, and don't want judgment, logic, solutions or rescuing, it may help to remind your spouse of that before you begin. Jim loves it when I tell him, "I need to talk. It's not your fault, and I don't need answers. Do you have time to hear me?" ("It's not your fault" is another way of reminding him that he doesn't have to assume responsibility to fix things for me.)

Caring, compassionate listening is one of the most kind, generous, loving things we can do for those we love.

If my SoulMate asks for my attention, and I am legitimately unable to give my full attention at that time, a response could be, "In three minutes I'll be able to give you my attention" or "I need to make two calls before 5 o'clock. As soon as those are off of my mind, I'll be glad to listen." Most tasks, however, can be postponed for a few minutes without any serious consequences. Caring, compassionate listening is one of the most kind, generous, loving things we can do for those we love.

After feelings have been heard, a problem solving conversation may be welcomed, but first ask:

♦ "Are you open to suggestions?"

♦ "I think I have an idea that might help. Do you want to hear it?"

♦ "Do you feel like brainstorming for some ideas now?"

If the answer is "No," or "Not now," honor that boundary. It is up to your partner (friend, child) to decide whether or not he or she wants suggestions or ideas for a solution to the problem. Remember, when advice is given without permission, it communicates doubt that the troubled person has the ability to find workable solutions. Bite your tongue rather than step over the boundary. Then all the good, safe feelings generated by being a good listener will be secure.

It is up to your partner to decide whether or not he or she wants suggestions or ideas for a solution to the problem.

❧

Jim: Nancy was upset. She began talking on our way home. After parking in the driveway, we continued to sit in the car so I could listen to her vent without interruption. I was sure I could fix the problem so easily. It was obvious to me what the situation needed, but when I asked if she was ready to hear some ideas, she answered "Not now." I bit my tongue. A few days later, however, she came back to me with, "If you still want to tell me your ideas, I'm ready to listen."

First of all, it felt so great to know and follow the "rules" for listening to venting, and then know I'd given her the respect she deserved by not forcing my answers on her. It felt even better when she came back and asked me for them later.

❧

School had always been easy for my son, Peter, but sometime after I'd begun to learn how to respond to venting with comfort, he enrolled in paramedic school. About once a week, Peter would call around 9:30 or 10:00 p.m. He'd tell me how hard it was. How many hundreds of formulas he was required to memorize. There was an unbelievable amount of data that must be learned. Classmates were dropping out or flunking. One of the professors was an unreasonable jerk! It was possible he wouldn't make it through.

I would listen, and say things like, "I'm so sorry. They ask too much! That professor is unreasonable. You must be so tired. It must seem impossible to learn all this. I don't blame you for being overwhelmed."

After about 40 minutes of this kind of conversation one particular night, Peter paused for a minute and said, "It feels so *good* for you to feel bad with me…"[2]

Corner Puzzle Piece # 3:
Always treat yourself and your partner with respect.

"I communicate respect for my loved one
as I listen and comfort without judgment or unwanted advice."

Venting and Problem Solving are two separate processes!
~ Jim and Nancy Landrum

Kindness makes a man (woman) attractive.
~ Proverbs 19:22

ENDNOTES

1   Nichols, Michael, Ph.D., *The Lost Art of Listening*, p. 159. New York: The Guilford Press. 1995.

2   Peter and about 20 others represented one third of the starting class who completed the course and received their certification as paramedics.

Chapter 17
Sailing the Seven SoulMate "C"s

*A husband bragged, "I talk. She listens. She talks. I listen.
We both talk. The neighbors listen."*

~ **Milton Berle**

This chapter maps out a seven-step strategy for supporting the rest of your relationship while working to resolve a difficult, long-standing issue. Each step begins with the letter "C." I've used the metaphor of sailing the seven seas as a reminder that these steps, when used as described, will make the process of sailing through a deeply entrenched issue as smooth an experience as possible.

In describing the first "C" of the trip, however, I'm using a different metaphor, one that evokes a vivid scene of a marriage's deterioration because of an unresolved, ever-expanding issue.

By the time we sought out and found a counselor that we trusted, we could hardly be in the same room without a fight erupting. Our counselor asked us to try to limit our "discussions" to certain times and, until we found some resolution, try to restore some of the good things about our marriage that we had lost while all of our attention was focused on the conflict. I couldn't imagine how to do that until this metaphor came to mind.

We liken our marriage to a two-story house. Downstairs there is the family room where Jim and I gather with our children. In the living room we enjoy mutual friends. Down the hall are bedrooms representing each of our children. There is a kitchen where many of the family birthday parties and holidays are celebrated. Off of the kitchen is a craft room that is primarily mine. In that room, I enjoy sewing and painting. I also keep my gardening tools there. The backyard garden is mostly mine as well, although we often enjoy meals, games and entertaining there. There is a game room where Jim keeps his golf clubs and where the guys watch football or boxing without grossing out the rest of us. Upstairs is our bedroom, the private part of our marriage. There is a sitting area where we enjoy a good book or talk things over. This is where we share our day-off activities like table games and movies. There is also our bed, where we share sleep, lovemaking and many late night conversations.

There was one particular, major issue between us that became so enormous that it could not be resolved in one or even a few mirroring sessions. Using the metaphor, it was as though the conflict had begun in one little downstairs broom closet. Over time, it leaked out until it covered the downstairs floor and eventually crept up the stairs like the green slime of a horror flick. In time it covered our bedroom floor and threatened to climb the walls, rotting the house from the inside. The odor was foul and the gunk stuck to us no matter where we went to try to escape. It tainted the relationships with each of our children. It stuck to us even when we were working or on a date. It smeared itself across our bed, taking what used to be a safe area for closeness and pleasure and turning it into a tentative, guarded place.

What our counselor was asking us to do, metaphorically, was sweep up all the green slime, dump it in a big bucket, and stuff it back into the broom closet. Then we could reclaim the parts of our marriage that had originally been safe and enjoyable. Combining that directive with the other things we were learning, we eventually worked out a strategy for dealing with this enormous conflict. For those of you who may find yourself in a similar situation, we share this strategy for sailing the first "C" with you.

1. CONTAIN THE CONFLICT

The strategy of shoving it back into the closet requires two steps:

A. Agree to take the issue out of the closet only during times specifically set aside for mirroring that issue. This is not the same as "sweeping it under the rug." Dates are made for the purpose of taking the mess out of the closet and using the mirroring format to hack away at it. Other than during those dates, both agree to leave it "in the closet." Dates may be spontaneously made, when something triggers the issue between you, but most dates are deliberately made ahead of time. In fact, no mirroring session is left before another date is made to continue the work. For a major, on-going issue, it would be appropriate to have two to three dates per week for mirroring until it is resolved.

In addition, the skill of being able to set an issue aside to work on later is a skill that is often needed in every marriage. It isn't always convenient or even possible to postpone other demands while you stop to "mirror" an issue. Although you may never have an issue that takes five years to resolve, you may occasionally have one that cannot be resolved in one or two sessions.

In a recent workshop, one young bride asked, "How does one deal with the hurt and anger during the times when the issue is in the closet? I would be refusing to speak to him until we completed the resolution of the problem!"

This skill requires some mature management of priorities, beliefs and feelings. The self-talk would go something like this: "The marriage is basically good and I love this person. We will work on resolving this issue again tomorrow. In the meantime, I will focus my attention on his (her) great qualities and remind myself that we will work this out. *I do not need to feed my anger in order to guarantee that I'll be heard.* My turn will come."

B. **Refocus your attention on things you used to like to do together.** It seems to be true of human nature that when something goes wrong, our attention becomes entirely consumed by that problem, blocking our awareness of whatever is going well. We no longer talked about anything other than "the issue." We had lost sight of every reason that we loved each other. We'd forgotten how to laugh together. We'd nearly forgotten how good it felt just to cuddle.

For awhile, it was hard to talk about much that was personal without inciting the need for a formal "issue discussion," so we thought of things we could do together that required little talk. While we did those things, we practiced the mental discipline of leaving "the issue" in the closet in order to just be together. We would go see a movie. Movies were safe because we could both enjoy them without needing to speak to each other. We would go out to dinner. He would take his crossword puzzle, penciling in answers while I was reading a novel about some woman whose love life always turned out great by the last chapter.

We planned dates to places he liked such as a baseball game. I went and enjoyed the upbeat atmosphere and a hot dog. I brought along a book to read or an embroidery project. He'd tell me if anything interesting happened. Baseball was a safe, neutral subject. We also went

The skill of being able to set an issue aside to work on later is a skill that is often needed in every marriage.

Learn the skill of managing priorities, beliefs and feelings.

to specialty nurseries or interesting shopping malls where we would stroll until he'd had enough. He'd park on a bench and read the paper while I wandered around until I'd seen all I wanted to see.

These activities were soothing. It felt good to be together without conflict. It helped remind us that there was more to our relationship than "the issue." These dates gave us back some balance so when we went to the closet and pulled out "the issue" for another mirroring session, we had some good feelings in reserve that helped us work on it more patiently.

A similar strategy to refocus attention was used by a woman whose letter appeared in "Dear Abby."[1] She wrote, "My husband and I had been fighting a lot. One night I couldn't sleep because I was so upset with him. I decided to think instead of all the things that I loved about him. I wrote them on a piece of paper, put it in an envelope, and placed it in his briefcase. The next morning, he called me from work to tell me how much he loved me…We seldom fight anymore. I get love notes weekly and kisses daily."

2. CAREFULLY SET THE STAGE

A. **State Your Need.** We found it helped to approach each other in a way similar to this: "I need to discuss an issue (or "the issue"). It's important to me to be heard. Would you mirror me?" Jim and I both appreciated knowing at the outset whether the issue was an upset between us or in regard to something else. It was also helpful to know how serious it was based on a scale of 1 to 10, with 1 being a minor annoyance and 10 being a very, very big issue.

B. **Make a Date.** Continue the invitation by asking for a specific time when neither of you will be distracted. "Would 2:00 this afternoon be a good time for you?" If the date was to continue working on a long-term issue, we would say something like this, "Do you feel up to taking 'it' out of the closet for awhile this afternoon at two o'clock?" We would tell each other how much time we thought we could work on it. One of us might say, "I think I have enough energy for about 15 minutes," or "I'm willing to stay with it as long as I can." Because working on this was so intense, whoever ran out of gas first could call a halt and set another date for the next session.

Making a date relieves anxiety in the one who's upset because a specific time is set aside when the partner will hear and respond to it. Putting the issue on the calendar takes some of the pressure off. Making a date also gives the partner a chance to prepare. Mirroring isn't always easy to do, and with a long-standing conflict, it is especially taxing. Having this information helped both of us mentally and emotionally prepare for the mirroring date by putting on a mirroring "hat." We would use the intervening time to plan the "I feel…" messages, gather the self-control required to stay with the mirroring format and prepare to listen empathically.

C. **Affirm Your Belief in the Outcome.** I always sighed with relief when Jim added, "I believe in us. I know we'll be able to respectfully work this out." It's an essential part of the process to begin and continue to nurture a belief in your ability to resolve conflicts satisfactorily.

D. **Keep the Date!** All the trust and expectation of success will be sabotaged if the date is forgotten or superceded by something else unless a change is respectfully requested and agreed upon by both partners.

3. COMMIT TO MIRROR! MIRROR! MIRROR!

The goal is to resolve the issue in a way that is acceptable for both partners. That may require several sessions of mirroring. With our primary "issue" we took nearly five years to hammer out a resolution.[2] In the meantime, we struggled along the best that we could, using the seven "Cs" plus the additional concepts included in this book. One would hope that, with this book and other resources that are available, nothing you're experiencing will take that long, but be committed to the process for whatever length of time it takes until it is satisfactorily resolved.

4. CALL "TIME OUT!"

A "time out" is needed when either partner becomes upset to the point that respectful methods of communication are about to be abandoned and replaced by any of the disrespectful, defective communication tools. It's ideal if each partner is willing to be responsible to say "I'm about to lose control. I need a 10-minute (or 2-hour or 24-hour) 'time out.'" Both SoulMates need to honor each other's limits. Neither one should continue talking or pushing the issue after a "time out" is called.

There are two more reasons to call a time out. (1) We gave each other permission to call a time out if I was nervous about Jim's ability to stay within respectful limits or he was apprehensive about mine. (2) We called time out if we simply ran out of available time or energy for continuing the session.

A "time out" is needed when either partner becomes upset to the point that respectful methods of communication are about to be abandoned.

Before you leave this session, a new date is set to resume the mirroring. A new time could be a few minutes from now or next Thursday at 7 p.m.

5. COMFORT EACH OTHER

In the intimacy of marriage, conflicts cause discomfort at best and excruciating pain at worst. It is soothing to comfort each other for the pain being experienced even before a resolution is reached. It isn't necessary to give up your "position" or "point of view" in order to hug your partner and say, "I know this is hurting you. I am so sorry that you are hurting."

Your two-year old is threatening to take over if you're tempted to retort, "If you were *really* sorry, you'd change what you're doing and see it *my* way!" Being a SoulMate means appreciating the compassion offered and receiving the comfort. A graceful reply would be something like, "Thank you for caring that I hurt. I know you're hurting, too. We'll keep going until we work this out in a way that's good for both of us."

We hadn't made any attempt to comfort each other because it seemed ludicrous to comfort Jim for an issue with *me* that was creating pain for *him* and visa versa. When we realized we could do this, there were several times when we lay in bed, holding each other, sobbing, and comforting each other for the depth of the pain we were both feeling. It felt so good to be comforted in Jim's arms and to comfort him. Often during our mirroring sessions on "the issue," one of us would be in tears. The other would stop and say, "I'm sorry this is hurting you so badly." It was soothing. Comforting each other began the process of healing the enormous wounds we each suffered long before the issue was finally resolved.

6. CANVAS FOR SOLUTIONS

There is always more than one solution to a problem.

A. Brainstorm Alternatives. There is *always* more than one solution to a problem. When we are rigid about our points of view, there are often solutions we don't see. It helps to employ the major rule of brainstorming: No idea is discouraged! Every idea, no matter how crazy, is added to the list. Many times a satisfactory solution evolves from this creative game. It's wise to stretch your mind to consider possibilities that may have been formerly unacceptable in your family traditions. Traditions were begun to serve the needs of the family. If the family's needs have changed, then the traditions may need to change as well.

For example, in a previous chapter I spoke of my extended family's desire that every person be present for family gatherings on holidays. Traditionally, Easter was a holiday on which my parents, sisters and their families gathered. In spite of the fact that Jim usually arose at 4 a.m.

to prepare for an Easter sunrise service, and was busy with responsibilities throughout the morning, he came to the family dinner for the first few years of our marriage but he was exhausted and miserable. All he wanted was to get it over with so he could go home and take a nap. We finally agreed that I would go to the dinner if I wanted to and he would go home and to bed. I brought home a plate of leftovers for him to enjoy for dinner that evening. With this arrangement, I could stay and visit as long as I wanted, and Jim was taking care of his need by napping. We were *both* happier.

B. **Compromise.** In any partnership, compromises are negotiated to sustain the success of the relationship. Compromises keep the world moving. Often somewhere in the middle of alternatives is one that might not be the first choice of either partner but one that both can accept.

C. **Trade.** When a decision cannot be compromised but has to be an "either/or" choice, a trade is needed. An example is "I'm willing to handle this situation the way you want it handled, if you will handle this other one the way I want it done." Or, "This year we'll spend Christmas day with your family, and next year we stay home (or go skiing, etc.). This solution comes with two imperatives: 1) Once you agree on a trade, follow through without reluctance, resentment, pouting or in any other way extracting a "payment." When your partner has to "pay" for doing something his or her way, it was not a trade; 2) The same partner cannot always be the one to "give in." If that were the case, it was not a trade at all, but a pattern of one always being the "winner" while the other is consistently the "loser"—a perfect environment for growing resentment.

When a decision cannot be compromised but has to be an "either/or" choice, a trade is needed.

D. **Love Gift.** When it's possible to give without hesitation or resentment, do it his (her) way as a free gift.

E. **Counseling.** When a solution can't be found, consult a trusted third party to help you identify solutions that haven't occurred to you. Sometimes our thinking becomes stuck, preventing us from finding workable solutions. Also, it's appropriate to ask for the support of a counselor[3] who can coach or moderate the mirroring sessions until you have gained more proficiency and confidence. I have clients who practice mirroring on little issues or compliments at home but save the big issues for my office because they feel safer knowing I'm there to keep them within respectful boundaries.

7. CELEBRATE EVERY SUCCESS

Before you leave any mirroring session, give each other credit for any part of the process done well, or any improvement over previous attempts.

Before you leave any mirroring session, give each other credit for any part of the process done well, or any improvement over previous attempts. If nothing else, you can acknowledge each other for your willingness to keep mirroring. When you successfully reach a resolution to an issue, verbally acknowledge that success with statements like "We did it! We're becoming good at this!" Celebrate by doing something you enjoy together. If the session was grueling, do something that is soothing, either together or apart.

~

Work the Seven "C"s until the issue is resolved. It's a great system. It works if you work it! It's a strategy that won't be needed forever.

George Leonard wrote a jewel of a little book called *Mastery*.[4] His original training was in the mastery of sports performance, but he found the principles applied to any part of life where success is desired. He said about the marriage relationship, "The ability to surrender to your art is a mark of the master, whether the art is martial or marital. Can you let go of an outworn behavior pattern without knowing exactly what will replace it? Are you willing at times to yield totally on some long-standing dispute for the sake of growth and change in your relationship? The tricky part is learning to lose your ego without losing your balance. The stronger you are, the more you can give of yourself. The more you give of yourself, the stronger you can be."

Corner Puzzle Piece #3:
Always treat yourself and your partner with respect.

"I will do my part to use this practical seven-step strategy
for maintaining the healthy areas of our marriage
while respectfully staying with the issue until we find a resolution."

There are no conflicts that cannot be resolved,
only people who will not resolve them.
~ Gary Chapman[5]

If you want a happy, good life,
keep control of your tongue...
do good.
Try to live in peace
even if you must run after it to catch and hold it!
...the Lord is watching his children,
listening to their prayers.

~ I Peter 3:10-12

Postscript:

Two or three times during the most desperate years, we did something that is, perhaps, unique to Judeo-Christian traditions. We walked throughout our home with a bottle of olive oil. We "anointed" each door jam with oil while we prayed for peace in our home. Each entrance to our house, every bedroom and bathroom, kitchen, living room, and family room, received a drop of oil and our heart-felt prayers. We were both asking for help and expressing our intention that there be peace in our home by the practice of this ritual. One of my clients sheepishly admitted to her husband that she had sprinkled salt on all their windowsills as a way of protecting their home from the "evil" of their unrelenting conflict. If a ritual would strengthen your intention to have peace in your home, do it!

ENDNOTES

1   *The Orange County Register*, February 7, 2000.

2   It took five long years because we had backed each other into such extreme corners that neither one of us was eager to give up our position. There has been so much more understanding developed about the unique issues of step-families since then. If we had known some of the rules that make step-families work, nearly all of our issues would not have occurred. For those of you who are "blending" families, I include a few suggestions and resources in *How to Stay Married & Love It Even More*. Meanwhile, check out the stepfamily resources listed in the Bibliography.

3   Refer to Chapter 1 for suggestions on finding a counselor.

4   Leonard, George, *Mastery*, page 149. New York: Plume Books. 1992.

5   Quoted from "Marriage Works by Communicating, Not Running" by Art Toalston, *The Baptist Messenger*, October 5, 1995.

Corner Puzzle Piece #4:
SoulMate Commitment

Chapter 18

About Divorce...

*The most important thing a father can do for his children
is to love their mother well.*

~ Theodore M. Hesburgh

When I was planning this book, I had no intention of writing about the long-range effects of divorce. As the book neared completion, however, I realized that it is not fair to make such a strong argument for doing the hard work of repairing a wounded marriage without at least investigating the option of divorce.

Up until the past two generations, popular American culture supported marriage for life and judged divorce as "bad." Although the stigma of divorce and ostracism of those who divorced was unfair, it served as a strong, negative support for staying in an unsatisfactory marriage. When no-fault divorce was introduced in 1969, dissolution of the marriage contract became the easiest way to deal with an unhappy or conflict-ridden marriage, and the frequency of divorce has increased by approximately 279 percent since 1970. As divorce became more common, the cultural stigmas have practically disappeared. In some circles, a first divorce is almost looked upon as a right of passage into "real" adulthood![1] Divorce is accepted by many as the best alternative to an unhappy marriage. But is it? I decided I'd better read up on the effects of divorce to see if my personal experience as well as family and religious biases had prejudiced me against a legitimate alternative to the relationship work I propose in this book.

Since no-fault divorce was introduced, divorce has increased by approximately 279 percent.

Before looking at the long-range effects of divorce, however, I want to acknowledge that some of you who are reading this have experienced, or are currently experiencing divorce. When the pain is unrelenting, your hope and your energy are exhausted, and your friends are encouraging you to give up, divorce often seems like the best option available. In some cases, by *anyone's* standard, it *is* the best option. I most certainly have understanding and compassion for what you have gone through. I have neither the right nor the desire to judge whatever decisions have been made in your past. As I have said before, I believe that we are each doing the best we know how to do each day of our lives. All of us deserve compassion.

This chapter, however, is addressed to those of you who may be struggling the way Jim and I were…those who are teetering on the fence of decision…those for whom the option of "freedom" is looking better and better. A few current beliefs about life after divorce make divorce seem so much more appealing than slogging through the mire of healing and rebuilding. See if some of these may be swaying you toward "greener pastures":

- ♦ I'll have more and better sex. Meeting lovers will be easy.
- ♦ Plenty of men (women) will be fighting for my attention.
- ♦ My life will be more glamorous and exciting.
- ♦ Being single has many more advantages—freedoms—than being married.
- ♦ I need to make my own decisions without consulting with anyone.
- ♦ He (she) is holding me back from all I could be.
- ♦ I need my…(independence, sexual fulfillment, career, whatever).
- ♦ I must pursue this chance with the "real" love of my life.
- ♦ I made a mistake and need to have a "fresh start."
- ♦ We are not compatible.
- ♦ We're always fighting.
- ♦ We've grown apart.
- ♦ He (She) is driving me crazy.
- ♦ I need to be appreciated.
- ♦ I can't make him (her) want me.
- ♦ He'll (She'll) be happier without me.
- ♦ I'll find someone better!

These "reasons" were identified in a book written by Diane Medved, Ph.D., a therapist who specializes in helping clients learn to make clear decisions. She has led workshops and written books about weighing the pros and cons of major life choices. Dr. Medved intended to write a dispassionate book to help individuals decide whether or not separation or divorce was a good choice, but the more she researched the documented results of divorce, and the more she heard from persons who had divorced (she conducted 300 interviews), the more her stance changed until the book became *The Case Against Divorce*.[2] Many of the interviewees agreed that they experienced momentary relief when separated from what they perceived as the source of their unhappiness. Most were surprised and unprepared, however, for the years of emotional devastation, cynicism, loneliness, loss of friendships, difficulty in finding desirable dating partners, and financial losses that came with the package of divorce. The reality of "freedom" did not live up to its promise. When asked, most admitted that if they had known what singleness or the challenges of re-marriage were going to be like, they probably would have stayed and worked harder in the first relationship.

The reality of "freedom" does not live up to its promise.

Dr. Medved wrote:

> *I discovered in my research that the process and aftermath of divorce is so pervasively disastrous to body, mind, and spirit—that in an over whelming number of cases, the "cure" that it brings is surely worse than the marriage's "disease." Of course, there are exceptions:*
>
> ◆ *When physical or mental abuse exists.*
>
> ◆ *When emotional cruelty or neglect becomes intolerable.*
>
> ◆ *When one partner adamantly refuses to stay in the marriage or withdraws to the point where in reality you're alone.*
>
> *I used to think that the range of situations when divorce is appropriate encompassed quite a bit more than that. But when I look at the balance of the bad and the good that divorced individuals endure, my only possible conclusion is that people could be spared enormous suffering if they scotched their permissive acceptance of divorce and viewed marriage as a serious, lifelong commitment, a bond not to be entered into—or wriggled out of— lightly. (Emphasis mine.)*
>
> *Although surviving the trauma of divorce forces many to develop more self-reliance, most "might have blossomed even more had they gathered the gumption to stick with and heal the marriage."[3]*

As I studied the research on divorce, I found six primary areas that affect the adults involved in the decision of whether to stay or to leave:

SEX: Sexual satisfaction, physically and emotionally, sometimes isn't that frequent or that great between partners who are in conflict. Even when we consider ourselves advertising-savvy, the movies, beer commercials, and Victoria's Secret ads insidiously lead us to assume that finding desirable sex partners and having passionate sexual escapades are easy without the dead weight of a marriage. So *is* there an exciting, glamorous world awaiting you out there?

Results of the latest research indicate probably not. In the giddy first year of "freedom," 20 percent of men and 45 percent of women who were surveyed reported dysfunctional lack of sexual desire. Thirteen percent of the men and 20 percent of the women said they were now unable to achieve orgasm, while eight percent of the men said theirs came prematurely. When asked if the media's portrayal of the single's lifestyle was accurate or distorted, the respondents overwhelmingly replied that "distortion is not only rampant but also produces some damaging myths."[4]

Without considering moral or safety issues, a sexually active single averages sex less frequently than the average married couple.[5] The most obvious reason is because of convenience. In marriage, going to bed together is usually part of the daily routine. Reaching for each other to relieve sexual tension or express emotional closeness is facilitated by proximity. A single person must put him or herself in a setting with other singles, do the wining, dining, and getting acquainted routine, and then hope to "get lucky." The only singles who average sex more frequently than married couples are those with live-in partners. Often the purpose of co-habitation is the enjoyment of the sexual benefits of a regular partner without the restrictions of the full commitment of marriage.[6]

But how do singles and cohabitors rate in the area of emotional satisfaction from sex compared with married partners? Singles (men and women) score the lowest in emotional satisfaction from their sexual experiences. Cohabitors, in spite of greater frequency than married couples, score lower in emotional satisfaction. Married couples consistently score the highest in emotional satisfaction from sex *and* the better the quality of the relationship and the longer the duration of the marriage, the higher they score!

"Both husbands and wives were more likely to see love and sex as intrinsically connected than either cohabiting or single men and women were… the data clearly show that commitment increases sexual pleasure for both sexes…The emotional content of the relationship was just as important

Without considering moral or safety issues, a sexually active single averages sex less frequently than the average married couple.[5]

Married couples consistently score the highest in emotional satisfaction from sex and the better the quality of the relation-ship and the longer the duration of the marriage, the higher they score!

to men as to women…A permanent commitment to one's sexual partner makes a big difference to both sexes' sexual satisfaction.[7]"

The conclusion derived is that when a couple makes a lifetime commitment to each other, they have more at stake in pleasing one another. A husband may see his efforts at eliminating some undesirable habit as an investment that will pay dividends in the bedroom. A wife may learn that when she prepares her husband's favorite meal, he has more patience with meeting her needs while making love. This is not a cold-blooded exchange, but simply the way a good relationship is built.[8] In addition, knowing one will spend the rest of one's life with this person, there is greater motivation for learning how to be in "sync" with each other and how to please each other sexually.

With the marriage vow of sexual exclusivity and the expectation of "'til death do us part" come more confidence in the fidelity of my partner and less anxiety about occasional sexual disappointments. Tomorrow brings another opportunity. After our 20 years together, Jim and I are living with the blessings of this long view. There are occasional disappointments—he's hot, I'm not, or visa versa…or we go through a stressful time like during my mother's final illness and death when we think we've probably forgotten how—but our overall enjoyment of and satisfaction with each other sexually makes those rare "misses" insignificant.

HAPPINESS: In the past couple of generations, marriage has been labeled a bad rap for both men and women. Men are sometimes perceived as burdened, limited or trapped by the responsibilities of marriage. When sirloin steak is chosen off of a dinner menu, halibut, lasagne or lobster are left behind! All choices come with the denial of other choices. Since the advent of the women's movement in the 1960s, marriage is sometimes judged as bad for a woman because it "prevents development of the true self" all the way to "it's an abusive, archaic form of enslavement." There's no question that there have been inequities perpetrated by our culture and in specific marriages that needed to be addressed. The women's movement has fought for and won many choices that in the past were withheld from women. But do these things mean marriage itself is essentially bad for men and women—an outmoded block to true happiness?

" …virtually every study of happiness that has ever been done has found that married men and women are happier than singles. The happiness advantage of married people is very large and quite similar for men and women and appears in every country on which we have information…"[9] 97 percent of husbands and 95 percent of wives rated their marriages as "pretty happy" to "very happy."

Psychologists Scott Stanley and Howard Markman recently reported similar results when survey data were formulated to isolate the degree of dedication to the marriage by both husband and wife. As a culture, our tendency seems to be to believe that women care more about the state of the marriage and are more willing to invest energy in its welfare. It turns out this was another false assumption. Stanley and Markman found that husbands and wives reported being equally dedicated to the welfare of their marriages. Only one significant difference was found: the tendency of men to withdraw in the face of conflict.[10]

When one is drowning in the morass of pain experienced in a conflicted marriage, it's tempting to fantasize about the relief that would come without one's marital partner and his or her hang-ups or demands. A break-up brings a different set of baggage, however. The psychological upheaval engendered by divorce is "...revealed by the fact that divorced men and women exhibit more symptoms (such as 'nervous breakdown' and 'inertia'), and to a more serious degree, than do persons of other marital statuses (married, single, widowed). Divorced and separated people have the highest admission rates to psychiatric facilities, and this holds true across different age groups, for both sexes, and for blacks and whites alike."[11]

Abigail Trafford estimated that it takes a minimum of five years to get through the worst of the emotional trauma and begin to rebuild your life.[12] In her personal interviews of 300 separated or divorced persons, Diane Medved concluded that seven years was closer to the average. "...many respondents wrote that twenty and thirty years after terminating their relationships, they are still reeling from the emotional wallop."[13] In his book, *Marital Separation*, Robert Weiss noted that characteristics of "separation distress" are desolation, apprehensiveness, anxiety and panic, leading to tension, vigilance, insomnia, depression and feelings of worthlessness.[14]

Unhappy marriages do not necessarily stay that way.

Unhappy marriages do not necessarily stay that way. Twenty-thousand married men and women have been questioned over the past several decades as part of the General Social Survey. Eighty-six percent of those who rated their marriage as unhappy in the late eighties and *who were still married five years later, said their marriages had become happier.*[15]

I find it interesting that the same five to seven years researchers reported were needed to recover from divorce can be spent waiting out the "bad patch" of a marriage and working to resolve the issues, resulting in a happier marriage with the same partner. When I complained that the emotional work I was doing in therapy was so painful, my counselor advised, "You can choose the pain of staying where you are or the pain of recovery. With the first there is little chance

"You can choose the pain of staying where you are or the pain of recovery..."

of getting out of pain. With the second there is hope that a better quality of life is ahead."

"The very worst marriages showed the most dramatic turnarounds… Permanent marital unhappiness is surprisingly rare among the couples who stick it out.[16]"

"Marriage and family provide the sense of belonging…the sense of loving and being loved, of being absolutely essential to the life and happiness of others. Believing that one has a purpose in life and a reason for continued existence, that life is worth the effort because one's activities and challenges are worthy comes from having other people depending on you, counting on you, caring about you. Married people have a starring role in the lives of their spouses; their shared universe would cease to exist if something happened to one of them. When the shared universe includes children, the sense of being essential, of having a purpose and a full life expands as well. Marriage improves emotional well-being in part by giving people a sense that their life has meaning and purpose.[17]

Financial issues are rarely the cause of a divorce, but become enormous in the aftermath of divorce.

EARNINGS AND WEALTH: Financial issues are rarely the cause of a divorce, but become enormous in the aftermath of divorce, especially if child support is required. Men and women both suffer after divorce, but the causes are often different. The authors of a study of the impact of California's no-fault divorce laws found that women's standard of living drops a whopping 73 percent after divorce. Lenore Weitzman says, "…the major economic result of the divorce law revolution is the systematic impoverishment of divorced women and their children."[18] Poverty, for many women, begins with single parenthood. "Joint custody" and "child support" sound fair, and some fathers honor their responsibilities to the children they helped bring into the world. Many others find the emotional and financial abandonment of their children convenient when their attention and resources are going into the building of a "new" life.

A woman's standard of living drops a whopping 73 percent after divorce.

Women who have postponed their own educations or careers in favor of putting hubby through school, or who have stayed home while children were young, are at a disadvantage when it comes to supporting themselves (and their children) after a divorce. Often the family home is ordered sold and the asset divided, meaning that the wife and children not only must face the emotional distress of a husband and father no longer in the home, but also the upheaval of moving to a less expensive neighborhood, and often to poorer schools.

If the former husband decides to remarry, the money leaving the bank account for alimony and child support payments often causes resentment from the new wife. In her book, *Second Wife, Second Best*, Glynnis Walker warns the second bride, "You will probably have to go out to work, not to make ends meet for your family but to help your husband make ends meet for his. Seventy-four percent of the second wives in the survey worked, while 60 percent of their husbands' ex-wives did not."[19]

Lenore Weitzman concluded that the reported economic benefit to men is artificial. "The dollar incomes of both divorced men and divorced women declined, while the income of married couples rose. Divorced men lost 19 percent in income while divorced women lost 29 percent. In contrast, married men and women experienced a 22 percent rise in income."[20]

Other researchers have shown that not only does the income stream diminish, but over-all net worth shrinks as well, which is clearly understandable as the assets have been divided as part of the divorce rulings. The reduction of assets sometimes means the loss of years worth of retirement savings or even the necessity of starting over.

In contrast, married men consistently make more money and enjoy a higher standard of living than do single or divorced men. The reasons have to do with the quality of home life and a different set of values. Most single men tend to have wilder lifestyles that mean greater absenteeism, less productiveness at work and less devotion to behaviors that result in promotions. Single and divorced men tend to devote more of their money and energy to dating and "toys" than do married men. Men going through a divorce show all the classic symptoms of extreme stress—lack of focus, easy distractability, and increasingly volatile emotions—making them unlikely choices for "Employee of the Year" awards at their companies.

Typically, a married man has some greater degree of stability at home and therefore has more mental and emotional energy to devote to his job, making him a better candidate for promotion than the single fellow. "The earnings advantages of marriage for men are even greater in the later years of marriage than in the first few. The close working relationship between a man and woman in marriage seems key to increasing men's earnings."[21]

An overwhelming majority of first generation millionaires are happily married to their original spouses. It seems that stability at home makes it possible to focus energy on wealth building enterprises. And it isn't because the spouse and family are neglected, either. Research confirms that they lead well-rounded lives with significant amounts of time invested in family activities.[22]

In addition, built into most marriage partnerships is the benefit of specialization. Each partner does what he or she does best, or what the partners together have decided will be done by each, so that neither of them must "do it

"The dollar incomes of both divorced men and divorced women decline, while the income of married couples rise…"

Married men consistently make more money and enjoy a higher standard of living than do single or divorced men.

An overwhelming majority of first generation millionaires are happily married to their original spouses.

all." With singles, separated or divorced men or women, and most cohabiting couples, each one is on his or her own. There is not the sharing of the responsibilities that makes a marriage partnership so much more efficient.

The research data reveal that because most cohabiting couples have not made a commitment to stay together "for life," they tend not to invest in their future together. Therefore, after three years of cohabiting, most couples have little savings or personal assets, but after three years of marriage, most couples are saving toward well-defined goals such as a home, or starting a family or retirement. The married couples are investing in the future they plan to enjoy together.

> "How much wealthier are the married? In Lingxin Hao's study, young married families had accumulated the most money, with a median net worth of almost $26,000. Remarried families were almost as well off ($22,500) as were single-dad families ($22,930.) At the bottom of the heap were both single mothers and cohabiting couples who, in marked contrast to married couples, had a median wealth of just $1,000. Single mom's typically had no assets at all."[23]

The relation between marriage and money for women is a little more complicated although women, as well, tend to earn more while married than as a single.

There is absolutely no doubt, however, that a woman's over-all standard of living and financial condition are better while married than if single. Unless a woman is willing to forego marriage and children in order to devote all her attention to a career, the division of a woman's energy and attention often takes its toll on her earning power.

If accumulating wealth or avoiding poverty are important to you, the evidence clearly proves that investment in making your marriage work is a smart move for both men and women.

If accumulating wealth or avoiding poverty are important to you, the evidence clearly proves that investment in making your marriage work is a smart move for both men and women.

HEALTH: The health benefits of married life are more evident for men than for women. Single women tend to take better care of themselves than single men, and most do not take dangerous risks with their lives. The benefits of marriage for men, however, show up clearly in their lowered risk of serious accidents, better general health attributed to less drinking, more adequate sleep and better professional health care.

The health penalties of divorce for both men and women are quite dramatic. "Divorced people have more illness, higher mortality rates (in premature deaths), higher suicide rates and more accidents than those who are married. In fact, the marital status of a person is one of the best predictors of his or her health, disease and death profile."[24]

Looking at age-standardized death rates, Professor Harold Morowitz of Yale University found that divorce seemed to be about as dangerous to a man's health as picking up a pack-a-day cigarette habit.[25] Although married men evidently enjoy *greater* health benefits, marriage is a healthy choice for both men and women. "Compared to married people, the non-married...have higher rates of mortality than the married: about 50 percent higher among women and 250 percent higher among men."[26] This author agreed with Lenore Weitzman that both men and women live longer if they are married than if they are not.

Although men enjoy greater health benefits, marriage is a healthy choice for both men and women.

A safer, saner, more stable lifestyle is an obvious difference between married and single men. There are more subtle assets, as well, as this quote reports:

> "Another health benefit men get from being married stems from the emotional support they receive, which can have profound effects on physical well-being. The emotional support of a spouse seems to help people recover better when illness strikes or to manage a chronic disease (such as diabetes) better over the long term. There is even intriguing evidence that social support of the kind marriage provides can actually boost the immune system, making the married less likely to catch even the common cold...While both men and women benefitted from marriage in this way, men were more likely to depend exclusively on their spouses for emotional intimacy."

Marriage can provide a boost to the immune system.

> "Not all marriages are equal, of course. The quality of the relationship between the spouses makes a difference:...both men and women who displayed more negative behavior during conflict had immune systems that functioned relatively poorly. *Men and women who used positive or supportive problem-solving behaviors showed no immunological or blood-pressure changes. As a marriage improves over time, so does the reported health of the husband and wife.*"[27] (Emphasis mine.)

I think those statements speak clearly to the health benefits of marriage over singleness, and a happy marriage with good problem-solving skills over a marginally happy marriage with negative expressions of conflict!

VIOLENCE: "Domestic violence" is a term that often includes cohabitors or sleep-over boyfriends as well as married couples. When statistics are lumped into "domestic violence," rather than separating "wife abuse" from non-married incidents, the statistics blur, a practice that suggests marriage puts women at heightened risk of violence. Only about 1.7 percent of wives and less than 1 percent of husbands are attacked even once each year. Michael Johnson argues that there are two kinds of spousal abuse: "'Common couple violence' happens when ordinary arguments get out of hand, involves aggression by both partners, happens relatively infrequently, and does not usually escalate." In fact, the occasional occurrence may frighten both partners into exhibiting more self-control in future encounters. "'Patriarchal terrorism,' by contrast, is a means by which a small proportion of men control 'their' women; the beatings are always initiated by the men; most women do not fight back; and the violence is frequent, severe and escalates over time."[28]

In contrast, a 1994 Justice Department report, based on the National Crime Victimization Survey, showed that single and divorced women were four to five times more likely to be victimized in any given year than married women. Single and divorced women were almost three times more likely than married women to be the victims of aggravated assault and ten times more likely than wives to be raped.

Boyfriends and cohabiting male partners appear to be less committed than husbands, so may have less reason to show restraint in their expressions of anger. "Marriage seems to help men desist not just from domestic violence, but all forms of lawbreaking. A study of five hundred chronic juvenile delinquents, which was conducted by researchers who tried to figure out why some youngsters ceased criminal activities and others continued piling up arrests into their early thirties, found that a good marriage made a dramatic difference."[29]

Marriage itself seems to help curb domestic violence. "Men with a stake in conforming to the social rules are more likely to be deterred from violence when they are shown (by an arrest) how seriously society frowns on domestic violence. Cohabiting men, by contrast, appear to rebel against social control by inflicting more pain on their partners. Cohabiting men have less to lose from being publicly identified as an abuser than do married men."[30]

Married men are less often victims of violent crime than unmarried men. Marriage appears to be the safest place to be for both men and women!

～

"If you are still tempted to think that divorce is the answer to your problems, that the 'same old you' will simply be freer and able to express yourself in a more liberated setting, you're wrong. It won't be the same *you* facing the world. Divorce inevitably changes you—it diminishes your moral perspective, staggers you emotionally for months or years, forces a change in address or living standards, and eliminates the friendships of half the names in your address book. Still there are some things that, unfortunately, it does not

A 1994 Justice Department report showed that single and divorced women were four to five times more likely to be victimized in any given year than married women.

Marriage appears to be the safest place to be for both men and women!

automatically affect: the patterns in your behavior that led to your marital problems in the first place. And those are precisely what need to be changed most."[31]

Despite every intention to choose more wisely the second time around, without addressing your own personal issues and those of your former marriage, chances are you'll choose someone on the opposite end of the spectrum from the problems you found in your former spouse, or you may look for a replacement spouse that fits you in the same old unhealthy way as your former spouse, repeating your patterns.

Several years ago a friend of mine left his wife stating that he needed to "find himself" and experience "sexual freedom." He cited all the faults of his wife and declared their marriage unworkable. He began an affair with a married woman at his work. She eventually left her husband, divorced and married my friend. Three or four years later he confided to a mutual friend that he was basically back where he started…the same issues that had surfaced in his first marriage were surfacing in his second. In addition to the original personal work he needed to do, there was trail of emotional and financial devastation left behind with which he had to cope. The first few years of leaving his wife and beginning a new life with a new wife were exciting and felt like progress to him. It took several years for the reality to appear that he had only gone in a big circle—and had never really left his starting place at all.

WHAT ABOUT THE CHILDREN? When California adopted a no-fault divorce law, all 49 other states quickly followed. We embarked on a gigantic social experiment without any idea about how the next generation would be affected. Now that there have been a good two generations of children of divorce, what does the research reveal about the long-term effects *on them?*

In a landmark study that exposes as false the popular myths about the minimal effects of divorce on children, Judith Wallerstein, Julia Lewis and Sandra Blakeslee have written *The Unexpected Legacy of Divorce.* In this book the authors document the childhoods, adolescences and ongoing adult experiences of children whose parents divorced.[32] The first myth is that if the parents are happier, the children will be happier as well. When parents are in so much pain that divorce looks like a welcome relief, it's easy to use this argument to support the decision to leave. If one spouse is already involved with a "new" person, and is in the throes of new passion, it's even easier for that partner to rationalize the decision to leave by arguing that the children will be happier if the parent is happy.

"…the patterns in your behavior that led to your marital problems in the first place need to be changed most."[31]

For children, having both Mom and Dad under the roof with them is the primary building block of their self-esteem.

Children are resilient and resourceful especially when the foundation of their world remains steady, and it seems clear that having both Mom and Dad under the roof with them is a primary building block of their self-esteem. *That Mom and Dad are happy with each other is ideal, but I am convinced that it is more important that each parent is there, accessible to the child.* Recently Jack, Sue and their three almost-grown children stopped at the table in the park where we were playing dominoes. They enjoy a great marriage and have three children who appear to be confident and happy. (Imagine! Three mid-to late-teens being glad to take a walk with mom and dad on Saturday morning!) In exchanging catch-up news, we told about our nearly finished book. Jack said, "As an adult, I realized that my mom and dad were not very happily married, but, you know, as a kid that didn't matter to me. All I knew was that I had a home, a family and food on the table. That made my childhood secure."

There are exceptions, but they are very few, and these include when there is extreme and prolonged conflict such as patriarchal tyranny or sexual abuse. In those cases the children show an immediate improvement in mental state after separation. "Psychologically, at least, children in very high-conflict marriage families experience their parents' divorce as a relief. When marriages of more middling quality end, however, *children experience the family breakup as an unmitigated and inexplicable disaster.* The bad news is that in this country, the majority of divorces involving children apparently are not ending terrible marriages but marriages that are, from a child's point of view, at least 'good enough.'"[33] (Emphasis mine.)

For children, the fallout from divorce never ends.

The second myth is that the divorce itself is a temporary blip in the lives of those involved and within a reasonable length of time, the ex-partners and children will recover and move on with their lives. The authors of *The Unexpected Legacy of Divorce* propose that for children, the fallout from divorce never ends.

"It's the many years living in a post-divorce or remarried family that count, according to this first generation to come of age and tell us their experience. It's feeling sad, lonely and angry during childhood. It's traveling on airplanes alone when you're seven to visit your parent. It's having no choice about how you spend your time and feeling like a second-class citizen compared with your friends in intact families who have some say about how they spend their weekends and their vacations. It's wondering whether you will have any financial help for college from your college-educated father, given that he has no legal obligation to pay. It's worrying about your mom and dad for years—will her new boyfriend stick around, will his new wife welcome you into her home? It's reaching adulthood with acute anxiety.

Will you ever find a faithful woman to love you? Will you find a man you can trust? Or will your relationships fail just like your parents' did? And most tellingly, it's asking if you can protect your own child from having the same experiences in growing up.[34]"

The children's feelings come from the predictable consequences of many divorces. They no longer have easy access to both parents. Often the extended families of one or both parents are less accessible as well. Both parents are going through the "crazy time" that follows the emotional upheaval of divorce, so are less emotionally available even if physically present. A physical move is often necessary, frequently to a neighborhood inferior to their previous home. Usually that means a change in schools and the loss of friends, as well. A mother who used to be home after school, is often at work, and may be exhausted when she gets home to all the household chores now hers alone. The bottom line is that significantly less time is available to pay attention to the needs of the child.

One feeling that seems to be common among children of divorce is anxiety—always waiting for the next disaster to strike without warning. It's as though they can't let themselves feel too much happiness for fear of what may be coming.[35]

The stresses of divorce not only negatively affect the health of the adults involved; one researcher found divorce made it 50 percent more likely a child would have health problems.[36]

In the long-range health scene, "Parents' divorce knocked four years off the life expectancy of their adult children, according to one study that followed the life course of a group of highly advantaged kids—white, middle class, with an IQ of at least 135—through their seventies. Forty-year-olds from divorced homes were three times as likely to die from all causes as forty-year-olds whose parents stayed married."[37]

And what about school performance? "The education gap begins early and persists into adulthood. One quarter of children in mother-only and remarried families repeat a grade in school, compared to 14 percent of those in married families. Twenty-three percent of kids in mother-only families and 18 percent of children in stepfamilies have been suspended or expelled, compared to less than 10 percent in mother-father families. Fifty-two percent of children in mother-only and 48 percent in remarried families are in the bottom half of their class, compared to 38 percent of children whose parents are still married. Living in a single-parent family approximately doubles the risk that a child will become a high-school dropout, and children whose parents stay married are also more likely to get a college education."[38]

One feeling that seems to be common among children of divorce is anxiety—always waiting for the next disaster to strike without warning.

Living in a single-parent family approximately doubles the risk that a child will become a high-school dropout.

How do these kids compare with others in drug use and sexual activity? Judith Wallerstein chose 131 children of divorced parents and followed them through 25 years with an in-depth interview every five years.

"One in four of the children in this study started using drugs and alcohol before their fourteenth birthdays. By the time they were seventeen years old, over half of the teenagers were drinking or taking drugs. This number compares with almost 40 percent of all teenagers nationwide. A majority used these substances for more than five years and several were seriously addicted by the time they reached their twenties.

"Early sex was very common among girls in the divorced families and has been described in several national studies. In our study, one in five had her first sexual experience before the age of fourteen. Over half were sexually active with multiple partners during their high school years. In the comparison group, (the comparable children of conflicted parents who remained married) the great majority of girls postponed sex until the last year of high school or their early years in college. Those who engaged in sexual activity did so as part of an ongoing relationship that lasted an average of a year.

"These young women are anxious to turn the tables on what they understand to be the natural pecking order between men and women. One said, 'From age eighteen on I was a man. I was being like my dad. Men use, they're powerful and they're smart. Women are stupid and want men. I get a kick out of being sexy, smart and using people.' Several told me that they enjoyed seducing their girlfriends' lovers. These young women were motivated by a frank vengeance against men that was startling in its passion. They were driven to use sex as an arena for playing out unfinished business with their parents—especially anger and longing for their fathers and defiance of and competition with their mothers. Sex is a way to get even with both parents.[39]"

Children in any family without a married-to-each-other mother and father, experience more delinquency, perpetrate more crime and suffer significantly more physical and sexual abuse.

Children in any family without a married-to-each-other mother and father, apparently experience more delinquency, perpetrate more crime and suffer significantly more physical and sexual abuse. With evidence of the serious disruption of divorce in their lives, it would be surprising if children of divorced parents were able to participate in a stable, lasting marriage. Children of divorce "are less likely to be happily married and more likely to divorce than children whose parents got and stayed married."[40]

In her research of teenage motherhood, Judith Musick found that, "Divorce in one generation leads to a big increase in illegitimacy in the next. Parental divorce also almost tripled the chances that young women left home early because of friction and doubled the chances that they cohabited before marriage.[41]

"When parents are unable or unwilling to build a good-enough marriage, the consequences may be felt not only by their children, but by their children's children who will be far more likely, as a result, to experience and pass on the deprivations of poverty, the trauma of fatherlessness, and the health risks and economic handicaps of living outside of marriage.[42]

"The startling results of Amato and Booth's investigation, one of the largest and most well-designed studies of its kind, led these two social scientists to make this unusually firm pronouncement: 'Spending one-third of one's life living in a marriage that is less than satisfactory in order to benefit children—children that parents elected to bring into the world—is not an unreasonable expectation.' Especially since, as they point out, 'Many people who divorce and remarry find that their second marriage is no happier than their first.'"[43]

In this book we propose an even better solution. We've given you the tools that we used to pull our own marriage back from the brink of divorce. These corner pieces of the puzzle form the foundation of a SoulMate marriage. The second volume of this set, *How to Stay Married & Love It Even More!* documents the remaining pieces of the puzzle that complete the building, and maintaining, of our SoulMate relationship. You can do it, too. Perhaps, one day, you'll have the experience I enjoyed just two days ago. Our daughter, Karen, called me to encourage me as she knew I was working on this difficult chapter. She confided that she and her husband, Matt, had often said to each other that any problems they have they will work out. Divorce is not an option. She added, "The example that you and Dad set for us is one of the reasons we know we can do this."

As I pointed out earlier, there are some circumstances, especially those where family members are endangered by violence, in which divorce is the appropriate solution, but there are many marriages where couples can, if they are determined, work out the issues that tear them apart. Divorce needs to be the last, rather than the first, resort.

Ellen Byron interviewed couples who had reunited after separations and even divorces for a February, 1986 *Redbook* magazine article entitled, "Will You Marry Me—Again?" These couples said that their rekindled love is even more precious: "There's a cherishing of one another that's so much better than before." (p. 146)

If you are teetering on the brink, or if your partner is threatening divorce or has even already left, a book by Michele Weiner Davis offers practical strategies for your "critical emergency" status. She has been helping broken marriages heal for more than 20 years. *The Divorce Remedy*[45] is the result of refining and clarifying the successful emergency measures she taught in her first best seller, *Divorce Busters*. Get it now, and do what she recommends if you want to save your marriage. *Then* add the recommendations in *this* book!

"Surmounting a marital crisis is an 'annealing' process. Like steel that must be heated red hot, almost to the melting point, and then cooled repeatedly to become strong, your relationship and your character are transformed into stronger, more durable entities as a result of your ordeal."[46]

Jim and I are confident that the steel we forged between us is strong enough to last forever. We *know* that we can work *anything* out. We have. The last chapter encourages each of you to take the final step that provides the power for making all the skills work together in the most effective way. Turn the page…

Corner Puzzle Piece #4:
Commit to this partner, this marriage, for life.

"I trust the research and wisdom of others to help me make a choice
that considers the long-range welfare of my children, as well as myself.
Unless the safety of my children or myself is at risk,
I choose to devote my energy to *healing* this relationship
rather than to *recovery* from tearing it apart."

You cannot compare the depth of a relationship
that has lasted for two years
to one that has been nurtured for twenty.
Even those tinged with conflict are more romantic because
the phases of encountering and resolving problems
bring the partners ever closer
and add enhancing nuances to a core of dedication.
~ Diane Medved[47]

Above all else, guard your affections
for they influence everything else in your life!

~ Proverbs 4:23

ENDNOTES

1 Medved, Diane, Ph.D., *The Case Against Divorce*, p. 12. New York: Ballantine Books. 1989.

2 IBID, p. 1,2.

3 IBID, p. 4.

4 Carroll, David, and Simenauer, Jacqueline, *Singles: The New Americans.* New York: Simon & Schuster. 1982.

5 Cool, Lisa Collier, "Am I Normal?" *Good Housekeeping*, p. 71-74. New York: Hearst Magazines Division., and "The National Sex Study," based on interviews in 1992 with 32,500 men and women between the ages of 18 and 59, by Edward Laumann, John Gagnon, Robert Michael, and Stuart Michaels at the University of Chicago. March, 2001.

6 Stanley, Scott and Markman, Howard, "Marriage in the '90s: A Nationwide Random Phone Survey." Denver, Colorado: PREP, Inc., 1997.

7 Gallagher, Maggie, and Waite, Linda, *The Case for Marriage*, p. 82-87. New York: Doubleday. 2000.

8 These building blocks of romance are covered in *How to Stay Married & Love It Even More!*

9 Gallagher, Maggie, and Waite, Linda, *The Case for Marriage*, p. 168. New York: Doubleday. 2000.

10 Stanley, Scott and Markman, Howard, "Marriage in the '90s: A Nationwide Random Phone Survey." Denver, Colorado: PREP, Inc., p. 23. 1997.

11   Weitzman, Lenore, *The Divorce Revolution*, p. 349. New York: Free
      Press. 1985.

12   Trafford, Abigail, *Crazy Time: Surviving Divorce*, p. 124. New York:
      Harper & Row. 1972.

13   Medved, Diane, Ph.D., *The Case Against Divorce*, p. 196. New
      York: Ballantine Books. 1989.

14   Weiss, Robert, *Marital Separation.* New York: Basic Books, 1975.

15   Linda Waite's tabulations from the "National Survey of Families and
      Households," 1987/88 and 1992/94.

16   Gallagher, Maggie, and Waite, Linda, *The Case for Marriage*,
      p. 148-149. New York: Doubleday. 2000.

17   IBID, p. 75.

18   Weitzman, Lenore, *The Divorce Revolution*, p. 10. New York: Free
      Press. 1985.

19   Walker, Glynnis, *Second Wife, Second Best*, p. 10. New York·
      Doubleday. 1904.

20   Weitzman, Lenore, *The Divorce Revolution*, p. 337. New York: Free
      Press. 1985.

21   Gallagher, Maggie, and Waite, Linda, *The Case for Marriage*, p. 104.
      New York: Doubleday. 2000.

22   Stanley, Thomas J., Ph.D., *The Millionaire Mind.* Kansas City, MO:
      Andres McMeel Publishing. 2000.

23   Hao, Lingxin, *Family Structure*, p. 269-92.

24   Weitzman, Lenore, *The Divorce Revolution*, p. 349. New York: Free
      Press. 1985.

25   Morowitz, Harold, "Hiding in the Hammond Report," *Hospital
      Practice*, 10, p. 35, 39. 1975.

26   Ross, Catherine E., Mirowsky, John, and Goldsteen,Karen, "The
      Impact of the Family on Health: Decade in Review," *Journal of
      Marriage and the Family,* 52, p. 1061. 1990.

27 Gallagher, Maggie, and Waite, Linda, *The Case for Marriage*, p. 56-57. New York: Doubleday. 2000.

28 Johnson, Michael P., "Patriarchal Terrorism and Common Couple Violence: Two Forms of Violence Against Women," *Journal of Marriage and the Family*, 57, p. 283-94. 1995.

29 Gallagher, Maggie, and Waite, Linda, *The Case for Marriage*, p. 158. New York: Doubleday. 2000.

30 IBID.

31 Medved, Diane, Ph.D., *The Case Against Divorce*, p. 207-208. New York: Ballantine Books. 1989.

32 Wallerstein, Judith, Lewis, Julia, and Blakeslee, Sandra. *The Unexpected Legacy of Divorce*. New York: Hyperion. 2000.

33 Gallagher, Maggie, and Waite, Linda, *The Case for Marriage*, p. 147. New York: Doubleday. 2000.

34 Wallerstein, Judith, Julia Lewis and Sandra Blakeslee. *The Unexpected Legacy of Divorce*. p. xxv. New York: Hyperion, 2000.

35 IBID, p. xxvii.

36 Mauldon, Jane, "The Effects of Marital Disruption on Children's Health," *Demography* 27, p. 431-46. 1990.

37 Gallagher, Maggie, and Waite, Linda, *The Case for Marriage*, p. 131. New York: Doubleday. 2000. Derived from Joan S. Tucker, Howard S. Friedman, Joseph Schwartz, Michael Criqui et al., "Parental Divorce: Effects on Individual Behavior and Longevity," *Journal of Personality and Social Psychology*, 73: p. 381-91. 1997.

38 Zill, Nicholas, "Understanding Why Children in Stepfamilies Have More Learning and Behavioral Problems Than Children in Nuclear Families," in *Stepfamilies: Who Benefits, Who Does Not?* Eds. Alan Booth and Judy Dunn (Hillsdale, NJ: Lawrence Erlbaum Associates), p. 97-106. 1994.

39 Wallerstein, Judith, Lewis, Julia, and Blakeslee, Sandra. *The Unexpected Legacy of Divorce*. p. 188-189. New York: Hyperion, 2000.

40   Amato and Booth, *A Generation at Risk*, p. 84-119, Flewelling and Bauman, "Family Structure as a Predictor," p. 171-81.

41   Musick, Judith S. *Young, Poor and Pregnant: The Psychology of Teenage Motherhood*. New Haven: Yale University Press. 1993.

42   Gallagher, Maggie, and Waite, Linda, *The Case for Marriage*, p. 137. New York: Doubleday. 2000.

43   Gallagher, Maggie, and Waite, Linda, *The Case for Marriage*, p. 148. New York: Doubleday. 2000, and Amato and Booth, *A Generation at Risk*, p. 238.

44   Davis, Michele Weiner. *The Divorce Remedy*. New York: Simon & Schuster. 2001.

45   Medved, Diane, Ph.D., *The Case Against Divorce*, p. 255. New York: Ballantine Books. 1989.

46   IBID, p. 247.

Chapter 19

Closing the Back Door

Commitment involves a decision to work with
(the) fears and rigid patterns that arise in a relationship.
Conscious commitment is to being together, not just staying together.
~ John Welwood, Ph.D.[1]

I began this book by giving you a glimpse into the ugliest of the many ugly scenes that were common to us the first several years of our marriage. To help illustrate the essential role of full commitment—the fourth corner of the SoulMate puzzle—Jim and I invite you to view more of that scene with us:

~

Jim: That day we had been fighting…again. I was lying on our bed. Nancy was sitting in an overstuffed chair against the opposite wall. Neither of us wanted to be physically close enough to touch. Nancy challenged something I'd done with one of the boys. I got defensive. She replied sarcastically. I accused her of some offense to get the heat off of me. She yelled. I began my "hopeless talk" routine. We did what we had learned to do so well—attack. Both of us reached for our favorite "defective communication tools." We hadn't caught on yet that these defective communication tools only made things worse. They *never* helped us reach any lasting, satisfactory resolution. We were bruised and bloodied.

I felt like a cornered animal. More than anything I wanted to hurt Nancy. On an impulse, I yelled, "Well, I'll just divorce you, then!"

The room reverberated with the shock of those words. Until that moment, in spite of the unrelenting conflict, we were still confident that both of us *wanted* to find a way to make it work. Neither of us had ever spoken the "D" word. Nancy turned white and buried her face in her hands, crying. We were silent for a long time, both of us painfully aware that an invisible line had been crossed. With that word, all kinds of fearful and painful possibilities erupted between us.

Nancy: I felt a rush of weakness flood my body. I had trouble breathing. My heart was responding as though I had a vicious lion charging at me. Finally a deep certainty emerged from my wild thoughts. I spoke. Quietly. With determination. "If that's what you're going to do, then pack up your mother and your son and get out today. I can stand any amount of pain if I know that we are both going to hang in here until we find our way through; but if you're going to bail on me, I don't want to go through one more day of this. You decide."

The silence seemed to last forever. I couldn't look at Jim. I was bracing myself, waiting for him to tell me that he was leaving. In one way it would have been a relief. In another, I couldn't even imagine the unbearable pain of losing someone I had once been so blissfully happy to marry.

After many minutes, some small sound caught my attention. I risked a glance. Jim was weeping.

Jim: When I could speak, I said, "I don't really want to divorce you. I just wanted to hurt you. I'm so sorry. I love you. I won't leave. We'll keep trying until we find a way to make this work. Please forgive me."

Nancy: Since that day I've learned that an impulsive ultimatum such as this one is unwise. We were fortunate that Jim was able to realize that divorce was not what he really wanted. If he had reacted differently to my ultimatum, the momentum may have begun toward a divorce that neither of us would have had the wisdom to stop. As mentioned before, Michelle Weiner Davis suggests many useful strategies that would have been safer than this ultimatum for coping with an angry spouse in her book, *The Divorce Remedy*.

Jim: What neither of us immediately realized was that the speaking of the word "divorce" had slashed a giant gap in our resolve to find a way to be happily married. Now, in spite of my reassurances, Nancy wasn't sure she could trust me to stay. If I got too angry, would I threaten again to divorce her? Next time would I follow through and do it? Nancy's survival mode kicked in. She wanted to pull back and protect herself from that possibility.

Nancy: That Jim would even *threaten* divorce was such a shock to me. It tainted my image of the man I thought he was. Before, I knew we were having a bad time, but I thought he was a man who would, without question, stay and work it out. Now, I wasn't sure who he was. The possibility of total loss was very real.

Jim: Looking back, we realize that the introduction of that little word, "divorce," opened a back door of escape from our relationship that hadn't previously existed. Before, we were dealing with hurt and frustration that sometimes escalated to anger. That was bad enough, but now, the possibility of divorce allowed truckloads of distrust and fear to rush in. It took a long time to rebuild what was broken by just a few seconds of hurtful retaliation.

～

It is easy to say, "I do." It is much harder to say, "I'm here for the long haul. We may be having some problems now, but I'm staying to work it out." It is even harder to *mean* it and *do* it.

Remember the analogy of a marriage being like a house with many rooms?[2]

For the person who's marriage-house has a back door, thoughts like these will show up when the going gets rough: "If this doesn't work out, I'll just leave. I can find someone else who will love me." Or, "He (she) must prove to me that I'm most important or I'm out of here." Or, "Every girl (guy) needs a little secret money put aside just in case." Or, "Susie's husband brings her flowers. (Brad's wife never nags him for watching too much football.) I could do better than this." It's as though the husband or wife has one foot outside the back door, daring the partner to push too hard. Even if the words aren't spoken, the reality is sensed that he or she is poised to bolt. This condition is the equivalent of *partial* abandonment. Even more damaging, the threat of bolting is a form of

> *It is easy to say, "I do." It is much harder to say, "I'm here for the long haul."*

blackmail. The partner is afraid that honest dialogue will result in *total* abandonment rather than precipitating resolution and increased SoulMate love.

When you maintain a back door, a large portion of your energy is withheld from the process of healing and resolution. Your energy is leaking out the back door.

When you maintain a back door, a large portion of your energy is withheld from the process of healing and resolution. Your energy is leaking out the back door. Your partner will sense your lack of full commitment to the marriage, and tend to protect him or herself by holding something in reserve. *That same* portion of energy and commitment is exactly what is needed to tip the scales toward success.

Building a successful marriage takes 100 percent involvement. Anything less means the marriage will be less than it could be. Nailing a board across the door is not enough. The back door must be torn out, the door jam disassembled, new studs secured to the space, and the opening plastered up.

Once the escape door is eliminated, and all your energy is focused on doing your part to make the marriage work, then magical things begin to happen.

Mysteriously, or perhaps very logically, once the escape door is eliminated, and all your energy is focused on doing your part to make the marriage work, then magical things begin to happen. When you *know* that this is the person with whom you will spend the rest of your life, the motivation to use healthy communication tools shoots way up. The choice to safely vent out-of-control anger becomes easier. The focus of your attention is on the long-run rather than getting your needs met immediately. It becomes possible to put your desire to be heard "on the shelf" long enough to hear your partner's point of view, feel your partner's feelings, and soften in your willingness to compromise. Finding a way to express your own feelings and needs respectfully becomes a welcome challenge.

As you experience successful communication sessions and satisfactory resolution of issues, the level of intimacy deepens and the benchmark of the quality of the relationship rises, opening up new vistas for the marriage. When a higher level of relationship is experienced, your tolerance for anything *less* decreases…the richer the flow of love between you and your partner, the more motivation there is to quickly resolve any issues that arise in order to return to the peace and joy of the better relationship.

SoulMate love, once experienced, is seductive.

SoulMate love, once experienced, is seductive. The day comes when it is so painful to be in conflict that it no longer matters who makes the first move toward healthy resolution. All that matters is that the oneness you treasure is restored. Your partner truly is your SoulMate. Eventually, you realize that no temporary loss of temper, no petty remark, no fleeting thrill with someone else, *nothing* could possibly be worth the loss of this precious treasure.

The treasure we describe is characterized by two persons, each of whom has assumed full responsibility for the healthy management of his or her own feelings. Each is willing to be held accountable for communicating respectfully.

Both desire solutions to issues that are fair and mutually satisfying. Both share equal responsibility for the quality of their relationship. As the need for love and security are met, the couple is available to work in partnership for the good of both. Both receive encouragement and support for the expression of their unique contributions to the world. SoulMate loving becomes a way of life. The home is a peaceful respite from the world "out there"—a haven for safety, renewal, and celebration.

Have we drawn the picture vividly enough? Do you see it? Are you willing to do whatever it takes to have it? Are you ready to sign this commitment and share it with your partner? If so, we personally guarantee you the greatest adventure of your life with unimaginable rewards!

∾

I choose you. I choose you *for life*. I will make every effort to hear you, learn your needs and be the partner you deserve. I do this because I know that in the working out of our lives together, I will become the best I am capable of being. I will reap the greatest personal rewards as our relationship flourishes.

Signed_____Signed_____

Date_____Date_____

Corner Puzzle Piece #4:
I am fully committed to this partner,
this marriage, for life.

Until one is committed there is hesitancy…
the moment one definitely commits oneself,
then Providence moves too.
All sorts of things occur to help one
that would never otherwise have occurred.
A whole stream of events issues from the decision,
raising in one's favour all manner of unforeseen incidents
and meetings and material assistance,
which no man could have dreamt would have come his way.
~ William Hutchison Murray[3]

These words were spoken by an eight-year-old boy to his father
on the eve of his dad's second marriage,
"Dad, this time when you make a promise,
I want you to keep it…[4]"

Two can accomplish more than twice as much as one,
for the results can be much better. If one falls, the other pulls him up;
but if a man falls when he is alone, he's in trouble.
Also, on a cold night, two under the same blanket
gain warmth from each other,
but how can one be warm alone?
And one standing alone can be attacked and defeated,
but two can stand back-to-back and conquer.
~ Ecclesiastes 4:9-12

…and the two shall be one…
~ Matthew 19:6

ENDNOTES

1   Welwood, John, Ph.D. *Journey of the Heart,* p. 103, p. 101. HarperCollins Publishers: New York, 1990.

2   Chapter 17, "Sailing the Seven SoulMate 'C's."

3   Murray, William Hutchison, *The Scottish Himalayan Expedition*. New York: J.M. Dent & Sons Ltd. 1951.

4   Relayed to me by my client, the father to whom the words were spoken.

Bibliography and Recommended Reading

GENERAL REFERENCES:

Angelou, Maya, (1997). *All God's Children Need Traveling Shoes*. New York: Random House.

Beattie, Melody, (1987). *Codependent No More*. New York: Harper Collins Publishing.

Bradshaw, John, (1995). *Family Secrets*. New York: Bantam Books.

Breathnach, Sarah, (1995). *Simple Abundance: A Daybook of Comfort and Joy*. New York: Warner Books.

Cameron, Julia, (1992). *The Artist's Way*. New York: Putnam Publishing.

Chopra, M.D., Deepak, (1991). *The Unconditional Life: Mastering the Forces that Shape Personal Reality*. New York: Bantam Books.

Covey, Stephen, (1989). *Seven Habits of Highly Effective People*. New York: Simon & Schuster, Fireside.

Hillman, James, (1996). *The Soul's Code: In Search of Character and Calling*. New York: Random House.

Hummel, Charles E., (1977). *Tyranny of the Urgent*. IL: InterVarsity Press.

Leonard, George, (1992). *Mastery*. New York: Plume Books.

Murray, William Hutchison, (1951). *The Scottish Himalayan Expedition*. New York: J.M. Dent & Sons, Ltd.

Orman, Suze, (1997). *9 Steps to Financial Freedom*. New York: Crown.

Perruci, Piero, (1982). *What We May Be (Techniques for Psychological and Spiritual Growth Through Psychosynthesis)*. New York: G.P. Putnam's Sons.

Piper, Watty, 1930. *The Little Engine That Could!* New York: Platt & Munk Publishers.

Pipher, Mary, Ph.D., (1996). *The Shelter of Each Other, Rebuilding Our Families*, p. 225-226. New York: Ballantine Books.

Reeve, Christopher, (1998). *Still Me*. New York: Random House.

Roberts, Monty, with Lawrence Scanlan, (1998). *The Man Who Listens to Horses*. New York: Random House.

Sheehy, G., (1977). *Passages*, p. 353. Massachusetts: Dutton & Co. Publishing.

MARRIAGE SUPPORT: RECOMMENDED READING:

Chapman, Gary, (December, 1992). *The Five Love Languages*. Chicago: Moody Press. This is a great guide for discovering why certain actions make you feel loved, while your spouse may need different actions from you in order to feel loved.

Cloud, Dr. Henry, and Townsend, Dr. John, (1999). *Boundaries in Marriage*. Grand Rapids, MI: Zondervan Publishing House. A wealth of wisdom about how to assume appropriate responsibility in your marriage with Biblical support for those who struggle with a misunderstanding of what it means to love someone unconditionally.

Boundaries in Marriage Workbook. Grand Rapids, MI: Zondervan Publishing House. This is a self-study guide for an individual or a couple to work through together for the purpose of establishing and clarifying healthy boundaries in a marriage. Remember, healthy boundaries reduce or eliminate resentment! (Addressed in *How to Stay Married & Love It Even More!*)

Cloud and Townsend are the best-selling co-authors of several other books and tape series, including *Changes That Heal*, *Safe People*, *Hiding from Love*, and the Gold Medallion Award-winning *Boundaries*, and *Boundaries in Dating*, all published by Zondervan Publishing House.

Davis, Michele Weiner, (2001). *The Divorce Remedy, The Proven 7-Step Program for Saving Your Marriage*. New York: Simon & Schuster. This book is the sequel to her best seller, *Divorce Busting*, in which she has refined and clarified the principles that have helped thousands save their marriages. It is written in a personable and conversational style. She proposes solutions to locked-in problems that are refreshing, supremely practical, and that work!

It isn't necessary to be on the brink of divorce in order to benefit from her "do what works" plan.

Harley, Dr. Willard F. Jr., (1992). *Love Busters*. Grand Rapids, MI: Flemming H. Revell Publishers. Dr. Harley identifies the five most common habits that destroy romantic love and teaches how to eliminate them once and for all.

5 Steps to Romantic Love: *A Workbook for Readers of Love Busters* and *His Needs, Her Needs*. (7th Printing, 2000). Grand Rapids, MI: Flemming H. Revell Publishers.

Hendricks, Gay & Kathlyn, (1992). *Conscious Loving: The journey to co-commitment, a way to be together without giving up yourself*. New York: Bantam Books. The personal example of their own marriage makes this call to deeper intimacy and healing especially powerful. A great resource for advanced relationship work.

The Conscious Heart: 7 Soul Choices That Inspire Creative Partnership. (Feb. 1999). New York: Bantam Books.

Hendrix, Harville, (1990). *Getting the Love You Want*. New York: Harper & Row, Publishers. This book is rich with exercises that, by the time we completed them, gave us profound appreciation for the inner wisdom that brought us together.

Nichols, Michael P., Ph.D., (1995). *The Lost Art of Listening*. New York: The Guilford Press. The entire book is about the importance of listening to the process of real communication. He explores why it is hard to listen, and the benefits to all relationships if listening skills are improved. The book is full of pithy little nuggets of listening truth, which is why I quote him so often.

Notarius, Richard and Howard Markman, (1993). *We Can Work it Out: Making Sense Out of Marital Conflict*. New York: G.P. Putnam & Sons Publishing. A groundbreaking account of research that pinpoints the behaviors that make relationships work over a lifetime, and those that can predict failure.

Waite, Linda J., and Maggie Gallagher, (September, 2000). *The Case for Marriage: Why Married People Are Happier, Healthier, and Better Off Financially*. New York: Random House. This authoritative and provocative book reveals the benefits—emotional, physical, economic, and sexual—that marriage brings to individuals and society.

*In addition, we recently discovered a wonderful bi-monthly magazine that supports the ongoing process of creating a SoulMate relationship simply called: *Marriage*. Call 1-800-MARRIAGE to ask for a sample copy or to subscribe. Visit their web-site at www.marriagemagazine.org. Published by International Marriage Encounter, Inc.

MARRIAGE SUPPORT WEB SITES:

www.smartmarriages.com. Diane Sollee, who hosts this site, is director, and founder of the Coalition for Marriage, Family and Couples Education. The Coalition serves as an information clearinghouse on skills-based marriage education. If you get on her free newsletter e-mail list, you will receive a wealth of the most current articles, research, news, and legislation in the field of marriage and family welfare.

www.marriage.rutgers.ed. "The National Marriage Project's purpose is to strengthen the institution of marriage by providing research and analysis that informs public policy, educates the American public, and focuses attention on a problem of enormous scope and consequence. Simply stated, marriage is declining as an institution for childbearing and child rearing, with devastating consequences for millions of children." Co-directed by Barbara Dafoe Whitehead, Ph.D., and David Popenoe, Ph.D.

www.CloudTownsend.com. Dr. Henry Cloud and Dr. John Townsend are popular speakers, psychologists, co-hosts of the nationally broadcast "New Life Live!" radio program and cofounders of Cloud-Townsend Clinic and Cloud-Townsend Resources. A wide variety of relationship books and tapes are available via their web site.

APPLYING THE PRINCIPLES of "How to Stay Married & Love It!" TO CHILD-REARING:

Chapman, Gary, (1997). *The Five Love Languages of Children.* Chicago: Northfield Publishing. (2000). *The Five Love Languages of Teenagers.* Chicago: Northfield Publishing. These books teach us how to identify the primary way that each child receives the message, "I am loved." These are enormously helpful concepts to make sure that the love we feel for our children is being communicated in a way that is easiest for each child to receive.

Jones, James J., www.familyhood.com. His tapes are very humorous, very informative, and very practical. The book, *Parenting Magic; Your Children Will Whistle While They Work!,* is full of specific, practical ways to help children become self-responsible. Angela Meyers, M.A. Trainer of Parenting Instructors says, "I've studied them all and this is the best!" Their

Mission Statement is "Familyhood is dedicated to strengthening individuals, marriages and family relationships by teaching the correct principles upon which healthy and loving relationships are established."

Major, Jayne A., Ph.D., (2000). *Breakthrough Parenting.* Quality Publishing. This book shows you how to: Discipline effectively, promoting willing cooperation from your children. Set appropriate and clear boundaries together with your children. Turn mistakes into positive learning experiences. Promote confidence and healthy self-esteem. Communicate so that everyone listens and understands. Help all family members accept personal responsibility for their actions. Resolve conflicts quickly and easily with win-win methods. Form a deep and lasting bond with your children. It can be ordered from Amazon.com or directly from www.Breakthrough parenting.com.

Sprague, Gary, with Randy Petersen, (1993). *Kid's Hope.* Colorado Springs: CO: Thomas Nelson Publishers. This book comes in different versions appropriate for different ages. These books are great for the biological parent (in the case of blending families) to go through with the child as a vehicle for helping the child talk about feelings. They are also appropriate for asingle parent, and a divorced or widowed parent.

FOR STEPFAMILIES:

The Stepfamily Association of America. www.stepfam.org. This is non-profit organization dedicated to helping stepfamilies live successfully by educating, supporting, and acting as an advocate.

Deal, Ron, M.MFT. *Building a Successful Stepfamily,* Audio Seminar. Nine hours of presentation on six tapes plus a 98-page seminar manual has over 150 practical ideas for strengthening your stepfamily. This set may be purchased at www.swfamily.org/stepfamily.

Dunn, Pastor Dick, M.MFT, (1997). *New Faces in The Frame.* Nashville, TN: LifeWay Press. Available from Amazon.com, general, or Christian bookstores. This is a workbook for studying and resolving marriage and parenting issues in the blended family.

Houck, Don and LaDean, (1997). *The Ex Factor.* Grand Rapids, MI: Flemming H. Revell Publishers. An excellent resource for learning how to successfully work with an ex-spouse.

www.steplife.com. This web-site promotes the education of stepfamily principles that increase the chances of successfully "blending." The site is hosted by a couple, Steve and Dena Sposato, who care passionately about the success of stepfamilies. They are part of the leadership of a support group for stepfamilies that meets in Orange County, CA.

DIVORCE INFORMATION:

Medved, Diane, Ph.D., (1989). *The Case Against Divorce*. New York: Ballantine Books. Discover the lures, the lies, and the emotional traps of divorce—plus the seven vital reasons to stay to- gether. Winner of the 1990 Christopher Award.

Wallerstein, Judith, Lewis, Julia and Blakeslee, Sandra, (2000). *The Unexpected Legacy of Divorce: A 25 Year Landmark Study*. New York: Hyperion. In depth interviews of 131 children every five years beginning 25 years ago after the divorces of their parents. Interviews with children with parallel lives who's happy or conflict ridden parents chose to stay together provide accurate contrast to the long-term effects of divorce into middle adulthood.

FOR CHILDREN OF DIVORCE:

Major, Dr. Jayne A. *Creating a Successful Parenting Plan, a Step-be-Step Guide for the Care of Children of Divided Families*. Steven A. Mindel, a Family Law Attorney, says about this book, "Finally someone has prepared a practical guide to developing a parenting plan which takes into account both the emotional and legal aspects of child custody and visitation." Deanie Kramer, a divorce mediator adds, "Parents working together to create a parenting plan are 80% more successful in carrying out the plan than when a third party, who does not know the family, dictates what they should be doing." This book may be ordered from Breakthrough Parenting, Inc. 1-800-770-7935 or www.breakthroughparenting.com.

Rothchild, Gillian, (1999). *Dear Mom and Dad: What Kids of Divorce Really Want to Say to Their Parents*. New York: Pocket Books. 180 pithy words of advice from children to their parents who have divorced.

Sprague, Gary, with Randy Petersen, (1993). *Kid's Hope*. Colorado Springs: CO: Thomas Nelson Publishers. This book comes in different versions appropriate for different ages. These books are great for the biological parent (in the case of blending families) to go through with the child as a vehicle for helping the child talk about feelings. They are also appropriate for a single parent, and a divorced or widowed parent.

HOW TO STAY
MARRIED
&
LOVE IT
EVEN MORE!

Completing the Puzzle
of a SoulMate Marriage

Nancy Landrum with Jim Landrum

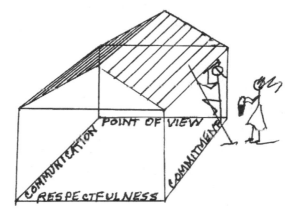

Love is what matters.
When all is said and done,
love is what we remember.
On your deathbed you won't say
"I wish I'd made more money,
I wish I had worked more."
You will grieve the lost opportunities for love,
and celebrate the ones you had.

~ **Pat Love**[1]

When I start a jigsaw puzzle, I like to get the four corners and the frame in place first. It defines the field, so to speak—letting me see the parameters within which the rest of the pieces will fit. *In How to Stay Married & Love It!* we "framed" the puzzle of a SoulMate marriage by defining the four most essential elements. Those elements establish the dimensions and foundation for a SoulMate marriage.

When I was eleven years old, my parents decided to build a new house. Up until then, the only home I had known was about 1200 square feet of squeaky hardwood floors, real plaster walls, wood framed windows and a little front porch. My two older sisters shared a small room. My younger sister and I shared a double bed in an even *smaller* room. All four of us shared a miniscule bathroom, the site of many squabbles.

The location of the new house was only about a mile away, so we visited the building site often. The first few weeks went by with very little observable progress. A tractor moved some dirt around. Sticks with red ribbons tied to them seemed to be randomly distributed over the area. Trenches were dug, big pipes laid and more pipes added. Some wires were strung about and hung from poles. It didn't look anything like a house to me. I wondered how the workmen knew what to do. It was a *huge puzzle*.

After several weeks of what appeared to be little change, I heard the excitement in my mother's voice when she said, "They're pouring concrete today!" I knew that meant a foundation. Maybe *now* it would start to look more like a house.

After the concrete hardened, we walked over the foundation as my mom described where the various rooms would be. I was afraid she'd made a big mistake. It looked so small. If we weren't going to have more room, why couldn't we stay in the old house that I loved? It was familiar. I was dreading the move. Mr. Dorming, the Swedish master-builder, assured me that the new house was considerably bigger than our current abode. Darn.

From that point on everything happened fast. It seemed that it became a real house overnight. The walls were framed in a blink. I could walk down a hallway, enter rooms and see where the long bathroom counter would go with two sinks and a huge mirror for my sisters and me. It was such a *long* walk from the back bedroom to the family room—how did the space become so big? The transformation felt like magic.

Since then I've explored many homes under construction. I've learned that the foundation *alone* appears deceptively small. Once the walls are framed, defining the various living areas, the true space of the house can be more accurately assessed.

When Jim and I were laying the foundation of our SoulMate marriage it seemed to take forever. It was tedious work. Progress was measured in inches. It was like a chaotic building site with trenches, pipes and wires randomly scattered about. The tools were unfamiliar and felt awkward to use. We knew that we *didn't* want to live in the old angry marriage anymore, but we had only a vague concept of what we were trying to build. The amount of work was daunting.

In addition, the dimensions of the foundation felt too small. The confines of *respectful* communication sometimes made me feel claustrophobic. Our agreement specifically barred sarcasm, yelling, attacking "you" statements and bringing up old business. Leaving in a huff, slamming doors, withdrawing in martyred silence and self-righteous accusations didn't fit within the parameters, either. Jim and I some times longed for the days when we said whatever we wanted to say without going through an internal check to see if the eminent words and tone of voice conformed to our chosen limits.

It was only after our relationship continued to improve and expand that we began to appreciate what a magnificent foundation we had. A lovely, spacious marriage-home was gradually taking shape. My parents had Mr. Dorming to insure that all the important pieces fit and the foundation perfectly matched the plans. We believe there was a *Master Builder* at work in our marriage. Although we hadn't known *what* we needed or *how* to read the blueprints, all the essential pieces of the foundation for a great marriage were in place. In review, they are:

1. Accept your partner's point of view as valid.
2. Communicate in ways that get the desired result.
3. Always treat yourself and your partner with respect.
4. Commit to this partner, this marriage, for life.

If you haven't read *How to Stay Married & Love It!* I urge you to put *this* book down and read *that* one first. The puzzle of a SoulMate marriage needs a clearly defined frame before the rest can be successfully completed.

As we learned to stay within the parameters of our marriage-foundation, we felt safe and secure. Our depleted energy resources were gradually restored. We gained confidence that we could live at peace and even joyfully with each other "'til death do us part." The remaining six pieces began falling into place to complete the multi-dimensional puzzle of a SoulMate marriage. Those are the qualities described in *How to Stay Married & Love It Even More! Completing the Puzzle of a SoulMate Marriage.*

Unlike cardboard puzzles, your marriage is a multi-dimensional puzzle—a living, breathing, changing organism. Every exchange—each separate act—influences the relationship in a negative or a positive way. A SoulMate marriage-house is built piece by piece, day by day, as the skills that express each of these ten qualities are practiced in relationship with your spouse.

Although not a physical house, this marriage structure provides shelter impossible for wood or stone to give. By putting into practice the skills recommended in *How to Stay Married & Love It!* you've been framing the puzzle—building from scratch or shoring up your marriage foundation. Keep going. Add these next six pieces to complete the puzzle of a SoulMate marriage. As you do, your marriage becomes a shelter safely housing a place of intimate belonging and romantic loving for you and your spouse for life!

It is in the shelter of each other that the people live.
~ Irish Proverb

There are three things too wonderful for me to understand—no, four!
How an eagle glides through the sky.
How a serpent crawls upon a rock.
How a ship finds its way across the heaving ocean.
The growth of love between a man and a woman.
~ Proverbs 30:18, 19

ENDNOTES

1   Love, Pat, Ed.D., 2001. *The Truth About Love*, p. 243. New York: Fireside

Index

FREE!

In exchange for your experiences in using the concepts in this book, we will send you a **LAMINATED COPY OF THE INSTRUCTIONS FOR MIRRORING** with the list of feeling words on the back. Sharing feelings or needs and effective listening are the core skills for building a SoulMate marriage. This aid will be invaluable while you are learning how to use the mirroring technique for resolving issues and deepening intimacy.

To receive this helpful gift, answer one or more of these questions as fully as you can:

1. Share the concept that has had the most powerful effect on your relationship and why. Share details of what your marriage was like before, how that concept was put into practice, and what difference it has made.

2. What has been your experience with learning to share your feelings rather than your opinions? What is the hardest for you? What has been the result in your interactions when feelings were shared? What effect has it had as a couple on your problem solving or conflict resolution?

3. What difference has the Commitment to Respect made in your relationship? What was happening before? How is that different now? In the past were you aware of the line between respect and disrespect?

4. How has the concept of the healthy management of anger changed your marriage? What safe method of venting are you using when you are not able to be respectful to your partner? What is your experience after venting? Are you able to address the issue respectfully with your partner?

5. Have you or your partner (or both) been able to "shut the backdoor?" What has changed since you made the commitment to this marriage, this partner for life?

6. Have you used these tools in other relationships? What has been the result?

Write your answer and send it by e-mail to staymarried@aol.com or mail to River Publishing, P.O. Box 27433, Anaheim, CA 92809-0114. Include your full name and complete address and phone number so we can mail you your free mirroring aid. Some stories will be used in my next book, *Becoming SoulMates*. (Your information will not be given to any other person or organization.) Thank you for taking the time to give us such detailed feedback about your successes with these concepts. Bless you!

Order Form

To order additional copies of *How to Stay Married & Love It!* please send this form, along with a Check or Money Order, made payable to River Publishing, to the address below.

River Publishing
P.O. Box 27433
Anaheim, CA 92809-0114

$17.95 plus $4.50 shipping for first copy ($1.50 shipping for each additional copy). CA orders please add sales tax.

Number of books _____

Shipping address: *(please print)*

Name: _____

Address: _____

_____

City: _____ **State:** _____ **Zip:** _____

E-Mail: _____

You can also visit us via our website: www.howtostaymarried.com or e-mail us at staymarried@aol.com. Secure credit card transactions available.

☐ Please notify me when the second volume, *How to Stayed Married & Love It Even More!* is available.